Financial Resource Management

Sport, Tourism, and Leisure Services

3rd edition

Russell E. Brayley and Daniel D. McLean

SAGAMORE ❖❖ VENTURE

©2019 Sagamore–Venture

Publishers: Joseph J. Bannon and Peter L. Bannon
Sales and Marketing Manager: Misti Gilles
Sales and Marketing Assistant: Kimberly Vecchio
Director of Development and Production: Susan M. Davis
Production Coordinator: Amy S. Dagit
Graphic Designer: Marissa Willison

Library of Congress Catalog Card Number: 2018965757
ISBN print edition: 978-1-57167-941-3
ISBN ebook: 978-1-57167-942-0
ISBN extext: 978-1-57167-945-1

Printed in the United States.

Sagamore-Venture
1807 N. Federal Dr.
Urbana, IL 61801
www.sagamorepublishing.com

Dedication

To Our Families

Renée, Doug, Austin, Erika, Natalie

–Russell Brayley

JoAnn, Donna, Jennifer, Suzanne, Timothy, Sally, Michael, Kristine

–Daniel McLean

Acknowledgment

To Dr. Ethan Strigkas, for his authorship of the original chapter on sponsorship

Contents

Section A: Financial Management in Context

Section B: Budgeting

Section C: Accounting and Reporting

Section D: Revenue Generation

Preface

Effective managers in sport, tourism, and leisure service organizations are required to have a wide variety of skills and a good understanding of all of the resources that they manage. Not only should they be competent as personnel managers, but they also need to know how to manage their physical facilities. In addition, they need to be effective in their management of time, for time is one resource that cannot be renewed. Good managers also need to know how to use their financial resources effectively. Throughout the history of our profession, there have never been times of such great prosperity that decisions could be made or practices maintained without consideration of their financial implications. Certainly, there have been situations where financial constraints have been minimal, but even then, some measure of financial accountability has been required of those who receive and spend an organization's money. Similarly, there has never been a time of such flexibility that some degree of planning was not required of resource managers. In fact, experience has shown that a lack of planning reduces flexibility, as choices are replaced by externally controlled consequences. Budgeting and long-term financial planning are areas of understanding and skill that every sport and leisure service manager must develop and magnify. This book has been written with the needs of the sport, tourism, and leisure service manager in mind. The authors have worked in a variety of sport, tourism, and leisure settings in several different parts of the United States and Canada and have discovered that there is no place to hide from the opportunity or responsibility to know about budgets, finance, and fiscal management. It has been written for the mathematically challenged, for the pre-professional, for the professional who received on-the-job training, and for the professional who is keenly interested in and dedicated to continuous improvement. Readers will learn important principles of economics and finance. They will also learn the skills necessary to prepare, present, and manage budgets, as well as generate revenues for capital development and day-to-day operations. Discussions include examples from the "real world" and offer illustrations to facilitate the learning of some of the more complex or technical points.

About the Authors

Daniel D. McLean is a professor emeritus from the UNLV College of Hospitality Management where he served as vice-dean. A career-long park and recreation professional, Dr. McLean graduated from California State University, Sacramento, and served as a recreation supervisor in Ventura, California, before completing advanced degrees from Brigham Young University (M.A.) and Kansas State University (Ph.D.). He served on the faculties of Iowa State University, Indiana University, and Kansas State University prior to the University of Nevada, Las Vegas. He also served as a recreation director for the city of Cedar Rapids, Iowa. His 46 years of experience was both academic and as a practitioner. He retired in 2017.

Russell E. Brayley is a professor at George Mason University where he has served as Director of the Division of Sport, Recreation, and Tourism. After and between earning bachelor's and master's degrees in Recreation Administration from Brigham Young University, Dr. Brayley worked in community recreation leadership and as a government consultant in Alberta, Canada. He earned his Ph.D. degree at Texas A&M University and subsequently held faculty and administrative positions at the University of Manitoba, Indiana University and George Mason University. Dr. Brayley is an active, internationally recognized researcher in tourism management and has written many scholarly and professional articles, and spoken at conferences throughout the world. Dr. Brayley has served as the president of the Resort and Commercial Recreation Association and is very active in family and community service.

SECTION A

Financial Management in Context

The two chapters in this introductory section present a discussion and comparison of the different sectors in which and sport, leisure service, and tourism organizations operate. Specific industries are examined from the perspective of basic financial management principles and practices. After an examination of the general differences between sport, tourism, and leisure service organizations that operate in public, private, nonprofit, and commercial environments, a brief chapter is dedicated to primary financial functions and related organizational structures.

Sector and Industry Comparisons

Introduction

Approaches to the management of financial resources in sport, tourism, and leisure service organizations vary greatly, depending on the mandate and goals of the organizations, as well as the political environments in which they operate. However, almost every sport, tourism, or leisure service organization can be classified as either a public, private nonprofit, or commercial enterprise, and each type of organization has unique and uniquely common features that relate directly to financial management and budgeting.

This chapter examines the finance-related differences between the three types of sport, tourism, and leisure enterprises and explores related legislative/legal parameters, social roles/expectations, market management techniques, indicators of success, and particular financial management opportunities and challenges. The chapter also addresses competition and cooperation between sport, tourism, and leisure service organizations of different types. In devoting this discussion to the unique characteristics and differences among public, private nonprofit, and commercial sport, tourism, and leisure service organizations, there is a danger that their many important similarities will be ignored. Such is not the intent of this chapter. Although it is important to understand the differences, it is just as important to acknowledge the common principles, practices, structures, and competencies associated with financial management.

Public Sector Enterprises

A sport, tourism, and leisure service enterprise operating in the public sector generally has a broad mandate to provide services that directly or indirectly benefit an entire community. The organization is usually an arm of government (e.g., a municipal recreation department, a public educational institution, or a convention and visitors bureau) that is charged with enhancing the quality of life of its patrons by providing enriching experiences and remedying social problems. The "public" nature of the organization is not only emphasized in its nondiscriminatory offering and delivery of services, but also in the nondiscriminatory way by which its operating funds are expropriated. Public sport, tourism, and leisure service organizations receive their base financial resources from the public through taxation. They may also charge fees and receive gratuitous income from private sources, but the foundation of their support is the ability of government to meet its operational goals by taxing its constituents or those who fall within its taxation jurisdiction.

Legislative/Legal Parameters

In order for the governing body of a public sport, tourism, or leisure service organization to compel its constituents to contribute funds to support the operation of that organization, it must first win a legal right to levy taxes and to use those taxes for such purposes. The United States Constitution sets the legal parameters for the federal government to collect and use public funds for sport, tourism, and leisure services. The federal system also provides for the establishment and public funding of state and local governments and government programs. State governments must have their own constitutional provisions for taxation and public funding of sport, tourism, and leisure services. Local (i.e., municipal) governments, on the other hand, may extend public financial support to sport, tourism, and leisure services only if the state government already has enacted appropriate enabling legislation.

Social Roles/Expectations

Public sport, tourism, and leisure service organizations exist for the purpose of meeting social needs. The taxpaying public expects sport, tourism, and leisure service organizations to be engaged in enterprises and programs that use public funds for the common good and for community betterment. Within the community, there is general acceptance and tolerance of certain services receiving tax subsidies, and many low-cost or free (i.e. completely subsidized) services (e.g. neighborhood parks) are expected, demanded, and even required as basic elements of social order and as important tools in social engineering.

Market Management Techniques

Modern practices of sport, tourism, and leisure service organizations include market segmentation and target marketing. Public organizations use "need" rather than "profit potential" as the primary segmentation criterion in their marketing efforts. Products, prices, and promotional strategies are established in consideration of the desire to appeal to as many as possible in the community who need the service. Distribution considerations also reflect the priority of the public sector organization to ensure service delivery to as broad a market as possible. For example, when faced with a new private or commercial sector competitor, a public agency may choose to withdraw from the marketplace—not because it is unable to compete, but because the competitor has demonstrated that it can meet the same needs without tax support and, perhaps, with greater efficiency. The marketing objective of the public sport, tourism, or leisure service organization is either to provide the benefit or to accommodate its provision by another appropriate supplier.

Indicators of Success

Financial managers in the public sector measure their success by comparing their achievements to their goals. That is also true of financial managers in the private nonprofit and commercial sectors, but the goals of the latter organizations are more precisely associated with financial returns on financial investments. Public financial managers focus on achieving targeted levels of revenue and expenditure and on efficiently producing specific social and economic benefits through those expenditures.

Financial Management Opportunities and Challenges

Public sport, tourism, and leisure service organizations enjoy several opportunities that are unique to their sector. One opportunity is that of tax exemption. By convention, no government may charge taxes to a government at another level, which means that the local public agency has greater purchasing power due to being exempt from state or federal sales taxes. Another opportunity lies in the ability of the public institution to borrow money for capital projects. The government is a low-risk borrower, primarily because it can use its taxing power and its access to the taxable wealth of the community as collateral. A third opportunity enjoyed by the public sector is the goodwill and altruistic behavior of people in the community. Actively encouraged and supported volunteer programs provide human resources without draining the sport, tourism, and leisure service organization's financial resources.

A challenge experienced by financial managers in the public sector is the scrutiny of and accountability to the public and to other legislative/regulatory bodies. True to the democratic ideal, citizens voice their views about how their taxes are being used, and there is always someone who was not elected who is certain that he or she could do a better job. The close scrutiny of financial management also comes from other formal organizations or agencies whose job it is to ensure that the public treasury is being properly managed. This close scrutiny is usually facilitated by seemingly countless forms and reports which the financial manager must take time to complete. A second challenge comes in the form of changing political winds. Financial management in the public sector requires sensitivity to the political environment, and changes in political priorities may require readjustment of financial plans or management structures.

Other

Two other aspects of financial management in the public sector require a brief mention before looking at financial management in the private nonprofit sector. One aspect concerns the advantage that comes to the public sport, tourism, or leisure service organization by virtue of its taxing authority—an advantage over competitors or would-be competitors that cannot compete because they must raise capital funds at market prices and pay taxes to their competitor, the public agency. In many cases, the charge of unfair competition leveled at the public sector may be well deserved. The second aspect concerns the belief in the private sector that, because of the seemingly unchecked taxing power of government, the public sport, tourism, and leisure service organization has "deep pockets." Therefore, the reasoning goes, only public agencies can or should be expected to raise the capital necessary to build and maintain such major facilities as a 100,000-seat sports stadium or domed arena. Financial managers in the public sector are, however, quite aware of the limitations of public tolerance for taxation and have shortened their reach into the taxpayers' pockets. Sometimes this restraint has been self-imposed, and sometimes it has resulted from public pressure and sentiment, such as that expressed in several landmark propositions passed by voters in recent years.

Focus: Leisure Service Organizations in the Public Sector

The majority of sport, recreation, and tourism organizations that operate in the public sector are municipal agencies charged with providing a wide range of leisure services to their constituents. The following discussion focuses on the unique finance-related characteristics, opportunities, and constraints of public leisure service organizations.

Organizational Structure

There is no single organizational structure that is required of public leisure service entities. The most common structure is a combined parks and recreation department or division under municipal, county, or regional government administration. Separate, autonomous park or recreation organizations are declining in number. In a few states, park districts are organized with separate taxing power and, in some areas, the park districts have an elected board. In other cases an appointed board provides the policy direction for the public leisure service organization. The park board typically has

decision-making authority for organizational structure. State park organizations exist in all 50 states and are structured in a variety of ways. They may appear under a tourism umbrella or, more commonly, a natural resource structure.

It is unusual to find sport organizations as a part of the public leisure service structure. More often they operate as nonprofit organizations that have formal and informal links to public entities. The Indiana Sports Corporation, for example, is a nonprofit organization dedicated to bringing national and international sport championships to Indianapolis and Indiana. When putting a bid package together, they work closely with the city government and the local and regional tourism office. The sporting events they try to attract may use professional sport areas (e.g., FIFA World Basketball Championship), privately owned sport facilities (e.g., a professional golf tournament), public facilities (e.g., NCAA Swimming and Diving Championships), or a combination of the three (e.g., World Police Games). Sport organizations are discussed later in this chapter.

Tourism and commercial recreation enterprises do include some public organizations, such as city or state tourism development offices and local destination marketing organizations. However, these public organizations typically operate as if they are commercial entities and are also discussed further in this chapter.

Operational and Fiscal Authority

Almost all public leisure service entities report to policy or advisory boards. Policy boards typically carry decision-making authority and advisory boards provide input into operations and make endorsements, suggestions, and recommendations to the decision-making authority. Public entities are authorized to expend money only after the legislative body has formally approved a budget. Oversight authority for budget operations remains with the legislative body, and day-to-day fiscal operations and management is delegated to the leisure service organization.

Mandates or expectations of services and programs are articulated in the organization's enabling legislation at both the state and/or local level, the legislative body's vision and mission statements, and the leisure service organization's long-range plans. Fiscal operations are codified in state and local legislation and the public entity is reviewed, at a minimum, by a state auditing body on a regular basis. Organizations must operate within appropriate state and local codes that apply to fiscal operations.

Financial Objectives

The purpose of public leisure service organizations such as park and recreation departments is to improve the quality of life for residents, enhance the beauty of the community, and provide recreation and fitness-based activities and programs for individuals and groups. In some communities, public park and recreation entities are seen as social welfare agencies working in consort with other social welfare enterprises to improve individual opportunities for personal growth. The Boulder, Colorado Parks and Recreation Department mission statement is typical of many public entities and reflects the ideal of "public good."

The mission of the City of Boulder Parks and Recreation Department is to provide safe, clean, and beautiful parks and facilities and high-quality leisure activities for the community. These services shall enhance residents' health

and well-being and promote economic vitality for long-term community sustainability. We will accomplish this through creative leadership, environmentally sustainable practices, and the responsible use of available resources. (City of Boulder Parks and Recreation Department Vision Statement. Retrieved from http://www.bouldercolorado.gov).

Public entities serving the public good traditionally were not expected to generate a profit or even large amounts of revenue. They operated as public agencies with some or all of their funding coming from tax revenue. Contemporary public park and recreation departments, however, do actively generate revenue as part of their mandate. Public leisure service organizations, once almost wholly subsidized by compulsory income (see Chapter 9), now generate 15% to 100% of their operational funds through fees, charges, and entrepreneurial activities. Capital improvement funds for buildings and structures typically come from other sources (see Chapters 12 and 16).

Major capital investments such as parks, recreation centers, or specialized facilities are viewed as public commodities. Parks are typically not expected to generate revenue; however, recreation centers and specialized facilities within parks may be expected to produce varying levels of revenue (including profit) and are viewed as investment decisions. The decision to build a new facility is based on its revenue potential and the public good that it represents. For example, most public agencies that might construct a family aquatic center would expect the facility's revenue to cover its operations, partially or wholly contribute to the long-term debt incurred from construction, and provide additional funds to agency operations. By contrast, a skate park is seen as an opportunity to provide youth with a safer public outlet for their activities and may only be expected to recover part of its operating costs and none of its long-term debt.

Debt Management

Simply stated, the two main goals of the public leisure service organization are to serve the public and to maintain a sound financial foundation. Public agencies are dependent upon tax revenues, fees and charges, and enterprise operations for their operating revenue. They are not allowed to engage in deficit spending. Long-term debt is controlled by state and local legislation, and public organizations may not engage in debt-creating activities outside of those specifically permitted. For example, state financial codes typically limit the amount and type of debt that a city or an independent park district may incur. Public entities will engage in activities and types of activities that commercial enterprises often will not even consider, especially when it is justified as a public benefit. Parks, recreation centers, recreation programs, and similar activities frequently fit within the public benefit rationale. Louisville, Kentucky Metro Parks, for example, operates 13 recreation centers, many of them in lower socioeconomic neighborhoods where expectations of cost recovery are low. The recreation centers are seen as meeting a public good (benefit).

Accounting Management

Accounting management in public entities is similar to that of the commercial enterprise, with some important differences. Public entities operate under generally accepted accounting practices (GAAP) but, unlike in the commercial

sector, the use of the revenue may be restricted according to the source of the revenue. For example, a special tax may be restricted for a single use, such as reduction of long-term debt. Different than for commercial enterprises, revenue generated from a public program or a facility may go into the government general fund and be made available for use anywhere within the government, or it may go to a restricted fund that limits where the funds are used.

Pricing in the public sector is becoming more sophisticated, yet it is sometimes based on a mix of intuition and cursory analysis of limited measures of demand and willingness to pay. In the public sector, pricing is more often seen as a tool to recover partial rather than full costs. The need to provide for the public good and to maintain sound financial practices drives decision-making in the public sector. It is frequently seen as a conundrum for policy makers as they strive to provide for the public good and simultaneously ensure sufficient funds are available for the public enterprise.

Reporting

Public park and recreation entities are strongly affected by seasonal variations. Outdoor aquatic facilities typically have a 90- to 120-day season. Indoor sport, recreation, and fitness facilities are affected by seasonal shifts in sport, individual preferences for being outdoors or indoors, inclement weather periods, and public school calendars. For example, when public leisure service organizations prepare for summer operations they may spend up to 75% of their annual operating budget between May 1 and September 30.

Financial reporting usually occurs on a monthly basis and is supplemented by seasonal reports. Policy boards and advisory boards are trained to understand seasonal influences on revenues and expenditures, and historical reports are frequently provided to aid in that understanding. In addition, program reports are provided for each activity at the end of the season. The task of the chief executive officer and chief financial officer is to interpret financial data, generate reports, and educate staff, legislative officials, and lay board members about fiscal operations.

Performance Evaluation

Serving the public good is the primary goal of public park and recreation entities. From a financial perspective, auditors require assurance and proof that standard accounting practices have been followed. Policy makers require proof that funds expended have contributed to the public good. Park and recreation entities may respond to the two different reporting needs by providing data from performance goals and objectives, attendance reports, outcome measures, and other forms of data. Application of measures of effectiveness and efficiency are becoming more common, and it is generally believed that measuring outputs (such as the number of people served) is no longer an adequate substitute for measuring how people benefited from participation in programs and use of facilities or services. Performance measurement is becoming more sophisticated and it is more important than ever that public leisure service organizations provide effective evaluations.

Private Nonprofit Enterprises

The private nonprofit sector is composed of organizations that provide sport, tourism, and leisure services without the direct support of public funds and without the requirement to generate increased personal wealth for any owners or investors. These organizations are private in the sense that they are not owned or directed by government. They are nonprofit in the sense that they must generate income to at least cover their expenses, yet do not generate profits for the purpose of making anybody richer. They may make a profit from certain enterprises, but overall profit is not the goal, and any profits that are realized are used to maintain or enhance the viability of the organization. Private nonprofit sport, tourism, and leisure service organizations exist to meet the service needs of selected consumers in situations where the public sector is either unwilling or unable to function, and where commercial organizations are also either unwilling or unable to conduct business. Well-known examples of private nonprofit sport, tourism, and leisure service organizations include the YMCA, local church groups, community sport and athletic associations, recreation clubs, Boys and Girls Clubs, Boy Scouts of America, Girl Scouts, Chambers of Commerce, Historical Societies, and Destination Marketing Organizations.

Private nonprofit organizations receive financial resources from membership fees, fundraising projects, donations, grants, and user fees. Their need for money from such sources is reduced considerably by the ability of private nonprofit organizations to attract and keep committed volunteers. After religious organizations (which also offer many recreational programs), community sport and leisure organizations receive the greatest share of volunteer support in the United States and Canada.

Legislative/Legal Parameters

Private nonprofit organizations are permitted to operate because of several important laws that free them from some of the restrictive controls that otherwise encumber public and commercial operations. For example, most private nonprofit sport, tourism, and leisure service organizations enjoy a tax-free status. Additionally, the U.S. Postal Service and most commercial retailers and service suppliers offer specially reduced rates for recognized nonprofit organizations. Federal and state income tax laws also encourage individuals and corporations to donate to charitable nonprofit organizations by recognizing tax deductions or offering tax credits according to the amounts donated. In order for a donor to apply for such a tax benefit, the donation must go to an organization that is registered with the Internal Revenue Service as a 501(c3) Charitable Organization. Other state and federal tax law provisions also exist to support the valued work of private nonprofit organizations.

In addition to filing with the IRS, all private nonprofit sport, tourism, and leisure service organizations need to be properly constituted and registered as corporate entities. This registration may need to be with local, state, and/or federal agencies that regulate the operations of commercial and nonprofit organizations.

Social Roles/Expectations

Like public agencies, private nonprofit sport, tourism, and leisure service organizations exist to meet social needs. However, they are more selective in the needs that they try to meet. Usually, a private nonprofit organization is identified with a single "cause" or specific interest, such as helping at-risk youth, strengthening families, promoting mass involvement in camping, developing coaching skills for basketball, promoting literacy, encouraging historic preservation and interpretation, or promoting visitation.

Market Management Techniques

The relatively narrow focus of the nonprofit organization tends to restrict the scope of its market and dictate the techniques it must use to effectively and appropriately manage the consumption process. The identity of the client base is readily established by the needs or the shared interactions of the people with the target needs. Pricing decisions reflect the requirement to break even or generate modest profits when additional money is needed for other service activities of the organization. Service allocation for private nonprofit sport, tourism, and leisure service organizations is based primarily on need, with little regard for merit or profit potential.

Indicators of Success

Financial managers in the private nonprofit sector measure their success by comparing their achievements to their goals. That is also true of financial managers in the public and commercial sectors. The goals of the public organizations, however, are not at all associated with financial returns on financial investments, while the overarching goal of commercial sector organizations is to make as much money as possible for the owner(s). Private nonprofit financial managers focus on achieving social benefits while generating enough revenue and other resources (e.g. volunteers) to stay in operation and continue benefiting their specialized markets.

Financial Management Opportunities and Challenges

Public sympathy and affection are two important advantages enjoyed by organizations in the private nonprofit sector. This factor is particularly helpful both in fund-raising efforts and the recruitment of volunteers. Tax breaks and discounts also provide opportunities for private nonprofit sport, tourism, and leisure service organizations to get the most out of their financial resources.

One challenge that smaller private nonprofit organizations have is the lack of staff (or, at least, highly qualified staff) that can manage the financial resources in a consistent, accurate, and timely manner. Reliance on volunteers for financial management functions can occasionally have disastrous results for the organization. Another challenge is the relative risk associated with extending credit to an enterprise that depends so much on the popularity of its cause and the generosity of its supporters. Credit is based on confidence, and confidence is something that most small nonprofit organizations enjoy from conservative lenders. A third significant financial management challenge is that of protecting the financial resources of the organization from short-term governing bodies that do not always act with long-term wisdom. Many nonprofit sport and leisure service organizations have failed or struggled because a new board of directors decided to use their carefully developed cash reserves for an immediate program expansion or initiative that did not result in sustained or enhanced financial strength.

Other

Financial management in the private nonprofit sector requires many of the same skills and involves many of the same activities as those in the public sector. Sports, tourism, and leisure in the private nonprofit sector is likely to continue as a strong and viable part of community life. It will, however, need more sophistication in the management of its financial resources as every aspect of operating in a modern society becomes more complex.

Focus: Leisure Service Organizations in the Private Nonprofit Sector

Many leisure services are provided by nongovernment organizations that do not operate with a profit motive. The following discussion focuses on the unique finance-related characteristics, opportunities, and constraints of private nonprofit leisure service organizations.

Organizational Structure

Nonprofit organizations typically operate with a board of directors providing policy oversight to the organization. An executive director may be hired, especially in a larger organization, but in the absence of full-time staff, the president of the board and executive committee may provide day-to-day operational direction. Nonprofit enterprises come in all sizes, from the large National Parks Foundation with tens of thousand of members, to the small local swim club with 30 or less members. Nonprofit organizations typically have a narrow focus or purpose. For example, the Appalachian Mountain Club focuses on conservation, education, and outdoor recreation, with further concern for maintaining regional chapters, conservation activities, and lodging (all focused in the Appalachian mountains). As another example, a local youth swim club may provide a coach and the facilities in which members may swim, train, and learn about nutrition. All nonprofit organizations have a purpose and a focus that are stated in their articles of incorporation.

Financial Objectives

The financial objectives of a nonprofit organization are linked to its stated purpose. All nonprofit organizations strive to generate sufficient revenue to pay for their annual operations. They are not expected nor encouraged to generate a profit. The Internal Revenue Service provides guidelines for how nonprofit organizations might use their funds. For example, there are restrictions on the amount of money allowed for political lobbying. In moving beyond the Internal Revenue Service guidelines, nonprofit organizations jeopardize their nonprofit tax status.

The vast majority of nonprofit organizations do not have major capital investments, but those that do must manage them as efficient enterprises. Nonprofit organizations might also have unique cash-flow circumstances, such as would a Boy Scout camp that generates 85% of its camping revenue in the three-month summer period, but has year-round expenses. Nonprofit organizations are frequently dependent upon the good will of members or donors to provide funds for ongoing operations. A Boys & Girls Club operating in the inner city probably cannot charge sufficient revenue to cover the operating costs of the programs and facilities, so donors, the United Way, and revenue from programs are used to cover the costs.

Debt and Account Management

Nonprofit organizations work to maintain sufficient funds for operations.

Sources of income include programs, special events, donors, bequests, government grants and contracts, private grants, and the United Way. The United Way provides support to a limited number of nonprofit organizations that meet their minimum guidelines and are selected by a lay community-based board for inclusion in their funding model. Some self-reliance is required, as the United Way almost never provides 100% support to a nonprofit organization.

Nonprofit organizations have a wide range of financial solvency. The small, narrowly focused nonprofit organization may struggle from month to month to generate sufficient funds for operations. A larger nonprofit organization, such as the Appalachian Mountain Club, might have a budget in the millions with multiple sources of revenue and a strong endowment. In 2016, the Appalachian Mountain Club's operating budget was $31.1 million, and it maintained an endowment of almost $60 million (Appalachian Mountain Club, 2016 Annual Report, http://www.outdoors.org). The solvency contrast among nonprofit organizations is dramatic. Financial operations and debt management principles are consistent, but management of each will vary based on the size, solvency, and management competency of the nonprofit organization. In the absence of an ongoing income revenue stream, many nonprofit organizations adjust their operating budget on a monthly or seasonal basis to deal with operating revenue availability.

Reporting

Nonprofit organizations report on a monthly, quarterly, and annual basis. They often utilize more than one of the standard financial reporting formats that are discussed later in this book. Regardless, there should be a monthly reporting process, sometimes as a treasurer's report, and there should be an annual report, ideally certified by the nonprofit organization's account manager or an independent auditing body. The variety of nonprofit organizations, their size, scope of services, and management skills frequently determine the type and effectiveness of reporting. Nonprofit organizations with external funding sources require standardized reporting consistent with the expectations of the funding organizations. The United Way, for example, usually requires monthly reports and an annual external audit. In addition, they may conduct their own audit on a regular cycle, such as once every three years. Financial reports should be consistent with the principles presented in Chapter 7.

Performance Evaluation

For nonprofit organizations, the level of performance evaluation is dependent upon the expectations of the board of directors, leadership, and outside funding entities. Annual reports are commonly required and are primarily concerned with reporting on progress made toward achievement of goals and objectives. A United Way-supported entity frequently is required to measure outcome for funded programs, and continued United Way funding may be based on progress achieved toward intended outcomes. Foundations may also require specific evaluation products or performance indicators from an organization, such as completion of a project, publishing of a report or monograph, completion of a capital improvement project, or a formal assessment report.

Larger nonprofit organizations issue annual reports reflecting progress toward their vision, mission, goals, and objectives. The Appalachian Mountain Club's annual report identifies goals and annual progress toward those goals. Their goals pertain to the number of acres protected, the management of miles of trails, the number of outdoor experiences provided, the provision of outdoor education experiences, and the amount of literature about the environment distributed. The annual report also identifies income sources, expenditure categories, levels of income and expenditures, and the impact of the expenditures upon individuals, regions, and the goals of the organization.

From a financial standpoint, a common measure of efficiency is the percent of the operating budget spent for administration. Nonprofit organizations desire to maintain a low administrative cost, striving to spend the bulk of their operating budget on programs and services. The Appalachian Mountain Club, for example, spent 7.7% of its operating budget on administration in 2016 (Appalachian Mountain Club, 2018).

For comparison purposes, Table 1.1 summarizes the organizational features, sources of revenue, and measures of success for public and private nonprofit leisure service organizations.

Commercial Enterprises

Sport, tourism, and leisure service enterprises operating in the commercial sector are distinguished from the others previously discussed by their profit motivation. It is important to note that "profit motivation," rather than "profit generation," is given as the defining characteristic. Commercial sport, tourism, and leisure enterprises may not always produce profits (especially in the early stages of development or during off-seasons), but the commercial enterprise will only stay in business if, over a reasonable period of

Table 1.1

Public and Private Nonprofit Organizations Compared on Structure, Revenue, and Measures of Success

Sector	Public	Nonprofit
Examples of organizations	State park systems, county park systems, community park and recreation agencies	Boys & Girls Clubs, YMCA, YWCA, swim club, scouting organizations, conservation organizations, support groups for public agencies
Sources of revenue	Primarily taxes (property tax), dedicated taxes, fees and charges	Grants, membership fees, fund-raising, donors, fees and charges, government grants
Financial measures of success	Fees and charges generated, financial accountability	Achievement of goals, objectives, and outcomes

time, an expected return on the investment is eventually realized. These organizations do not exist out of a need for a particular type of service. They exist because satisfying the need for a particular type of service is profitable. Commercial sector organizations do not receive tax revenues—they pay taxes. Commercial sector organizations do not typically receive operating grants or other forms of gratuitous income—they are called upon to make donations. Commercial sector organizations do not use volunteers—they support them. Because the commercial sector exists to benefit certain individuals (investors), it does not have access to the major revenue sources utilized by public and private nonprofit agencies. Commercial sport, tourism, and leisure businesses must cover most or all of their costs of operating by charging fees, sell-

ing goods and services, and making other types of investments. Examples of commercial sector sport, tourism, and leisure service organizations include professional sports teams, resorts, amusement parks, meeting management companies, bowling centers, movie theaters, outdoor outfitters, and travel managers.

Legislative/Legal Parameters

There are many laws aimed at supporting and regulating commercial activity. Profit-motivated sport, tourism, and leisure service organizations are subject to those laws that apply to their particular situations. The application of some laws will vary depending upon whether the sport, tourism, or leisure business is set up as a corporation, syndicate, or partnership, or is individually owned.

Social Roles/Expectations

The primary social role or social expectation of the commercial sport, tourism, and leisure enterprise is to contribute to the economic well-being of the community. Proposals for new commercial enterprises often highlight community benefits such as diversity in leisure options, opportunities for social interaction, promotion of health, development of community pride, and educational enrichment, but the benefit that is most eagerly sought is described in terms of jobs created, household income produced, sales activity, and tax revenue generated. Of course, there is the basic expectation that the enterprise will be consistent with community social standards, but the economic impact of the venture is regarded with the most interest and concern.

Market Management Techniques

Market management in commercial sport, tourism, and leisure services is designed to do one thing: tap consumer spending power. Therefore, the only market that is of interest is the market that can pay enough and is willing to pay enough to help the organization realize its financial goals.

Responsiveness to market conditions is a key to success in commercial enterprises, and this responsiveness is often reflected in pricing strategies and in the use of advertising as a major promotional tool. Pricing strategies in the commercial sector focus on the total bottom line. That is, variation in pricing is frequently used to attract consumers by responding to price sensitivity on certain elements of the total service package. In a movie theater, for example, the admission price may be reduced to

a point where it barely covers the costs of providing the cinematic opportunity, and yet, the price of the popcorn may be kept at a level that consumers can accept and that make the whole movie-going event (movie + snacks) profitable for the theater operator. The commercial sector is usually more responsive and more flexible in pricing than organizations in the public and private nonprofit sectors. For similar reasons, the commercial sector is also more inclined than other types of organizations to use advertising (both institutional and product) to promote desired consumer responses.

Indicators of Success

Financial managers in the commercial sector measure their success by comparing their achievements to their goals. Unlike their counterparts in the public and private nonprofit sectors, managers of commercial enterprises set goals that focus on the financial growth of the enterprise and on the return on the investment made therein. The balance sheet and the income statement serve as the primary evaluation documents rather than participant evaluation surveys. There is concern for the quality of consumers' experience, but only so far as it affects the financial bottom line. The commercial sport, tourism, and leisure service organization also measures its success by comparing its financial ratios with standards established for the industry. Financial ratios are discussed further in Chapter 16.

Financial Management Opportunities and Challenges

Commercial sport, tourism, and leisure service organizations enjoy several opportunities that are somewhat unique to this sector. Because they are profit motivated, they are not required to prop up socially beneficial but financially ineffective programs and services and can, as a result, concentrate on maximizing the utility of their assets. They can more easily identify and avoid products that do not meet their standards of success. The entrepreneurial spirit has free rein in the commercial sport, tourism, and leisure business environment, and managers find excitement in the many opportunities to move resources from areas of low productivity to initiatives that offer greater results.

Challenges associated with financial management in the commercial sport, tourism, and leisure service organization include developing the knowledge and skill competencies required in order to be effective. Foremost among the skill requirements are investment management, bookkeeping, and financial forecasting. Effective financial managers continually add to their store of management abilities by reading and studying, attending conferences and workshops, and furthering their formal education in this discipline.

Focus: Sport Organizations in the Commercial Sector

Many sport organizations operate in the private nonprofit sector. There are, however, major organizations that are part of a vibrant and economically significant commercial sport industry. The following discussion focuses on the sport industry and addresses several key finance-related topics.

Sport as an Industry

The business of sport has a tremendous financial and cultural impact on contemporary society. Jobs in sports are not limited to intercollegiate athletics and major professional leagues. Opportunities for a career in sports cross over into other entertainment-related industries, from video gaming and fantasy leagues, to sport tourism and event hospitality. The growth of the sport industry in recent years can be attributed to (a) increased interest in sport from diverse market segments such as women, minorities, and aging individuals; (b) increased offerings of new and different forms of sports; (c) growth in corporate sponsorship; (d) increased coverage of sports and sporting events and on television, Internet, and the radio; (e) the influence of technology on sport-related goods, services, and training; and (f) increased numbers and variety of print and online media related to sports. This growth has influenced local job creation and entrepreneurial activity, but there is no consensus on the broader economic impact of the sport industry as a whole. The lack of consensus results, in part, from the fact that "sport" is not classified as an industry in the North American Industrial Classification System (NAICS—a system devised by the U.S. Census Bureau to identify industries based on the similarities of firms in economic activities). Without that classification, statistics are not collected nor analyzed in a way that readily permits independent examination of the economic contribution of sports and sport-related activities.

An industry is a collection of businesses and consumers that have similar products and markets, and that engage in similar economic activities. NAICS uses the similarity of economic activity to classify businesses in North America into 20 distinct sectors, including Arts, Entertainment, and Recreation.

NAICS industries are identified by a six-digit code in order to be placed in the hierarchical structure of the classification system. The first two digits refer to the industry sector, the third digit identifies the industry sub-sector, the fourth designates the industry group, the fifth refers to the NAICS industry, and the sixth digit designates the national industry (U.S., Canadian, or Mexican). Take, for example, the six-digit code for U.S. sports teams and clubs (711211):

71	Industry Sector (Arts, Entertainment, & Recreation)
711	Industry Sub-sector (Performing Arts, Spectator Sports and Related Industries)
7112	Industry Group (Spectator Sports)
71121	Industry (Spectator Sports)
711211	U.S. specific (Sports Teams and Clubs)

The definitions that NAICS provides for the North American Industry of Spectator Sports (71121), and the U.S.-specific Industry of Sport Teams and Clubs (711211) are:

71121 Spectator Sports

This industry comprises (1) sports teams or clubs primarily participating in live sporting events before a paying audience; (2) establishments primarily engaged in operating racetracks; (3) independent athletes engaged in participating in live sporting or racing events before a paying audience; (4) owners of racing participants, such as cars, dogs, and horses, primarily engaged in entering them in racing events or other spectator sports events; and (5) establishments, such as sports trainers, primarily engaged in providing specialized services to support participants in sports events or competitions. The sports teams and clubs included in this industry may or may not operate their own arena, stadium, or other facility for presenting their games or other spectator sports events.

711211 Sports Teams and Clubs

This U.S. industry comprises professional or semiprofessional sports teams or clubs primarily engaged in participating in live sporting events, such as baseball, basketball, football, hockey, or soccer, before a paying audience. These establishments may or may not operate their own arena, stadium, or other facility for presenting these events.

NAICS does not consider sport as a major economic activity, and does not designate commercial sport organizations as part of a stand-alone industry or industrial sector. The wide range of commercial sport-related activities is scattered across several of the 20 industry sectors, such as construction, manufacturing, wholesale and retail trade, real estate, rental and leasing, education services, arts, entertainment and recreation, and other services. This dispersion makes it difficult to reconcile sales or financial data (attributed to sport activities) from each of these sectors and, therefore, next to impossible to accurately estimate the economic magnitude of the sport industry. Since the government has no system in place to estimate the annual impact of sport on the U.S. economy, several analysts and scholars have tried to develop a reliable measurement for the sport industry. It is estimated that, in 2016, the direct global economic impact of the sports industry was $35 billion (approximately $18 billion in the United States) (Charaf, 2016).

The importance of the sport industry and the unique aspects of financial management in sport organizations are highlighted in the following discussions.

Public Subsidization of Sport Facilities

The significance of modern spectator sports is evident in the number of cities entering the race to build expensive new sport facilities (using, to a great extent, public money) for the purpose of attracting professional sport franchises. Proponents of such endeavors argue that hosting a professional sports team provides increased community visibility, enhanced community image, stimulated development, and higher levels of psychic income (emotional and psychological benefits of sports) for the residents of that community. As a result, local and state governments work closely together to either attract professional teams, or to prevent their existing professional sports teams from going elsewhere. In the first decade and a half of the millennium, local, state, and federal governments have allocated more than $12 billion of taxpayers' money to subsidize many new major league stadiums and arenas, and a larger number of minor league sport facilities (Farren, 2017). In the two decades since 1997, 20 National Football League (NFL) stadiums were built with the assistance of $5 billion of taxpayer funds (Foxsports, 2016). Experts have argued that the public subsidy is more like $15 billion when hidden and indirect costs are also considered. The practice of using public resources to support private and commercial sport enterprises is growing, and governments continue to spend to subsidize major sport facilities.

For example, construction of the Mercedes-Benz Stadium that is home to the NFL team Atlanta Falcons cost $1.5 billion, of which $700 million came from the public purse (deMause, 2017).

Critics have voiced concern about the spiraling costs that seem to be making the entire big league sports structure unworkable, and have challenged the assumption that publicly supported sports stadiums justify themselves financially. Advocates of sport facility subsidies argue that the use of public money to fund their development and operation provides the following benefits:

- Injection of substantial amounts of money into local economies
- Creation of new jobs
- Revitalization of urban neighborhoods.

The opposing claims have been thoroughly investigated. Economist Robert Baade conducted a study that investigated 30 U.S. cities that had built new sport facilities during the last 30 years (Baade, 1990). The findings were disappointing for proponents of subsidized sport developments. His study demonstrated that the development of new sport facility projects does not have a positive effect on local economies. In 27 of the cities examined, the effect of major sport developments on the per-capita income was not significant, and in the remaining three cases, the sport facility had a significantly negative impact on the local economy. Two explanations for these findings are offered: the substitution effect and revenue leakages (Coates and Humphreys 2003, 2004).

The substitution effect measures how much money is simply transferred from other entertainment, food, and retail venues in town, as fans may decide to spend their disposable income on stadium food and merchandise instead of at the local restaurants and retail stores.

Revenue leakage is a measure of the degree to which stadium spending is taken out of the local economy before it can be recirculated. Leakage is taking place because team owners and players usually live, invest, and spend money outside of the local economy.

The myth of new job creation attributed to sport facilities also collapsed under the weight of evidence found in this study. In testimony to a Congressional Committee on government reform, Neil DeMause pointed out that

> where good job-development programs can cost about $10,000 for each new job created, sport facilities typically come in at as much as $250,000 in public cost for each new job, a worse ratio than some of the most infamous corporate giveaways in history. (deMause, 2017)

Also, the belief that sport facilities can be used to revitalize urban neighborhoods was not justified, especially for seasonal operations such as baseball and football. There is no evidence that a new sport facility is going to attract further development such as restaurants, sport bars, retail space, and entertainment venues, especially when the facility is closed for most of the year.

Television Ratings and Broadcasting Fees

The entertainment value of sporting events is evident in the large fees that television networks are paying to rightholders in order to broadcast professional or intercollegiate sporting events. The amount of money that is paid is greatly influenced by the television ratings and shares that each professional league, game, individual athlete, and conference captures when the sporting event is aired for public consumption. A single rating point means that, of all television-equipped households in the country (118.4 million in 2016), 1% (1,184,000) were tuned in to the show being measured. A share indicates the percentage of all televisions being viewed that were tuned in to the particular show. High television ratings and shares are desirable because they mean that bigger audiences are watching the event. Advertisers and sponsoring companies are attracted to sporting events that capture high broadcast ratings and shares, and they are willing to spend large amounts of money to secure advertising space and time when these events are broadcast.

In the 2016 regular NFL season, a typical game was watched by 16.5 million people (13.9 rating, 27.3% share). That same season, the Super Bowl game attracted 172 million viewers and scored a 43.5 rating and 68% share. Similar success in securing high TV ratings was also experienced by the National Basketball Association (NBA) and Major League Baseball (MLB). Major League Baseball's World Series captured a 16.8 rating in 2016.

Television ratings are also used as a negotiation tool between network executives and leagues officials when contracts are just about to expire, or other media products, such as Internet broadcasting, pay-per-view sporting events, satellite sport packages, etc., are available for bid. The importance of broadcast revenue is evident in the 2014 deal between the NFL and four high-profile U.S. television networks (CBS, Fox, NBC, and ESPN). To share the broadcasting rights to NFL games between 2004 and 2022, the networks will pay the NFL $42.6 billion (Statista, 2018).

The NFL is not alone in realizing significant financial benefits from broadcast partnerships. The National Basketball Association (NBA) increased its revenue by $24 billion in 2016 by signing a 9-year extension to its broadcast agreement with ESPN and TNT (CBC, 2014).

Major League Baseball and the National Hockey League (NHL) also experienced success in negotiating their own television and broadcast contracts. For broadcast rights between 2014 and 2022, Fox, TBS, and ESPN will pay MLB $12.4 billion. From 2013 to 2025, the Canadian network Rogers Sportsnet will pay the NHL $5.2 billion (Settimi, 2012; Sportsnet, 2017).

There are also noteworthy developments in intercollegiate sports. Some National Collegiate Athletic Association (NCAA) conferences have established broadcast new channels dedicated to showcasing sporting events and other accomplishments of its member institutions. As joint ventures between the conference and broadcast networks, these channels produce and transmit programs that are designed to dramatically increase the visibility of the conference and, of course, generate additional revenue.

Franchise Values and Player Salaries

Additional evidence of the importance and magnitude of professional sports business can be found in skyrocketing values of franchises and player contracts. Franchises in almost all major leagues have experienced significant increases in their value and, by 2016, at least one (Dallas Cowboys [NFL]) was worth more than $4 billion. Another NFL team, the New England Patriots, experienced phenomenal growth in value: the franchise was purchased in 1994 for $172 million. It was a record high price to pay for a team but, by 2018, its value had risen to over $38 billion (Forbes, 2018).

Forbes magazine conducts an annual survey and publishes the actual market value of all professional sport franchises in the country. The survey takes into consideration a number of valuating factors, such as the franchise's annual operating income, the stadium/arena value, the size of the market in which the club operates, the aggregate value of the roster, etc. The highest valued teams in 2016 are shown in Table 1.2.

Players' contracts have also been increasing in value. In 2018-2019, the NBA paid the highest average player salary ($7.4 million) (Basketball Reference 2018). Its highest paid player was Stephen Curry, who received $37.5 million for his services (ESPN, 2018). The average salary for a MLB player in 2016 was $4.4 million, and Clayton Kershaw was the highest paid team member, earning $32 million. NHL player compensation in the 2016-17 season averaged $2.9 million. The highest paid man on ice was Anze Kopitar with a $10 million salary. Although NFL franchises are the most valuable, professional football players' average salary in 2016 was "only" $2.1 million. The highest paid gridiron star was Drew Brees ($31.25 million). The top earning Major League Soccer (MLS) in 2016 was Ricardo Kaka. He earned $7.2 million. The average MLS player salary was $309,000 (Badenhausen, 2016).

Attendance Costs of Sporting Events

Gate receipts for amateur, college, and professional sports significantly

Table 1.2

Highest Valued U.S. and Canadian Professional Sport franchises in 2017

Rank	Team / Value	Rank	Team / Value
	National Football League		**National Basketball Association**
1	Dallas Cowboys $4.2 billion	4	New York Knicks $3.3 billion
3	New England Patriots $3.4 billion	6	Los Angeles Lakers $3.0 billion
5	New York Giants $3.1 billion	16	Golden State Warriors $2.6 billion
6	San Francisco 49ers $3.0 billion	18	Chicago Bulls $2.5 billion
8	Washington Redskins $2.95 billion	26	Boston Celtics $2.2 billion
	Major League Baseball		**National Hockey League**
2	New York Yankees $3.7 billion	>40	New York Rangers $1.5 billion
10	Los Angeles Dodgers $2.75 billion	>40	Montreal Canadiens $1.25 billion
12	Boston Red Sox $2.7 billion	>40	Toronto Maple Leafs $1.4 billion
14	Chicago Cubs $2.68 billion	>40	Chicago Blackhawks $1.0 billion
15	San Francisco Giants $2.65 billion	>40	Boston Bruins $890 million

Source: *Forbes,* 2017

contribute to the multibillion-dollar impact the sport industry has on the U.S. economy. In 2015/16, the NFL averaged 69,487 spectators per game in its regular season (Statista, 2017). In the same year, MLB recorded an average regular season game attendance of 30,163. High average attendance was also recorded at regular contests in MLS (21,693), the NBA (17,849), and the NHL (17,548) (Statista, 2017).

With attendance in professional sports hitting an all-time high, there are some concerns about the escalating costs of attending a sporting event, especially for middle- and low-income individuals and families. The Fan Cost Index (FCI), a survey conducted annually by Team Marketing Report provides a measure of how much a family of four will likely spend during a night out at a professional sporting event. The FCI is simply the sum of costs for four average-price tickets; four small soft drinks; two small beers; four hot dogs; two game programs; parking; and two adult-size team caps.

According to the 2015 FCI, the most expensive sport facility hosting an NFL game was the Dallas Cowboys' AT&T Stadium. The average ticket price was $110.20. The Cowboys' 2015 FCI was $634.80 (which was almost $154 higher than the NFL average). The average NFL game ticket was priced at $85.83, while the league average FCI was $480.89. In 2015, the NBA average FCI was $333.58, and, in the same year, the National Hockey League (NHL) recorded an average FCI

$211.68. Sample FCIs for teams from four of the major professional leagues in the U.S. are presented in Tables 1.3–1.6. Item costs that contribute to the calculation of the FCI are also shown.

Table 1.3

Item Cost($) and Fan Cost Indexes (FCI) for Selected National Football League Teams (2016)

Team	Avg. Ticket	Beer	Soda	Hot Dog	Parking	Program	Cap	FCI
Dallas Cowboys	110.20	8.50	5.00	5.50	75.00	10.00	20.00	634.80
Chicago Bears	108.44	9.25	5.00	5.00	49.00	5.00	25.00	601.20
Atlanta Falcons	78.83	7.50	6.50	5.50	20.00	0	20.00	438.33
New York Jets	105.66	5.00	3.00	6.00	25.00	10.00	20.00	553.63
Pittsburg Steelers	83.97	8.00	4.75	5.25	40.00	5.00	19.95	481.78
NFL Average	**85.83**	**7.42**	**4.79**	**5.29**	**31.21**	**3.91**	**21.46**	**480.89**

Table 1.4

Item Cost($) and Fan Cost Indexes (FCI) for Selected Major League Baseball Teams (2016)

Team	Avg. Ticket	Beer	Soda	Hot Dog	Parking	Program	Cap	FCI
Boston Red Sox	52.34	7.75	5.00	5.25	35.00	--	25.00	350.86
Washington Nationals	36.02	6.50	5.00	5.25	10.00	--	12.00	232.08
Los Angeles Dodgers	28.61	6.25	6.00	5.50	10.00	--	18.00	218.94
Atlanta Braves	19.14	7.25	4.75	4.75	15.00	--	15.00	174.06
Arizona Diamondbacks	17.98	4.00	1.50	2.75	10.00	--	9.99	126.89
MLB Average	**28.94**	**5.98**	**4.07**	**4.39**	**15.89**	**--**	**17.12**	**211.68**

Table 1.5

Item cost($) and Fan Cost Indexes (FCI) for Selected National Basketball Association Teams (2016)

Team	Avg. Ticket	Beer	Soda	Hot Dog	Parking	Program	Cap	FCI
Boston Red Sox	52.34	7.75	5.00	5.25	35.00	--	25.00	350.86
Washington Nationals	36.02	6.50	5.00	5.25	10.00	--	12.00	232.08
Los Angeles Dodgers	28.61	6.25	6.00	5.50	10.00	--	18.00	218.94
Atlanta Braves	19.14	7.25	4.75	4.75	15.00	--	15.00	174.06
Arizona Diamondbacks	17.98	4.00	1.50	2.75	10.00	--	9.99	126.89
MLB Average	**28.94**	**5.98**	**4.07**	**4.39**	**15.89**	**--**	**17.12**	**211.68**

Table 1.6

Item Cost($) and Fan Cost Indexes (FCI) for Selected National Hockey League Teams (2016)

Team	Avg. Ticket	Beer	Soda	Hot Dog	Parking	Program	Cap	FCI
Boston Bruins	88.70	8.50	5.75	5.75	42.00	5.00	20.00	509.80
Pittsburg Penguins	73.59	5.25	3.00	5.00	18.00	0	18.00	390.84
San Jose Sharks	54.68	6.25	4.00	4.00	21.00	5.00	25.00	344.42
New York Islanders	49.21	9.75	5.00	6.25	8.25	0	15.00	299.59
Florida Panthers	33.39	8.00	5.00	6.50	20.00	0	20.00	255.55
NHL Average	**62.18**	**7.45**	**4.46**	**4.94**	**17.70**	**2.60**	**19.75**	**363.58**

Focus: Tourism and Commercial Recreation Organizations

By most economic standards, tourism is the world's third largest industry, and is, for many countries, states, regions, or cities, the most important income generator. Commercial recreation enterprises serve tourists and host communities alike and contribute significantly to local economies. The following discussion focuses on tourism and commercial recreation industries and addresses several key finance-related topics.

Scope and Cross-Sector Nature

Managing financial resources in tourism and commercial recreation enterprises requires most of the same skills that should be applied in sport organizations or public and private nonprofit leisure service agencies. The skills may be the same, but the purpose of the tourism and commercial recreation organization will likely differ significantly. Tourism and commercial recreation are industries. Each industry is comprised of corporations, businesses, and organizations that have a common goal of generating financial and economic benefits for the owners. Commercial recreation businesses are an important part of the community leisure service inventory, as well as to the local economy. Similarly, tourism enterprises are not public social services, but their contributions to the economic well being of a community are significant, and they are likely to have positive social impacts.

Unlike commercial recreation businesses, tourism organizations operate in the public, private nonprofit, and commercial sectors. In some situations, local, state, and national governments fund tourism agencies and attractions, and in other situations there are private nonprofit organizations that exist to support industry and community efforts

Table 1.7

Funding Sources and Measures of Success for Tourism Organizations in the Public, Private Nonprofit, and Commercial Sectors

Sector	Public	Private Nonprofit	Commercial
Examples of tourism organizations	State or city tourism department	Destination marketing organization	Attractions, hotels, transportation, and other profit-oriented businesses
Sources of revenue	Primarily taxes (general or lodging/meal taxes)	Grants, earned income, donations, tax transfers	Earned income (investment, sales, fees and charges)
Financial measures of success	Tax revenue generated	General "health of the industry," sales statistics	Liquidity, solvency, profitability, return on investment

to attract visitors and guests. Of course, commercial tourism enterprises are also plentiful. The sources of funding and financial measures of success for tourism organizations in each sector are outlined in Table 1.7.

Financial Objectives

Financial decisions and operations in the tourism commercial recreation industries must address the goal of creating added value (improving the bottom line), and all appropriate accounting methods and investment activities should be applied to that end. In spite of a financial manager's passion for the destination, attraction, activity, or amenity, and regardless of any genuine interest in providing good service just because good service is the right thing to do, managers in tourism and commercial recreation must remain focused on the ultimate goal of generating a measurable profit.

In these industries, decisions about facilities to build or services to offer are viewed as investment decisions. Whether or not a tourism or commercial recreation project is developed or a program is implemented depends on how well it will generate expected returns under expected risk conditions. For example, a waterpark feature at a resort is only worth building if it generates more short-term and long-term returns than would be realized by simply putting the required capital development funds in the bank in a nominal interest-bearing account. As exciting as the waterpark may be, it will not be built if the financial return is greater for some other profit-generating amenity on the same site. Furthermore, investments are made not just to satisfy markets but to attract and serve those markets with the greatest spending potential. Chapter 16 discusses

investment decisions and provides the tools for evaluating proposed initiatives.

Debt and Inventory Management

In tourism and commercial recreation businesses, financial managers have two major interests: liquidity and solvency. *Liquidity* refers to the corporation's ability to meet its short-term financial obligations. In other words, it must be able to pay its bills. Assuring the availability of sufficient cash (liquid assets) for the payment of bills is an ongoing management task. *Solvency* refers to the corporation's ability to meet its long-term financial obligations. Long-term obligations include debt to creditors and the owner's claim to the corporation's assets. The entire management team of the tourism or commercial recreation organization must be concerned with maintaining an appropriate level of debt and ensuring a suitable return on the owner's investment.

Financial managers in tourism and commercial recreation enterprises must also be concerned about inventory turnover. An inventory turnover ratio tells the manager how effectively the costs of delivery goods to customers are being contained. For example, a low inventory ratio indicates that there may be an overinvestment in inventory and, therefore, unnecessarily high storage or distribution costs.

Account Management

In the tourism industry especially, there are also some unique situations that affect the way accounts are managed. In a hotel or resort, for example, each guest has an account to which charges and payments may be made at any time of the day or night, any day of the week. Thousands of those accounts may be opened and closed each day at one property. Additionally, payments for tourism services such as cruise ship passage or air transportation may be made in advance of the service being provided, or may include some sort of deposit. Payments received and expenditure commitments made before and after a service is delivered affect cash flow and must be managed carefully. A third unique aspect of managing financial resources in tourism organizations is the use of foreign currencies. Guests come from many parts of the world and may have limited ability to submit deposits or guarantees in local currency. Furthermore, the enterprise itself may have overseas operations that use a different currency. Not only is there the need to convert currencies, but the fluctuating exchange rate and government regulations on the cross-border flow of funds will also impact financial management in the tourism enterprise. Finally, tourism services are notoriously susceptible to differential pricing strategies. That is, many different prices may be applied to a service that differs in no substantial way between consumers or production/delivery costs. Airline ticket pricing is a well-known and somewhat mystifying example. Chapter 11 should help to demystify the application of differential pricing in businesses such as airlines and hotels. The tourism financial manager must be able to work with highly variable revenue models based on differential pricing.

Reporting

In many organizations, sales and expenditures are predictable and sometimes steady. This is so for tourism and commercial recreation organizations that know their markets, can control demand, and successfully attract a loyal clientele. In such cases, financial activity reports and statements of financial outcomes can be prepared relatively infrequently and for comparable periods of time. For example, monthly reports and statements may be sufficient for monitoring financial progress at a year-round reception center, even though there may be some peak periods around wedding seasons and traditional holidays.

Special events and tourism destinations, attractions, or amenities that serve many people for short periods of time usually need more frequent reports of financial activity. Reports may be required as often as hourly in some cases. At resorts and hotels, for example, it is a common practice to prepare a daily operations report, an event report, and a night audit.

Performance Evaluation

Profit is the goal in tourism and commercial recreation enterprises, and the ultimate evaluation criterion will always be the amount of profit generated with respect to the amount of the investment made, or in other words, the return on the investment. It would, of course, be foolish for any manager of a tourism or commercial recreation enterprise to simply wait until the end of a fiscal period and then look at the investment return for that period before deciding how well the business is doing. Along the way, there are many other ways to assess the financial health and vitality of the organization.

One important evaluation criterion that is widely used and is unique to the lodging side of the tourism industry is known by the acronym RevPAR. It focuses on revenue and lodging room availability, and measures how effectively the resort or hotel fills rooms during the low-rate off-season, as well as during the high-rate peak season. RevPAR, identifies the Revenue Per Available Room, and differs from other measures that consider revenue per occupied room. Discussed further in Chapter 11, RevPAR is a valuable indicator of management effectiveness and is used by franchise companies, hotel owners, lenders, and management companies.

A Comparison

Although public, private nonprofit, and commercial sport, leisure service, and tourism organizations are alike in many ways, there are important differences among the three sectors with respect to financial management goals and practices. The foregoing discussion of differences is summarized in Table 1.8.

Cross-Sector Competition and Cooperation

Although there are important differences among sport, tourism, and leisure service organizations operating in the public, private nonprofit, and commercial sectors, this does not mean that these sectors never relate to each other. In one respect, they may be competitors trying to serve the same markets, provide the same kinds of services, or compete in other ways. In another respect, they may be cooperating in enterprises and activities that provide mutual benefits. It would not be unusual, for example, to see similar aquatics programs offered to a community by the YMCA, the local college, and the city recreation department. In this case, the three agencies (representing public and private nonprofit sectors) are competing directly for customers. On the other hand, the city and the YMCA may also have an agreement that youth soccer

leagues will be offered exclusively by the YMCA, while the city recreation department will offer all softball and baseball programs in the community. Furthermore, a commercial local sport management firm might be contracted by both agencies to train and manage the officials and the umpires for both the soccer and baseball leagues, or cooperate with public and nonprofit organizations in hosting a tourism-generating regional or national tournament.

Competition among public, private nonprofit, and commercial agencies provides a number of benefits. They include the following:

- Greater choice for consumers (e.g., variety in program features, scheduling, location, price)
- Greater attention to high-quality service (necessary for maintaining competitive advantage)
- Greater ability to respond to increasing demand
- Greater opportunity to focus on specific market segments (i.e., establish a market niche)

Cooperation among public, private nonprofit, and commercial sport and leisure service agencies also provides some benefits. They include the following:

- Operational efficiency (by reducing duplication of physical and human resources)
- Synergism (i.e., the total benefit of agencies working together can be greater than the sum of the benefits provided by each alone)
- A coordinated approach to the delivery of sport, tourism, and leisure services in the community (ensuring that a full range of needs and interests are considered)

Table 1.8

A Summary of Finance-Related Similarities and Differences among Public, Private Nonprofit, and Commercial Sport, Tourism, and Leisure Service Organizations

Area of Contrast	Public	Private Nonprofit	Commercial
Ownership	Usually government	Private organization	Private corporation
Legal Authority	Through enabling legislation	Through enabling legislation and designation of tax status	Through incorporation (state and federal government recognition, regulation, and protection)
Mandate	Serve social welfare and commonwealth needs of all citizens	Serve specific social welfare needs or leisure interests of a specific population	Realize maximum return on investment through service to most profitable market
Source of Funds	Taxes, grants, donations, earned income	Grants, memberships, donations, fundraising activities, earned income	Investors, creditors, earned income
Market Management	Market limited to geographic/political constituency Market segmented on basis of need Might not compete	Market defined by particular need	Market composed of those who can pay Defined by merit
Success indicators	Social change	Social change Financial viability	Profitability Growth Return on investment
Opportunities	Tax exemption Volunteers Bulk purchasing and discounts	Tax exemption Volunteers Public concern	Entrepreneurship Support for eliminating financially unsuccessful products
Challenges	Public accountability and scrutiny Changing political directions	Relative uncertainty Reliance on gratuitous income and volunteers Limited, qualified staff Inconsistent leadership	Developing and maintaining skills

- Conversion of competitive energy to service energy

Summary

The delivery of sport, tourism, and leisure service in the community is achieved through a system that includes organizations operating in the public, private nonprofit, and commercial sectors. The purpose of financial management in public and nonprofit entities is to enhance programs, service, facilities, and areas for the public good, to improve the quality of life of community members or people in general, and to meet the goals of the organization in an effective and efficient manner.

Public agencies have a clear social mandate and are supported by public funds, especially tax revenues. Public entities, while conforming to some commercial business practices, are nonprofit enterprises and generally are not expected to generate excess revenue. There are a few exceptions to this rule. Public organizations operate within legislatively mandated guidelines, reporting to elected or appointed lay and professional individuals.

Private nonprofit agencies do not receive tax dollars to fund their operations, but rather seek funding through donations and enterprise activities. They may, through service fees and other fundraising activities, generate profits; but those profits are used to maintain the organization and sustain other nonprofitable activities or services. Private nonprofit organizations have an internal structure for reporting with the Internal Revenue Service that, in turn, provides some external review for financial accountability. Financial success is defined in terms of solvency while impacting positive perceptions of the community, meeting social needs, providing opportunities for involvement, and reinforcing perception of value in the sport, tourism, or leisure service.

The purpose of financial investment in tourism and commercial recreation enterprises is to generate added value for the business or industry. Financial decisions, management procedures, and reporting mechanisms must address the achievement of this purpose. Tourism and commercial sport and recreation businesses have some unique circumstances that make managing financial re-

sources a challenging task. Accounts may be numerous and may be opened and closed in short periods of time. Short-term and long-term financial decisions require up-to-date data, thus requiring accurate and frequent reports. Corporate success in the tourism and commercial sport and recreation industries is measured primarily in terms of efficiency and effectiveness in generating profits and enhancing investments.

Although the three sectors differ in other ways, those differences do not deny them opportunities for direct competition and cooperation in service delivery.

References

Appalachian Mountain Club. (2018). Consolidated financial statement years ended December 31, 2017 and 2016. Tonneson & Co.

Baade, R. (1990). The impact of stadium and professional sports on metropolitan area development growth and change. *A Journal of Urban and Regional Policy, 21* (1– 14).

Badenhausen, K. (2016, December 15). The average player salary and highest paid in NBA, MLB, NHL, NFL and MLS. *Forbes.* Retrieved from https://www.forbes.com/sites/ kurtbadenhausen/2016/12/15/ average-player-salaries-in- major-american-sports- leagues/#6153d9321050

Badenhausen, K. (2017, July 12). Full list: The world's 50 most valuable sports teams 2017. *Forbes.*

Basketball Reference. (2018). 2018-19 NBA player contracts. Retrieved from https://www.basketball-reference. com/contracts/players.html

CBC Sports. (2014). NBA TV deal: How the new $24B contract stacks up against other leagues. Retrieved from https://www.cbc.ca/sports/basketball/nba/nba-tv-deal-how-the-new-24b-contract-stacks-up-against-other-leagues-1.2790143

Charaf, T. (2016). The importance of sport from an economic and social point of view. Retrieved from https://www.linkedin.com/pulse/importance-sport-from-economic-social-point-view-dr-tarek-charaf

Coates, D., & Humphreys, B. R. (2003). Professional sports facilities, franchises and urban economic development. *Public Finance &Management, 3*(3), 335.

Coates, D., & Humphreys, B. (2004, October). *Caught stealing: Debunking the economic case for D.C.* Baseball. CATO Institute.

deMause, N. (2017, September 29). Why are Georgia taxpayers paying $700m for a new NFL stadium? *The Guardian.* Retrieved from https://www.theguardian.com/sport/2017/sep/29/why-are-georgia-taxpayers-paying-700m-for-a-new-nfl stadium

ESPN (2018). NBA salaries. Retrieved from http://www.espn.com/nba/salaries

Farren, M. (2017, July 3). America's priciest national pastime. Sports subsidies aren't worth the cost to taxpayers. *USA News and World Report.* Retrieved from https://www.usnews.com/opinion/economic-intelligence/articles/2017-07-03/sport-subsidies-are-a-terrible-deal-for-american-taxpayers

Forbes. (2018). Sports money: 2018 NFL valuations. Retrieved from https://www.forbes.com/teams/new-england-patriots/

Foxsports. (2016, March 31). Taxpayers have spent a staggering amount of money on NFL stadiums in the last 20 years. Retrieved from https://www.foxsports.com/nfl/story/nfl-new-stadiums-public-funding-how-much-atlanta-san-diego-minnesota-los-angeles-033116

Settimi, C. (2012, October 12). Baseball scores $12 billion in television deals. *Forbes.* Retrieved from https://www.forbes.com/sites/christinasettimi/2012/10/02/baseball-scores-12-billion-in-television-deals/#32429d7771d3

Sportsnet. (2017). Rogers and CBC sign new 7-year deal for Hockey Night in Canada. Retrieved from https://www.sportsnet.ca/hockey/nhl/rogers-cbc-sign-new-7-year-deal-hockey-night-canada/

Statista. (2017). Average per game attendance of the five major sports leagues in North America 2015/16. Retrieved from https://www.statista.com/statistics/207458/per-game-attendance-of-major-us-sports-leagues/

Statista. (2018). Total value of NFL national TV broadcasting rights deals from 2014 to 2022 (in billion U.S. dollars). Retrieved from https://www.statista.com/statistics/615678/nfl-national-television-broadcast-deals/

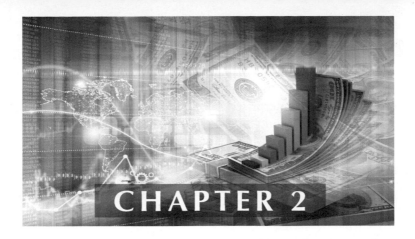

CHAPTER 2

Functions and Organization

Introduction

Effective management of financial resources in the sport, tourism, and leisure service organization requires the assumption and recognition of responsibility, as well as the deliberate assignment of authority and duties to the appropriate departments, offices, and individuals. Those who are responsible for the financial well-being of the organization are the financial decision makers. They are the ones who are the sources of authority, and they are the ones who are ultimately held accountable for the consequences of their decisions. Those to whom they delegate authority may make financial decisions within the parameters of their stewardships, but they typically function with limited responsibility as financial administrators. Financial administrators are those in the organization who are authorized to implement financial policies and follow established financial management procedures. They have specific duties and authority and are responsible not for the financial well-being of the organization,

but rather for how they perform their duties and exercise their authority.

This chapter examines the elements of organizational structures that are designed to facilitate the integrated efforts of financial decision makers, financial administrators, and program/facility managers in sport, tourism, and leisure service agencies. It also describes the roles of the different types of financial managers in a variety of settings, including public agencies operating at all three levels of government; private nonprofit agencies with local, regional, and national programs; and commercial sport, tourism, and recreation enterprises of different sizes.

It also discusses the relationship of the department of finance to other organizational units, including those that also have some financial management roles. Additional discussion is devoted to developing an understanding of the extent to which financial management duties are shared by different people within typical organizations in public parks and recreation agencies, school athletic departments, private nonprofit organizations, and tourism enterprises.

Functions

Functional distinctions between the individuals or units within an organization are most evident on the vertical dimension of the organizational chart. Specifically, those who occupy positions at the top of the organizational chart are the financial decision makers, while those at the bottom of the chart are, in varying degrees, the financial administrators. For example, the owner of an indoor sports complex in a responsive market will, as the financial decision maker, establish policies about such things as cost recovery targets, free services, employee compensation, etc. However, the implementation of those policies is left to the financial administrators: program managers (who set prices and incur program costs), cashiers (who collect admission fees or check passes), and clerical staff (who handle the payroll).

Financial Responsibility

In the preceding example, the owner is responsible for her decisions, regardless of the outcomes. If she sets the cost recovery target too low, authorizes too many free passes, or pays her staff too well, then she may not make a profit. On the other hand, if she has instituted sound policies on cost recovery, complementary services, and employee compensation, then she is likely to enjoy a suitable return on her investment. The owner is responsible for either outcome.

In order to realize her financial goals, the sports complex owner will delegate authority and assign duties to her staff. The likelihood of her realizing a profit is dependent on her staff exercising that authority and performing their duties in

the way she expects. If they exceed the limits of their authority or fail to do their duty, the staff members are responsible for those offenses only; however, the owner is still responsible for the resulting profit or loss. In financial management, as in any other area of management, authority can be delegated, but responsibility cannot.

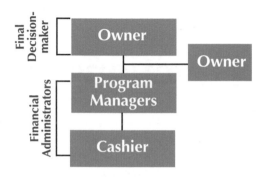

Figure 2.1. Financial Management Functions and Roles within the Organizational Structure

Financial Functions of the Organization

Sport, tourism, and leisure service organizations facilitate two primary financial functions: controlling and acquiring. *Controlling* is an internally oriented function that involves recording, monitoring, and managing the financial consequences of past and current activities. *Acquiring* is an externally oriented function that deals with securing financial resources required to meet current and future needs. The organizational chart of a sport, tourism, and leisure service agency will usually reflect these two functions by designating a *controller* and a *treasurer*. In large organizations, there may be many people working in both a controller's office and a treasurer's office; in smaller organizations, the two functions might be handled by the same person. Furthermore, that single controller/treasurer may also have other non-financial duties. Although desirable in certain situations, there is usually no requirement that a crowd of financial managers be included in the organizational structure. These two primary functions should, however, be adequately addressed in the structure.

The major financial management functions in the sport, tourism, and leisure service organization are handled by skilled individuals who have specific areas of responsibility. Several key positions and their functions are described below.

Director of finance. The duties of the director of finance include supervising and coordinating the activities of the department of finance. The director of finance serves as a financial adviser to decision-making bodies within the organization and often serves as the chief budget officer.

Controller (also called "Comptroller"). The controller's duties include describing (by using generally accepted accounting principles [GAAP]) the financial events that have occurred within a certain period of time. The controller develops and maintains a management information system and prepares financial forecasts for use by financial decision makers. Additional duties include pre-auditing purchase orders, handling receipts and disbursements, and issuing all payments and invoices. The controller may also be charged with maintaining inventory records.

Treasurer. The duties of the treasurer focus on the acquisition of funds needed for the operation of the sport and leisure service organization. Private funds may come from a variety of sources, thus requiring the treasurer in the private or commercial setting to maintain and nurture relationships with lenders, stockholders, security markets, and regulatory agencies. In contrast, the treasurer in a public agency works primarily with tax collection and fund generation through special assessments. In addition to collecting all revenues, the treasurer plans cash flow, invests available funds, and recommends pricing policies/strategies that will help to achieve funding objectives.

Assessor. Public sport, tourism, and leisure service organizations receive much of their funding from tax revenues. Property taxes are collected according to assessed property values, and the establishment of those values is the duty of the assessor. Working closely with the treasurer, the assessor applies relevant state laws, studies property values, and assesses property for taxation purposes.

Purchasing agent. The duties of the purchasing agent go well beyond processing paperwork for ordering materials, supplies, and equipment. An effective purchasing agent establishes standards for regularly purchased items and prepares specifications for each item to be purchased. By maintaining relationships with vendors and suppliers, the purchasing agent can economize on certain bulk or special order purchases, as well as advise program managers on new services or materials that are available. The purchasing agent purchases all materials, supplies, and equipment for the organization and then receives and inspects them to ensure that specifications have been met.

Significant monetary savings can also be realized through the purchasing agent's maintaining of warehouse storage and commodity distribution systems.

Auditor. Though not incorporated in the finance department, the auditor has a position of great importance to the financial well-being of the organization. The task of the auditor is to periodically provide an independent, objective evaluation of financial management systems and practices. The independent auditor serves as a check on executive officials by determining whether any errors (unintentional misstatements) have been made or whether there are irregularities (deliberate misstatements or unauthorized/illegal use or depletion of financial resources).

The auditor thoroughly reviews procedures and statements to determine and report whether the following are true:

- The financial statements present fairly the organization's financial position
- The financial statements accurately present (in accordance with GAAP) the results of agency operations
- The financial activities of the organization are in compliance with local, state/provincial, and federal laws and regulations
- The organization has established an adequate system of internal accounting and control
- There are questionable expenditures
- There is evidence of waste, abuse, or fraud

Since the finance department is the primary administrative body (and subject to input by executive officials), it would be unwise for the auditor's position to be too closely associated with that department. To avoid the appearance of the finance department checking up on itself, auditors are usually directly accountable to the chief executive officer or directing authority (board of directors, city council, etc.) and may not even be an employee of the agency. Many large and small sport, tourism, and leisure service organizations contract with or retain an independent accounting firm to serve as their auditor. In a few local governments, the audit function is carried out by an independently elected auditor or controller.

Organization

Financial management functions are the responsibility of specific financial officers (at least a controller and treasurer) and individuals within program units that receive revenues or make and approve expenditure commitments. Financial officers in large organizations might be housed (with respect to organizational structure) in a department of finance or similarly named unit.

Organization for Financial Management in the Public Sector

Figure 2.2 presents a basic organizational chart for a local government (e.g., a city, county, or town). Detailed in the chart are the relationships of the independent auditor to the elected governing body, and the Department of Finance to the institutional hierarchy and other civic departments. This model also represents the general structure of state/provincial and federal governments in the United States and Canada. Note that the responsibility and full authority to manage public finances is vested in the elected governing body. In a representative democracy, this authority comes from the people, and it is to them that the elected body is accountable.

Figure 2.2 shows an independent auditor who reports to the financial decision-making body. It is a standard practice and often a legal requirement for local, state/provincial, and federal governments to have auditors who submit public reports of their reviews to their respective legislatures. As much as possible, these auditors operate independently and without regard to personal or partisan politics.

Also shown in this basic organizational chart is the position of general manager. The general manager is the senior civil servant to whom all department heads report and through whom government policies are articulated. The director of finance reports to the general manager; thus making the latter an important figure in the financial management system. That importance is underscored by the dual role that the general manager, at times, appears to play. This top official is effectively both a financial decision maker and a financial administrator.

Technically, financial decision-making or policy setting does not exist at the level of the general manager; however, it must be recognized that this person is in a position to provide selective information that leads the elected body to make certain decisions. Thus he or she has *effective* decision-making power without having formal decision-making authority. The general manager is also the top financial administrator in the government and oversees the work of the director of finance. In this oversight role, the general manager interprets the policy decisions of the elected governing body and, thereby, has further opportunity to broadly influence financial management in the organization.

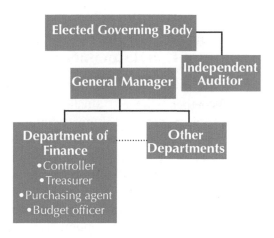

Figure 2.2. Basic Organizational Chart Emphasizing the Financial Management Unit

Figure 2.2 uses a dotted line to represent the relationship between the department of finance and the other governmental departments. The dotted line indicates that one department does not take direction from the other(s), but rather, departments must communicate and work together to ensure proper management of financial resources. In reality, the department of finance is a support unit to the other program-based departments, yet it does maintain control over most procedures pertaining to budget implementation. In some organizations, financial administrators working within program-based departments actually report both to the program department head and to the department of finance. This matrix structure can be an efficient way to manage financial functions with a degree of consistency, as well as avoid duplication that occurs when other departments feel the need to keep their own financial records and develop their own financial management information systems.

Organization for Financial Management in the Private, Nonprofit, and Commercial Sectors

Whether large, small, private nonprofit, or commercial, most nonpublic organizations will have a similar basic structure to the government organization typified in Figure 2.2. Instead of from an elected governing body, the private nonprofit agency will receive policies and directives from an appointed board of directors. In the commercial sector, the decision-making body will be the owner(s) or board that represents the shareholders.

The value of an independent auditor is just as great for nonprofit organizations as it is for public entities. The independent auditor position is frequently mandated by the organization's charter or bylaws. Some small, private nonprofit sport, tourism, and leisure service agencies rely on local volunteers to conduct their financial audits, while major commercial enterprises may have large in-house auditing departments.

As in the public agency, the day-to-day management of the private nonprofit or commercial organization is entrusted to the general manager. The title used for this top management position varies, but the most common alternatives are "chief executive officer" or "president."

Finally, the finance division is also an important part of private nonprofit and commercial sport, tourism, and leisure service organizations. In these nonpublic settings, the finance division continues to fulfill the basic functions of acquiring funds and controlling internal financial activities while relating in a supportive way to the organization's program-based departments.

Program Unit Involvement in Financial Management

Though not designated as financial managers, some individuals in the sport, leisure service, and tourism organization do manage financial resources. They are most likely program personnel who recommend and implement pricing strategies, collect fees, make expenditure commitments, and ensure that program activities are consistent with established fiscal parameters. In a public leisure service organization, for example, the Parks and Recreation Superintendent is responsible for developing and implementing an operating budget. The recreation manager makes purchases and wages commitments, as does the parks manager. The administrator and positions within the administrative support unit manage financial resources by controlling petty cash, purchasing, accounting, and reporting.

Figure 2.3. Units Within a Public Leisure Service Agency that are Involved in Managing Financial Resources (Shown as Gray Boxes)

In a school or college setting, an athletic department has a director who oversees all operations, including the use and acquisition of financial resources. The athletic director develops and implements a budget for athletic operations and oversees other areas that also manage finances. One important area for school athletic departments is fund-raising and development. The associate athletic director for external affairs spends a great deal of time and effort identifying and recruiting donors and sponsors, thus assuring an important source of income for the school. Managers of the athletic fund record and account for revenues into and expenditures from that account, but are also involved in helping the fund grow (through additional donations and investment). The associate athletic director for administration and finance makes certain that all bills are paid and that earned income is properly managed. This individual and others in subordinate units handle a wide variety of expenditure accounts, such as travel, lodging, licensing, staff compensation, marketing, administrative operations, accreditation/affiliation, etc. Income accounts that they manage include ticket sales, sponsorships, concessions, licensing, merchandising, etc.

In a private nonprofit sport, tourism, or leisure service organization, the executive director prepares and implements the budget. This individual also has a somewhat unique responsibility for encouraging fund-raising success and philanthropic support. In representing the nonprofit organization, the executive director works closely with the development manager to nurture giving relationships with individuals, foundations, and corporations. The facility manager manages financial resources as an expenditure officer and is expected to keep costs down and enhance the revenue potential of the facilities. The office manager records financial transactions, makes payments, issues invoices, receives revenue, handles payroll issues, and generates financial status reports and projections. The program coordinator provides programs while making expenditure commitments within the limits of the approved budget. The program coordinator is also involved in financial management when setting prices and determining the number and nature of revenue-generating programs and services.

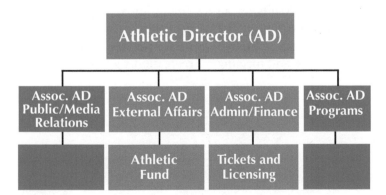

Figure 2.4. Units Within a School Athletic Department that are Involved in Managing Financial Resources (Shown as Gray Boxes)

Figure 2.5. Units Within a Private Nonprofit Organization that are Involved in Managing Financial Resources (Shown as Gray Boxes)

It is reasonable to expect that, in a commercial setting, financial resource management is shared by a wider range of positions within the organization than would be the case in public or private-nonprofit sport, tourism, and leisure service organizations. The general manager (GM) of a resort hotel, for example, must make the property earn a profit. The GM's job depends on it. Financial management becomes the primary concern of the GM, and he or she ensures that all subordinate managers and staff share that interest. The use of profit centers in resort hotels and other commercial enterprises pushes the concern for and involvement with financial procedures and results to all levels of management. The role of the human resources department is limited to salary and benefit issues, and meeting

the costs of training requirements. The accounting office is involved in financial management in an obvious way, and the marketing and sales department spends money for marketing and generates revenues through group and individual sales. Marketing and sales goals are expressed almost entirely in monetary terms. The food and beverage division plans and follows a budget for every catered event and for the operation of the restaurant, lounge, snack bar, café, food vending machines, and room service. Food and beverage managers must be smart purchasers and experts in limiting expenses by accurately estimating demand and consumption. The rooms and guest services unit generates revenue through the services they provide. This area includes resort recreation services, to which appropriate

Figure 2.6. Units Within a Hotel/Resort Organization that are Involved in Managing Financial Resources (Shown as Gray Boxes)

pricing structures should be applied and for which expenses should be kept to an appropriate minimum. The staff in each of these areas is usually keenly aware of the impact of their activities on the management of financial resources. Many of their operational decisions are, in fact, financial decisions.

Figures 2.3 to 2.6 illustrated the slight differences in organizational structures in sport, leisure, and tourism settings. There are very few organizations, if any, that do not decentralize the management of financial resources, at least to some degree. Likewise, there are probably no sport, tourism, and leisure service, and tourism organizations that leave all financial management activities up to just one office or person.

Politics and the Financial Management Organization

Managers of public sport, tourism, and leisure service organizations are generally quick to point out that there is no work environment where politics so much influences day-to-day management as it does in government agencies. Private nonprofit managers would likely disagree and describe the many frustrations that they experience in their own politically sensitive positions. Further claims to the title of "most political organization" could also be made by managers of commercial sport, tourism, and leisure service organizations who feel that too much of their time and energy is spent on keeping the owners happy rather than doing the job properly.

A reality of management life is the constant exposure to and influence of corporate politics: It is a part of public service management. It is a part of management in the private nonprofit sector. It is a part of how the commercial sport, tourism, and leisure service organization operates. It is natural, and it is not necessarily bad.

Financial decision makers are usually in such a position because their political viewpoint is consistent with that of the power base (i.e., the voters or the shareholders). It is believed that the management philosophy of the financial decision maker will lead to desired results, and the decision maker is, therefore, empowered to establish fiscal policies for the organization. Financial administrators are expected to reflect that management philosophy in their implementation of the fiscal policies. In reality, it is just as important for the financial administrator to be responsive to the political context as it is to be efficient and effective in performing the technical finance functions of the organization. To underscore the importance of this responsiveness, most financial administrators serve "at the pleasure of the board," and their job security depends on how well they reflect political ideologies and achieve desired results.

In some public organizations, however, there is a stated need for and an interest in achieving nonpartisan, technical competence in financial management. In other words, the voters want to be sure that their tax dollars are managed by the most competent financial administrator, regardless of their political party affiliation. In such cases, the organizational structure may include a variety of autonomous or semiautonomous elected fiscal agencies (ranging from boards of tax appeal to boards of assessors) and elected officers such as controllers, treasurers, and assessors. However, the more integrated financial system and organizational structure (with the general manager as the chief steward and distributor of authority) is most common in the public sector and almost universal in the private nonprofit and commercial sectors.

It should be noted that, while financial managers might not serve a political (i.e., policy-making) function in the organization, they are working in an environment that is influenced by political philosophies, structures, and behaviors. Financial management requires a set of skills that goes beyond accounting and forecasting, and includes interpersonal skills that allow the financial manager in sport, tourism, and leisure service organizations to respond to directives that don't always make the most financial sense. An important function of the financial manager is to advise about the "right" course, and about potential problems with politically motivated decisions. This responsibility is one that cannot be shirked, but it must be understood that the final decision is often made by somebody else in the organization.

Summary

The many aspects of financial management in the sport, tourism, and leisure service organization can most effectively and efficiently be addressed through an organizational structure that clearly defines the lines of authority and differentiates between financial decision-making bodies and financial administrators. Financial officers develop systems and apply standard procedures to monitor, control, and report on the financial position, activities, and future of the organization. They also implement policies that generate required financial resources, as well as relate to program-based departments. The general organization for financial management varies little between public, private nonprofit, and commercial agencies and maintains the same basic elements in both small and large enterprises.

Financial management specialists may be assigned to a distinct organizational unit and be directed to assist and support program units in such matters as payroll, invoicing, payments, and purchasing. Program specialists in other organizational units usually do have financial management responsibilities, but financial management is not the major skill that they possess, nor is it considered to be a defining element of their assignment.

A variety of organizational structures can support financial management relationships in sport, tourism, and leisure services. Typical structures vary and reflect the public, private nonprofit, or commercial nature of the enterprise. They also reflect the political realities of the corporate environment and emphasize the importance of hierarchy in financial resource management.

SECTION B

Budgeting

Budgets are important financial management tools, and the chapters in this section describe how budgets are prepared and managed. Operating and capital budgets are contrasted, and a description of the budget styles or formats that are most frequently used by sport, tourism, and leisure service organizations is presented. This discussion emphasizes the need for detailed attention to all aspects of planning to receive and spend financial resources. This section also provides helpful guidance in presenting a budget proposal.

CHAPTER 3

Budgeting Basics

Introduction

Individuals who are new to budgeting are sometimes overwhelmed with the expectation of putting numbers together to create meaning. As fewer people balance their own checkbooks, and more rely on computer programs, or choose not to track their finances, or pay others to manage their finances for them, the idea of taking on a task that requires even the most basic budgeting skills can seem daunting. Putting together a budget for a program, profit center, or an entire organization can be a challenging activity when budgeting skills and experience are lacking. This chapter addresses budgeting basics. It discusses simple, yet essential budget organization, articulates ground rules for developing program and activity budgets, and provides direction for structuring a larger budget document.

Most budgeting is a process of gathering, organizing, and reporting financial facts and plans in a format that is understandable to other individuals. It conforms to budgeting standards established by the parent organization and typically includes best and/or accepted practices. Every professional skill area has its own unique terminology as does budgeting. Budgeting, however, crosses professional disciplinary boundaries; that is, everyone has to do it! All organizations deal with budgeting, and thankfully, the basic concepts are common. Unique terms may be present within different industries and organizations, but the process of budgeting is much the same, whether for a small summer recreation program, a community festival, or the operation of a $26 million multisport complex.

Budget Construction Guidelines

There are some general rules that individuals, expert or novice, must follow when constructing budgets. Those new to budgeting would do well to apply these rules strictly. Those with budget experience understand the importance of following the rules and processes associated with budget construction.

One of the challenges with budgeting is that the individual constructing the budget rarely has all the information required to complete the process. Budgeting then, is a process that begins with gathering information that is readily available and seeking out the additional required information. Some of this information may be simple to acquire, other information may be more challenging. It is advisable to involve individuals who are directly impacted by the results of the budgeting process. If budgeting for a recreation center it would be prudent to include, for example, all the staff that have some element of budget responsibility. This might include the snack bar manager, the office manager, the facility maintenance manager, the program directors, and others who have some interaction with the expenditure or receipt of funds. The staff should gather budget information related to their areas of responsibility, such as the number of employees, their schedules, total hours worked, rates of pay, supplies consumed, unique expenditure needs, and other budget facts for the previous and current year, along with projected revenue and expenditure activities for the next budget period.

Gathering Information

All of the budget information should be organized and kept where it is readily available for use. Almost all organizations utilize computer software systems for data gathering, budget preparation, budget management, and budget reporting processes. The systems are becoming increasingly complex and provide a wealth of data to end users. Budget information should be gathered from previous budgets used for the same activity or program, from similar budgets available from other sources, or created by gathering information from previously unused sources. For example, salaries may be required, but how much to pay per hour may not be known. The organization may have a standardized pay scale for part-time and full-time salaries along with descriptions of how the salaries are to be applied. A budget for purchasing T-shirts could be based on an existing standing contract with a manufacturer, an outstanding purchase order, or a list of preferred vendors. There is almost always a source of information for gathering budget data. The challenge is to get the most accurate source. Modern budget systems are able to provide detailed data to the individual preparing the budget. It remains the preparer's responsibility to ensure that the information is accurate and relevant to their situation.

The budget data are organized around common categories. For instance, the most common categories for budgeting include salaries, small cost equipment, supplies, rentals, utilities, charges and services, and operations. Each of these categories might be subdivided. Salaries can be subdivided into full-time, permanent part-time, part-time, seasonal, contract, or others as specified by the organization. They can be subdivided again by type of function, such as a department or operating unit. An aquatics program may have the following seasonal or part-time employees classified as: lifeguard, head lifeguard, junior lifeguard, learn-to-swim instructor, assistant manager, manager, cashier, concession operator, concession manager, and so on. Each position most likely has a separate rate of pay that may fall within prescribed pay ranges. For example, the lifeguard might earn from $9.50 per hour to $17.00 per hour based on experience, number of years with the program, specialized training, and so forth. Figure 3.1 illustrates three

Figure 3.1. Sample Employee Categorization Scheme for Lifeguards

levels of categorization of lifeguards for the aquatic program described above (1) part-time employee to (2) lifeguard to (3) head lifeguard or lifeguard or junior lifeguard.

Anticipating costs associated with equipment can be equally challenging. Equipment falls into two different categories for purchasing. Some equipment, typically below a specific cost (such as $2,500) is considered operational (see Chapter 5) and appears in the operating budget. Equipment that is more expensive and may have a multiyear life-span is considered to be capital (see Chapter 16). Money for the operational and capital budgets comes from different income sources as discussed in Chapter 9. For a softball complex, chalk for lining the base paths, bases, pitching rubbers, lamps for field lighting, special soil for the field, field drying agents, grass for the sports field, fertilizer, trash cans, trash bags, and concession supplies are expendable (used up in a short time, such as one to three years) and appear in the operating bud-

get. Bleachers, benches, public address systems, parking lots, and signage are longer lasting and more expensive, thus they appear in the capital budget. For the same softball complex, utilities may include electricity, water, sewer, telephone, and Internet access, and are part of the operating budget.

Establishing the Budget Goal

Identifying what the final budget proposal should include and how it will be presented is essential information. If it is an activity or program budget, then the budget may include salaries, supplies, equipment, room rental, marketing, and other items, essential to the program. Most of the time the agency will define in advance what information the budget should include. By following the prescribed format and understanding what goes in each category, the budget will be consistent across different departments.

Essential Information

Invariably, after all the information has been collected, the individual preparing the budget has more information than immediately seems necessary. It is important at this point to ask, "What information is essential?" Essential information is that which allows the program manager to reasonably predict financial needs, project anticipated revenue, and establish defensible expectations.

Creating New Information

Gathering and organizing information into categories is the starting point. Organizing data should provide information that can be organized to create new information, such as the total cost of a program. Here's a simple illustration:

Unknown: The cost of Sample Program A

Known: The recreation program is going to meet for 6 weeks, 3 hours each week, and has 1 instructor at a cost of $11.50 per hour.

Calculation:
total cost = 6 weeks x 3 hours x 1 instructor x $11.50 per hour
total cost = 6 x 3 x 1 x $11.50
total cost = $207

Organizing the Data

Getting relevant financial information is the first step of the budget process. Next, it must be organized so that you and others can understand it. This is typically accomplished using a spreadsheet. The data labels on a spreadsheet should be short and descriptive of the information contained in the cells below the labels. These are usually prescribed by the parent organization, but frequently the budget preparer creates their own working spreadsheet that they can manipulate and revise before committing the data to the formal budget document. It is also appropriate to provide detailed footnotes to explain the data in the spreadsheet. In Figure 3.2 note how the data labels represent the known information. The same information that is presented above is included in the spreadsheet, except that it is listed so someone else looking at the data can see a snapshot of how the total cost was determined. In row 2, the data row, the precise information required was placed in the cells. A formula was used to arrive at the total cost in cell F2. In the examples in this chapter, all information will be depicted on spreadsheets.

In the following sections, the budget examples become increasingly complex. Each example is based on the guidelines previously discussed. Reference is made to the appropriate guidelines.

	A	B	C	D	E	F
1	Position	Number	Program Length (in weeks)	Hours per Week	Rate of Pay	Total Cost
2	Instructor	1	6	3	$11.50	$207.00
	formula	1 x 6 x 3 x $11.50				

Figure 3.2. Sample Data Organized and Presented in a Spreadsheet

Determining Costs: Three Examples

Three examples of recreation programs are presented below. Relevant financial and other data are presented on spreadsheets for the purpose of showing how essential information (total cost) is calculated. In the first example (data presented in Figure 3.3), the dance class meets once per week. In the second example of a dance class (data presented in Figure 3.4), most of the classes meet once a week, but some meet three times per week. The final example (data presented in Figure 3.5) provides a more complex budget for an aquatics center program.

Example 1: Simple Dance Program

Known Information:
1. There are 12 classes; all of the classes meet once a week for 8 weeks; each class period is 1-hour long.
2. The salary (rate of pay) for the instructor is $18.00 per hour; for the dance coordinator, $6.00 per class; for the room, $8.00 per hour.
3. There are 15 participants per class.
4. The program fee is designed to recover costs (it should neither lose nor make money).

Data Presented on a Spreadsheet:

	A	B	C	D	E	F	G
1	Position	Number	Number of Classes	F _ram Length (in weeks)	Hours per Week	Rate of Pay	Total Cost
2	Instructor	1	12	8	1	$18.00	$1,728.00
3	Dance Coordinator	1	12	8	1	$6.00	$576.00
4	Room Rental	1	12	8	1	$8.00	$768.00
5	Program Cost						$3,072.00
	formula	1 x 12 x 8 x 1 x $18.00 (Instructor rate - other formulas change rate of pay)					

Figure 3.3. Sample Data Organized and Presented in a Spreadsheet

Determining the Cost of the Simple Dance Program:

1. Total number of hours classes meet. This is determined by taking the product of 3 known items (number of classes, number of weeks, and length of individual classes):

12 classes x 8 weeks x 1 hour per class = 96 hours

2. Total cost of instructors, dance coordinator, and room rental. Multiply the cost of each by the total number of hours:

$$1 \text{ instructor} \times \$9.00 \text{ per hour} \times 96 \text{ hours} = \$1,728$$
$$1 \text{ coordinator} \times \$2.50 \text{ per hour} \times 96 \text{ hours} = \$576$$
$$1 \text{ room rental} \times \$5.00 \text{ per hour} \times 96 \text{ hours} = \$768$$

3. Total cost of program is determined by adding together the cost figures above. In each step, new information was generated that was used to calculate the total cost of the dance class:

$$\text{Total cost} = \$1,728 + \$576 + \$768 = \$3,027.00$$

Organizing the Data

The data in Figure 3.3 are organized similarly to Figure 3.2. One column was added to include the number of classes. Inclusion of the number of classes was an important new variable in this example. Table 3.4 illustrates a more complex budget using the same format and depicting more information, as discussed in Example 2.

Example 2: More Complex Dance Program

Known information:
1. There are 12 classes: 7 of the classes meet 1 time each week for 8 weeks; 5 classes meet 3 times per week for 8 weeks; all class periods are one hour in duration.
2. The rate of pay for the instructor is $18.00 per hour; for the dance coordinator, $6.00 per class; for the room rental, $8.00 per hour.
3. The agency has determined that indirect costs (or costs the agency has that the program needs to help pay for) should be charged at a rate of 12.5% of direct costs and added to the total cost of the program.
4. There are 15 participants per class.
5. The program fee is designed to recover costs (it should neither lose nor make money).

Items 4 and 5 are not essential information for this budget example. The purpose is only to determine the cost of the program. If supplies were being purchased based on the number of participants, then item 4 would be essential information. In item 3, above, the only information that is essential is the indirect costs at 12.5%.

Data Presented on a Spreadsheet:

		A	B	C	D	E	F	G	H
	1	Position	Number	Number of Classes	Program Length in Weeks	Meetings Per week	Hours per Class Meeting	Rate of Pay	Total Cost
	2	1-Time a Week Class Meeting							
	3	Instructor	1	7	8	1	1	$18.00	$1,008.00
	4	Dance Coordinator	1	7	8	1	1	$6.00	$336.00
	5	Room Rental	1	7	8	1	1	$8.00	$448.00
	6	Sub Total							$1,792.00
	7	Indirect Costs						12.5%	$224.00
	8	3-Times a Week Class Meeting							
	9	Instructor	1	5	8	3	1	$18.00	$2,160.00
	10	Dance Coordinator	1	5	8	3	1	$6.00	$720.00
	11	Room Rental	1	5	8	3	1	$8.00	$960.00
	12	Sub Total							$3,840.00
	13	Indirect Costs						12.5%	$480.00
	15	Total Cost							$6,336.00

Figure 3.4. Sample Data for Another Dance Class

Determining the Cost of the Program

The first question that the program manager needs to ask is, "What information is essential?" There may be information related to the program that is not essential. Essential information allows the program manager to determine the answer to each unknown piece of information. In this case, the essential and unknown information are as follows:

1. Total number of hours classes meet.

    7 classes meet 1 time per week
    5 classes meet 3 times per week (for those meeting 3 times a week, include the 3 as a new variable)

    total hours for 1 meeting per week classes = 7 classes x 8 weeks x 1 hour per class = 56 hours

    total hours for 3 meetings per week classes = 5 classes x 8 weeks x 3 times per week x 1 hour per class = 120 hours

    total program hours (classes in both formats) = 56 hours + 120 hours = 176 hours

2.   Total cost of instructors, dance coordinator, and room rental. Multiply the cost of each by the total number of hours:

instructor cost = 1 instructor x $18.00 per hour x 176 hours = $3,168

coordinator cost = 1 coordinator x $6.00 per hour x 176 hours = $1,056

room rental cost = 1 hour room rental x $8.00 per hour x 176 hours = $1,408

3.   Total cost of the program is determined by adding together the cost figures above. In each case, new information was generated that was used to answer the next question:

total program cost = $3,168 + $1,056 + $1,408 = $5,632

The indirect cost of the program is figured by multiplying the direct program cost by the indirect rate (12.5%): indirect costs = $5,632 x .125 = $704

Total cost of program is arrived at by adding the indirect costs and program costs: total program cost = $5,632 + $704 = $6,336

Organizing the Data

Presentation of the data in Figure 3.4 required a new column to include the number of meetings per week. In addition, the spreadsheet was divided into two groups, one identifying the classes meeting one time per week and a second for those meeting three times per week. Organizing the spreadsheet to show the two different class structures (meeting times) allows a clearer depiction of the data, providing clarity to the budget. The indirect costs were determined for each of the class meeting alternatives individually. Another approach would be to add the total costs and then multiply by 12.5 percent. The final total was calculated by adding the subtotals and the indirect costs for each program group.

Example 3: Aquatic Program

Known Information:

The public aquatic center is an outdoor facility operating five major programs during the summer over a 12-week period (June 5 to August 27). The program areas and management information are provided below, and illustrated in Table 3.5.

1.   The aquatics supervisor and maintenance worker are permanent full-time employees. All other employees are considered seasonal. This information

is important for employee benefits determination. Permanent employee benefits are an additional 28% of their salary. For seasonal employees, the benefits are an additional 9% of their salary.

2. The open swim program operates 7 days per week for 8 hours per day. Six lifeguards are on duty at all times at a rate of $12.50 per hour. Two concession staff are on duty at all times at a rate of $9.00 per hour. One cashier is on duty at all times at a rate of $9.00 per hour.

3. The family swim program operates 3 days per week for 3 hours per day. Two lifeguards are on duty at all times at a rate of $12.50 per hour. Two concession staff are on duty at all times at a rate of $9.00 per hour. One cashier is on duty at all times at a rate of $9.00 per hour.

4. Lane swim operates 6 days per week for 3 hours per day. One lifeguard is on duty at all times at a rate of $12.50 per hour.

5. The Learn-to-Swim program operates 4 days per week for 4 hours per day One lifeguard is on duty at all times at a rate of $12.50 per hour. Six learn-to-swim instructors are on duty at all times at a rate of $14.00 per hour.

6. The swim team meets 6 times per week for 3 hours per day. Two coaches are on staff for 4 hours each day (6 days) at a rate of $18.50 per hour. Two assistant coaches are on duty 3 hours each day (6 days) at a rate of $12.50 per hour.

7. The management team consists of the following: an aquatics supervisor who is and has a salary of $53,250 and has benefits charged at a rate of 28 % of the base salary; a maintenance worker who is and has a salary of $38,500 and has benefits charged at a rate of 28 % of the base salary; a pool manager position works 5 days a week, 8 hours per day, at a rate of $21.50 per hour; a head lifeguard position works 5 days a week, 8 hours per day, at a rate of $18.65 per hour; an assistant head lifeguard position works 5 days a week, 8 hours per day, at a rate of $16.00 per hour.

Data Presented on a Spreadsheet:

	A	B	C	D	E	F	G	H
1	Position	Number	Number of Classes	Program Length in Weeks	Meetings Per week	Hours per Class Meeting	Rate of Pay	Total Cost
2	**Open Swim**							
3	Lifeguard	4	1	12	7	8	$12.50	$33,600
4	Concession staff	2	1	12	7	8	$9.00	$12,096
5	Cashier	1	1	12	7	8	$9.00	$6,048
6	Sub Total							$51,744
8	**Family Swim**							
9	Lifeguard	4	1	12	3	3	$12.50	$5,400.00
10	Concession staff	2	1	12	3	3	$9.00	$1,944.00
11	Cashier	1	1	12	3	3	$9.00	$972.00
12	Sub Total							$8,316
1	**Lap Swim**							
2	Lifeguard	2	1	12	6	3	$12.50	$5,400
3	Sub Total							$5,400
1	**Learn-to-Swim**							
2	Lifeguard	1	1	12	4	7	$12.50	$4,200
3	Instructor	6	1	12	6	3	$14.00	$18,144
4	Sub Total							$22,344
1	**Swim Team**							
2	Coaches	2	1	12	6	4	$18.50	$10,656
3	Assistant Coaches	2	1	12	6	3	$12.50	$5,400
4	Sub Total							$16,056
1	**Management**				days/week	hours/day		
2	Aquatics Supervisor	1	1	1	1	1		$53,250
3	Maintenance Worker 1	1	1	1	1	1		$38,500
4	Pool Manager	1	1	12	5	8	$21.50	$10,320
5	Head Lifeguard	1	1	12	5	8	$18.65	$8,952
6	Assistant Head Lifeguard	1	1	12	5	8	$16.00	$7,680
7	Sub Total							$118,702
1	**Benefits**					benefits	total salary	
2	Full-time employees					28%	$91,750	$25,690
3	Part-time & Seasonal					11%	$130,812	$14,389
4	Sub Total							$40,079
5	**Total Cost**							**$262,641**

Figure 3.5. Sample Data for an Aquatic Program

Determining Salary Costs:

The information above provides detail about the type/classification and number of positions, rate of pay, hours per week, weeks for the season. The information that is still required includes how many hours per season each person works, what the total cost is of each position for the season, what the cost of employee benefits is, and what the total cost is of the salaries for the program.

The aquatic supervisor has 100% of the salary and benefits (28%) assigned to the aquatics budget. The maintenance worker has a salary of $38,500 salary and 28% benefits, which are also assigned to the aquatics program. Following the process discussed previously, the known information is the annual salary and the annual benefit percentage. The desired information is the cost of benefits and the total cost of the positions. The formulas for determining full-time employee costs (salaries and benefits) is:

full-time employee salary cost = sum of salaries = ($53,250 + $38,500) = $91,750

full-time employee benefits cost = (total salaries x benefits rate) = $91,750 x .28 = $25,690

total full-time employee salary and benefits cost = salaries + (salaries x benefit percent)

= ($91,750) + (($91,750)x .28) = $117,440

Figure 3.5 provides a structure that facilitates examination of program-specific employee costs. Note that, for convenience only, benefits costs for the part time employees will be added after all salaries/wages have been determined. With this program-specific approach, the first budget to be examined is open swim. The following formula is used for open swim and all other program areas. Note that the "number of classes" is not reported because in every case there is only one class. The first calculation applies to lifeguards:

total lifeguard cost = number of lifeguards per hour x number of weeks in season x days per week x hours per day x hourly rate of pay

number of lifeguards per hour = 4
number of weeks in the season = 12
days per week = 7
hours per day (reported as hours per class meeting) = 8
salary = $12.50 per hour

Placing the known information in the formula, the total cost can be calculated:

total lifeguard cost = 4 x 1 x 12 x 7 x 8 x $12.50 = $33,600

Throughout this example, known information is used to generate needed information. Pausing to reflect on how to set up the formula is essential. This should be repeated for each position until all costs are calculated.

The formula for computing the cost of concession staff salaries during open swim is:

salary cost for concession staff = number of employees per hour x number of weeks in the season x days per week x hours per day x hourly rate of pay

    number of concession employees per hour = 2
    number of weeks in the season = 12
    days per week = 7
    hours per day = 8
    salary = $9.00 per hour

    concession staff salary cost = 2 x 12 x 7 x 8 x $9.00 = $12,096.00

The same formula applied to the cashier during open swim looks like:

salary cost for cashier = number of cashiers per hour x number of weeks in the season x days per week x hours per day x hourly rate of pay

    number of cashiers per hour = 1
    number of weeks in the season = 12
    days per week = 7
    hours per day = 8
    salary = $9.00 per hour

    cashier salary cost = 1 x 12 x 7 x 8 x $9.00 = $6,048.00

The same approach is taken for each program area and the total cost for full-time staff is calculated as $91,750 and for part-time and seasonal staff it is $130,812. The costs of employee benefits are then added as follows:

    permanent full-time benefits = full-time total salaries x 28%
    seasonal part-time benefits = part-time salaries x 11%

or
    permanent full-time benefits = $91,750 x 28% = $25,690
    seasonal part-time benefits = $130,812 x 11% = $14,389

Organizing the Data

The data are organized by individual program area, followed by management staff, and then benefits. The total cost of the program is $262,641 and is shown in Figure 3.5.

Budgeting for Contingencies

Every effective budget preparer understands that a budget is an informed estimate and that unexpected variables are going to occur. The budget should include some flexibility to accommodate such contingencies. Contingency costs should be included in the budget at five percent or 10 percent of the total of the budget. When, for example, utility costs go up and the increase was not expected or provided for in the budget, the needed extra funds will be available in the contingency account. Contingency funds allow for emergencies, mistakes in the budget, and cost overruns. They should not be used as justification for poor planning, inadequate research, or whimsical spending.

Summary

Basic skills of budget preparation were discussed in this chapter. By deliberately moving from known information to new information will allow any individual working on a budget process to create the data that is needed to present a budget in an actionable form. Some budgets will be more complex than those demonstrated here but the basic principles that have been discussed are universally applicable.

CHAPTER 4

Budget Preparation

Introduction

Budgeting is a process that focuses on providing managers with information and tools to manage fiscal resources and operations. Well-constructed and well-understood budgets ultimately allow managers to make more informed decisions. In that context, budgeting is linked to organizational goals and objectives and is a tool to help achieve them. Further, budgeting allows sport, tourism and leisure service organizations to translate their organizational visions into realities. Budgeting, then, is an essential component of the larger management process of any organization. In today's competitive and changing society, sport, tourism, and leisure service organizations cannot function effectively without a clear understanding of how good fiscal management contributes to their day-to-day operational success. Few decisions facing sport, tourism, and leisure service organization managers are more daunting than those made concerning how to allocate limited fiscal resources. It is the decision-making in

these organizations, the allocation of human and fiscal resources that impacts the organization's ability to achieve its vision and mission. This chapter discusses the process of budgeting for sport, tourism, and leisure service organizations and should provide the manager with tools to measure and monitor the impact of budgeting on the organization.

Budget Processes

What Is a Budget?

Budgeting is one of the most essential tasks for a sport, tourism and leisure service manager. The budget is a financial plan that helps to move the operational and strategic plans of the organization into achievable activities over a specified period of time. This period of time is typically one year. A budget is a document that articulates the anticipated revenues and expenditures of an organization over a specified period of time. Budgets anticipate expenditures and revenue and are linked to organizational and individual work plans. Budgets provide direct benefits to organizations. Listed below are key benefits to budgeting, as identified by various public, nonprofit, and corporate organizations:

- In an environment where budgets are increasingly visible, budgeting helps an organization to maintain focus and establish priorities based on its core values and show responsiveness to public and end user needs and expectations.
- Budgets help to provide transparency of operations (valued in today's political and social environment), and are linked to performance and outcomes—measures that are visible to broad groups of stakeholders.
- Budgets provide guidelines to compare with accrual revenues and expenses throughout the year.
- Budgets indicate the amount of revenue that is expected to be available, which sets limitations on the amount of expenditures that can be supported.
- Budgets help to establish the acceptable costs of providing services and programs.
- The budget can be used for control of organizational priorities. Funding for projects can be approved, disapproved, shifted, based on the organization's internal and external expectations and influences.
- Budgets allow for systemization of operations, creating a structure where expenditures are tracked, measured against expectations, and become a tool for managers to measure expenditures, revenues, and match them to goals and objectives of the organization.

- The right type of budget structure can provide a flexible plan for operating the organization for an upcoming period of time.
- Budgeting promotes a future focus and planning within the organization.
- Budgets are constructed based on the organizations operational plan.
- Budgeting requires the presence of structure in an organization, and is a structure-reinforcing process, integrated into the organization's goals and objectives.
- Budgets identify priorities in allocating resources among the services and programs that the organization offers.
- Budgeting is a part of decision-making and helps to influence short and long-term plans. Budgeting is not the decision maker but can have a strong influence on actions.
- Budgets help to convert the organization's long and short-term plans and policies into services and programs.

The budget is a policy body's basic mechanism for fiscal control. Budgets are classified as two types: operating budgets and capital budgets. Operating budgets deal with current expenditures for a specified period of time, while capital budgets cover longer periods of time in attempting to address major projects requiring significant investments of dollars. Capital budgets are funded for more than one year at a time and are adjusted on an annual basis. Capital budgeting is discussed in detail in Chapter 16. Almost all managers work with operating budgets. Fewer work with capital budgets, yet they contribute to the construction of capital budgets in important ways.

The Budget Cycle

Budgets usually span a one-year period, called a fiscal year. A fiscal year is not always the same as the calendar year. The most common state and local government fiscal year period is from July 1 through June 30 of the ensuing year. The U.S. Government's fiscal year is October 1 through September 30. Most private nonprofit and commercial sport, tourism, and leisure service organizations use January 1 through December 31 as their fiscal year. It is acceptable and common to refer to a fiscal year by the year in which the budget ends. If a fiscal year begins July 1, 2021, and ends June 30, 2022, then the fiscal year is referred to as FY2022 (fiscal year 2022).

The importance of a fiscal year lies in the spending and accounting process. Money can be allocated, encumbered, and expended within a given fiscal year. Allocated monies are those dollars that the legislative/policy body has approved for use by the sport, tourism, and leisure service organization. Encumbered monies are those dollars that have been committed, but have yet to be paid out. For example, a municipal parks and recreation department requested funds for new sports equipment. When the budget was approved, those funds were *allocated*. In March, the department issued a purchase order to a vendor for the equipment. A purchase order is a commitment to pay for items when delivered. The department recorded the money as being committed or *encumbered,* but not spent. The sports equipment arrived, followed soon thereafter by an invoice from the equipment vendor. The department issued a check to the vendor, and the money was no longer

encumbered, but *expended*. Expended funds, then, are those funds paid out for services and items purchased, leased, and rented and for which invoices have been received and checks issued.

A fiscal year provides a fixed starting and stopping point for budget administration. Policy setting or legislative bodies and managers need to be able to establish time-limited budgetary guidelines for their organizations. The fiscal year is recognized as an accepted accounting standard. It allows organizations to accomplish fiscal planning within a fixed period of time. It allows government organizations to match anticipated tax revenues against projected expenditures. It allows commercial and nonprofit enterprises to plan for and manage revenues and expenditures.

Public sector budget cycles can be as long as 30 months; from initiation and planning, through administration, and until the final closeout of the budget. Figure 4.1 illustrates three fiscal years and includes the budget preparation time, the actual budget year, and the budget closeout period. The length of time required to construct a budget will vary from organization to organization and is usually mandated by the organization's governing body. It is conceivable that an organization could be working on three budgets simultaneously—preparation of next year's budget, implementation of this year's budget, and closing out last year's budget accounts. Accounting bodies prefer to finalize or close out an organization's end-of-the-fiscal year budget within 30 to 90 days. Even when some funds remain encumbered, budgets can be closed out with the knowledge that encumbered funds remain to be expended.

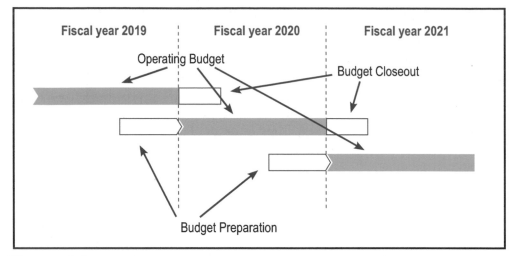

Figure 4.1. Budget Activities during a 3-Year Period.

Budget Preparation Cycle

A typical budget preparation cycle includes four tasks, as depicted in Figure 4.2. In a government agency, the budget cycle is usually prescribed by the legislative authority, such as a city council, a park board, a county council, or a state or provincial government. For nonprofit organizations, a board of directors defines the budget process. Nonprofit organizations that may depend on the United Way for part of their operating budget can anticipate following a United Way budget presentation process in full or in part. Commercial enterprises typically have their own set of instructions and procedures, or they may be flexible in their approach to budget development. Regardless of the type of sport, tourism and leisure service organization, there are some commonalities that each type of organization can follow in the development of a budget.

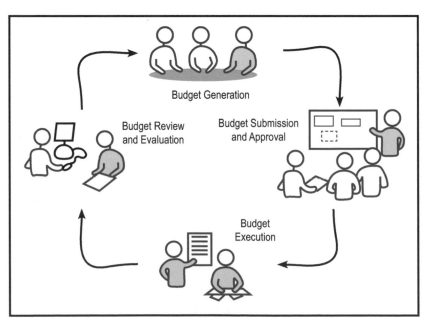

Figure 4.2.
Simplified Budget Preparation Cycle.

An example of a municipality budget cycle includes activities and deadlines. A budget preparation document includes such items as specific directives from the legislative body, any restrictions on budget growth, identification of budget deadlines, budget formats, budget decision guidelines, and specific instructions that either may be applicable only to this budget period or may be new to the organization. The guidelines are typically transmitted in a letter, along with support documentation from the head of the legislative body or her designated administrative officer. The organization is expected to comply with all of the guidelines prescribed by the legislative authority.

The budget guidelines include a budget calendar, which is an orderly chronological timetable showing the dates when necessary action must be taken in preparing the budget. A budget calendar may initiate the process as much as 12 months in advance of the start of the budget. (The example in Table 4.1 begins six months in advance.) The budget guidelines and calendar are provided so that the legislative, executive, and departmental entities will avoid encroachment on one another, and so that orderly performance in the budget preparation can be achieved. The development phase is the most critical phase of the budget process and the only phase for which completion dates are established. Dates should be established for the following:

- Distribution of budget planning documents

- Preparation of revenue estimates
- Preparation of proposed expenditures (using required forms)
- Return of the completed budget request forms (revenue and expenditures) to agency/organization director
- Completion of internal review of budget and preliminary preparation of work assigned to the central budget agency
- Open public hearings initiated budget
- Completion of executive review and executive determination of final budget content
- Submission of the budget to the legislative body
- Preliminary legislative determination of the content of the appropriation ordinance or budget to be approved
- Final action by the legislative body
- Executive approval or veto of the adopted budget and legislative action thereon
- Completion of administrative action, if any, needed to actuate budget appropriations
- Beginning of the fiscal year

The budget calendar should also include a schedule that shows the responsibilities of the various officials and departments with respect to specific budget preparation items. It should also include excerpts of legal and administrative rules that govern budget formulation and execution. These items should be shared with budget managers.

Table 4.1
A Sample Budget Preparation Calendar for a Local Government

Date	Actions to be completed
2 January (-180)	Mayor's budget policy letter requesting department heads to submit proposed work program and budget estimates for ensuing fiscal year. Necessary forms and revisions to budget manual are transmitted with the letter.
1 February (-150)	City Administrative Officer (CAO) approves staff budget assignments, which are thereafter distributed to the staff.
1 March (-120)	Service betterment budget estimates, if any, received from department heads.
10 April (-80)	CAO reviews tentative Capital Improvement Expenditure Program (CIP) and, upon approval, transmits it to the Public Works Priority Committee.
10 April (-80)	CAO submits annual salary recommendations to City Council.
10-30 April (-80 t0 -60)	Hearings conducted by the Public Works Priority Committee to determine final priority of capital projects to be included in CIP for ensuing year.
10-17 April (-80 to -73)	Preliminary budget hearing held by CAO and Budget Coordinator with the Assistant Budget Coordinator and staff analyst for each department.
18-28 April (-72 to -62)	CAO, assisted by Budget Coordinator, conducts departmental budget hearing with each department head, at which time the staff analysts' recommendations for that departmental budget are presented and the department head is given an opportunity to express his or her viewpoint.
1 May (-60)	Final date for submission by City Controller of the official estimates of revenue from all sources (other than general property taxes).
1 May (-60)	CAO submits official estimate of revenue from general property taxes.
1-5 May (-60 to -55)	Mayor, assisted by CAO, conducts budget conferences with each department head. Attended by council members, press, and taxpayer groups.
5-12 May (-55 to -48)	Final budget decisions made by Mayor, who is assisted by CAO.
12-31 May (-48 to -30)	Budget printed under supervision of CAO.
1 June (-29)	Mayor submits budget to City Council.
1-20 June (-29 to -10)	Council considers Mayor's budget and makes modifications, as it deems necessary.
20-25 June (-10 to -5)	Mayor considers any modifications made by City Council and may veto such changes.
25-28 June (-5 to -2)	Council considers Mayor's veto of any items and may vote to override Mayor's veto by a two-thirds majority.
1 July (0)	Beginning of fiscal year – budget takes effect.

It is recommended that each sport, tourism, and leisure service organization develop its own budget calendar using the legislative and administrative body's calendar as a guide. The calendar should provide information similar to that found in the legislative body's calendar but tailored to the tasks specific to the organization. Commercial or nonprofit organizations which may not have as formal a legislative process would be wise to develop a budget calendar along the same guidelines.

Case Study
The Las Vegas Convention and Visitors Authority Operating Budget

The Las Vegas Convention and Visitors Bureau is a dynamic example of how community convention and visitor bureaus (CVB) operate. It was established by state law, is funded by a county room tax, and is governed by an autonomous board of directors. The board of directors is composed of individuals from the private sector and county and city government sector representatives. Similar to many convention and visitor local organizations across the United States, the Las Vegas Convention and Visitors Bureau (LVCVA) has a core responsibility to promote Las Vegas and Southern Nevada as a destination for leisure and business travel. A key component of the business travel is conventions and meetings. In 2017, Las Vegas received 6.65 million convention visitors, representing 15.6% of all visitors. The Las Vegas, Clark County region has 160,000 hotel rooms and 10.9 million square feet of exhibit space. LVCVA's mission is to attract both business, including conventions, and leisure travelers. To do this, the LVCVA had an approved FY2018 budget of $354.9 million. The core of its operating budget comes from room taxes (83%), facility charges and services (15%), and other (2%). The 2018 budget is targeted for expenditures in marketing, advertising, and special events (73%), operations (17%), community support (10%), and general government (10%). The advertising budget for promoting southern Nevada is $101.3 million on visitations of 42.9 million showed an average cost per visitor of $2.36 for marketing. That is remarkably low for a community.

Sources: http://www.lvcva.com/what-we-do/; http://www.lvcva.com/includes/content/images/media/docs/FY-2018-Budget-in-Brief.pdf

Funds

Public and nonprofit budgets are constructed around fund accounting. Funds are categories into which income sources are placed. The revenue sources are the five that are discussed in Chapter 9. It is important to point out that not all income goes into funds. Organizations receiving revenue through public and private sources use a system of fund accountancy.

Fund accounting applies to the management and allocation of revenue that an organization acquires. The basic idea behind fund accounting is to monitor and document the use of assets that are donated by outside parties, including taxes, donations, grants, contracts, or other sources. Funds can include an independent fiscal source (e.g., donors, special revenue events, cookie sales, etc.), property taxes, or other income sources. They are segregated from the regular operating budget for the purpose of carrying out specific activities. Funds are a separate group of accounts that are managed independently of each other. Funds exist because government organizations have legal restrictions placed on them regarding how specific revenue may be expended. A local option hotel/motel tax may be restricted by state or city code for use to support greenways, greenbelts, or local tourism and convention and meeting facilities. These funds can be divided into three categories: governmental funds, proprietary funds, and fiduciary funds. Each is described below and depicted in Table 4.2.

Government Funds

Included within the three types of funds are sub-funds that are common to most public sport, tourism and leisure service organizations. Most government fiscal operations are conducted through the first four types of funds: general fund, special revenue fund, capital projects fund, and debt service fund.

Proprietary and fiduciary funds are also used in public agencies but the *general fund* is fund most common in the public sector. The general fund supports all operations that are not assigned to other funds. In public park and recreation agencies, this fund may account for 30 to 90% of the operating budget. Included in it might be personnel services, maintenance operations, supplies, contractual services, and more. Sources of revenue for the general fund at the governmental level are most frequently property taxes, but they also may include sales taxes, special taxes, intergovernmental grants, and licenses and permits.

The *special revenue fund* is made up of revenues from services that those revenues are specifically designed to support. User fees and charges are the primary source of revenue for special revenue funds. Fees collected from recreation and park programs and services are the most common source of revenue. These fees are deposited in the special revenue fund and used to pay for the recreation programs and services. The fund can also be used to partially defray or wholly pay for operating expenses, personnel services, supplies and material, etc. Use of these funds is typically governed by state law and will vary from state to state.

A *capital projects fund* (a governmental fund) focuses on the acquisition, design, and construction of capital or major projects that typically have an economic life of several years. These projects include aquatic complexes; recreation centers; sports complexes; ice arenas; city, county, and state parks; and other build-

Table 4.2

Types of Government-Based Funds (Aronson & Schwartz, 1996; Reed & Swain, 1998)

Governmental Fund Types	Proprietary Fund Types	Fiduciary Fund Types
General Fund Special Revenue Fund Capital Projects Fund Debt Service Funds Special Assessment Funds	Enterprise Fund Internal Service Funds	Expendable Trust Funds Nonexpendable Trust Funds Agency Funds

ings and structures. It also includes the purchase of major pieces of equipment. Funding for a capital projects fund can come from a variety of sources, including special taxes, intergovernmental grants, and proceeds from the sale of revenue or general obligation bonds. Chapter 9 provides more detail on revenue sources.

A *debt service fund* is used to pay the organization's long-term debt and, in the case of government, the general obligation debt from the sale of bonds. Any organization involved in capital projects of significant size has probably engaged in long-term debt. In the public sector, revenue for the debt service fund primarily comes from taxes, grants, special assessments, and intergovernmental grants. In other sectors, it comes from donations and/or revenue-producing services.

A *special assessment fund* consists of money targeted for a specific project or task. Assessments are made to selected individuals or organizations for an identified service or benefit that they will receive. On occasion, special assessment funds have been employed when a specific group or geographic area received a specific benefit, such as a downtown corridor that is beautified with trees, grass, shrubs, or with the creation of public spaces.

Proprietary Funds

Funds of the proprietary type are designed to provide self-sustaining operation and activities. An *enterprise fund* receives the bulk of its revenue from user charges, but typically supports a major operation or enterprise and, by definition, only needs to generate 50% of its operating budget. Examples of enterprise fund operations include civic centers, aquatic complexes, and major parks, zoos, and sports complexes. The distinction between a special revenue

fund and an enterprise fund may be clouded by various state codes.

Internal service funds transfer money between different departments within the same organization for services rendered. For example, if the program division at the YMCA needed 8,500 brochures, and its printing services department provided the brochures, the program division would be billed internally for the cost. This fund allows organizations to track the cost of services provided internally.

Fiduciary Funds

Funds of the fiduciary type are used to account for assets received and held in trust by either a government or an organization. The organization can be perceived as a trustee, custodian, or agent for the funds. Three types of funds are common to fiduciary funds.

The *nonexpendable trust fund* requires that the principal remain unspent, but allows the expenditure of income generated from an investment of the principal. The income may be spent in the general fund or assigned to specific programs or other funds. A nonexpendable trust fund may accrue income to the principal from a variety of sources, such as donations, grants, and bequests.

An *expendable trust*, by contrast, allows spending from the principal. Art endowment and zoo endowment programs are common examples of expendable trusts. Individuals are encouraged to contribute to a specific endowment, and the agency uses the money contributed for day-to-day operations or for special projects.

An *agency fund* allows an agency to have specific control over a set of designated monies. Examples might include lottery revenues used to finance parks and recreation or a boat tax for fish and wildlife.

Less common funds include annuity funds, endowment funds, loan funds, and operating funds. An *annuity fund* holds funds that remain after an annuity contract has expired. These funds can be used in any manner so deemed by the organization unless specific restrictions are placed upon them. An *endowment fund* is most frequently used by nonprofits, but has the same characteristics as a nonexpendable trust. A *loan fund* is a separate fund set aside with the monies available for loan for specific functions or services. An *operating fund* is made up of all those monies that are available to a nonprofit board for use. The operating fund fulfills the same role as the general fund in a government.

Budget Presentation Format

There are many different ways to format and present a budget. Table 4.3 provides information for 12 commonly used budget formats. Each budget format provides decision makers with different kinds of information. Depending on the goals of the sport, tourism and leisure service organization, one or more appropriate budget formats are selected. The object classification budget is the most common format for public, nonprofit, and commercial organizations. It is a budget format that allows managers to use the budget as a tool to accomplish goals and objectives. Expenditures are classified into a specific category (called a code). However, as government and nonprofits become more entrepreneurial and develop revenue-generating operations, the object classification budget cannot meet all of the requirements and is frequently paired with another budget type, such as the program budget. The object classification budget remains a standard accounting format within finance op-

erations, even when a different budget format is utilized. (Chapter 5 discusses selected budget formats in more detail.)

Budget Preparation Activities

Budget preparation is the responsibility of the chief executive officer (CEO) of the sport, tourism, and leisure service organization. This person may be the director, the executive director, the superintendent, the manager, or the owner. The CEO sets the agenda and the tone for budget preparation for all members of the organization. Budget preparation should be a cooperative endeavor among the organization's members and the external budget agency, if one is present. Cooperation among participants in the budget process is a key element in the success of the organization. It should be viewed as a cooperative process rather than a competitive process.

Effective budget preparation engages all members of the organization. Budget preparation should be taken to the lowest levels of the organization, thus fostering understanding, input, and commitment from its members. This process may necessitate training for members of the organization, as well as an enhanced level of trust. Decentralizing budget decision making to the lowest possible levels results in an increased commitment to the budget and to the organization's purpose and direction. Ultimately, the CEO defines each member's role in the budget's preparation and sets the tone for budget operations. One individual should be formally designated as the budget preparation officer (BPO). The BPO ensures conformity in the budget preparation, collects and collates all of the data submitted by different budget managers, identifies discrepancies, and resolves disputes. The BPO also

Table 4.3
Comparison of Commonly Used Budget Formats

Type of Budget	Description	Purpose/When Used	Advantages	Disadvantages
Object Classification Budget	Looks at operations as categories (objects) and classifies expenditures into those categories	Most common of budget types in use by government and nonprofit corporations and provides ease of budget classification and management	Relatively easy to establish / Process is uniform and follows standardized procedure / Category development is predetermined	Does not provide for flexibility to meet needs / Requires detailed cost elements at the program level / Categories too generalized to provide budget detail
Line Item Budget	Similar to object classification the item represents a specific object and is placed in a line for classification purposes	As common as object classification, provides similar ease of budget classification/management	Allows for multiple system utilization / Allows for budget adjustment with minimal difficulty	Requires detailed planning and preparation / Some loss of reporting accuracy because expenditures collapsed into lines
Activity Budget	Budget areas are divided into "activity areas" and focus on cost to perform a specific function	Allows agencies to have a clearer delineation of the of costs associated with different functional activities of the organization	Clearly defines services as activities / Allows comparison of costs between activities / Provides clear picture of where budget funds are allocated	Can be difficult to set up and requires detailed accounting system / Some budget activities don't comfortably fit / Reduces some levels of flexibility
Function Budget	Similar to the Activity budget this allows the agencies to group activities under major functions	Grouped activity budgets are tracked and administrators are able to view their change in costs across time	Comparison of functional costs available / Helps budget agency understand where money allocated / Provides for comparison of costs across functions	Budgets may not lend themselves to easy comparison / Uses Object Classification concept and suffers from same disadvantages
Performance Budget	Used to measure end results of activities based on performance outcome measures	Similar to the program budget most frequently used with operations that can have repetitive measures, such as maintenance operations and other reoccurring operations	Highly standardized units of measurement and cost / Provides for high control and detailed accuracy / Effectively integrated with computer based management of operations	Requires high level of sophistication in organization reporting procedures / Not particularly useful in nonrepetitive situations / Fixed approach to budget management and decisions

Table 4.3 (cont.)

Type of Budget	Description	Purpose / When Used	Advantages	Disadvantages
Planning, Programming Budgeting System	Implemented by the Kennedy administration and identifies the relationship between costs and end results of programs	Used to measure explain the outcomes of budget operations. Focus is on the end result rather than the cost of the program.	Focuses on service goals; Focuses on end results rather than just costs; Provides for a comparative analysis of programs and services	Requires equitable measurement system to be established; Difficulty determining importance of need and value; Not always able to make comparisons across the entire organization
Zero Based Budget	Focuses on actual cost of programs assuming that all programs must be regularly justify all operations	When the agency needs to assess operations and to justify those operations retained to decision makers	Encourages regular review of value/ importance of programs; Provides for increased flexibility and creativity; Enhances difficult decision making about service elimination; Facilitates orderly review of operations and services	Increased justification and reporting required; May increase competition within the organization; Tends to increase tension within the organization at expense of morale
Program Budget	Focuses on explaining why expenditures are required and tied to agency goals and objectives	Used when there needs to be a fuller explanation of the programs and when costs can be clearly identified along with identification of outcomes	Provides narrative justification; Focuses on values of programs/ services rather than just costs; Creativity and flexibility are enhanced	Requires a level of sophistication in the delivery of services and accounting; Limited budget-cost detail provided; May sell program beyond its ability to deliver
Fee Budget	Determines actual cost of providing services or operations and allocates to specific categories	When the budget operation requires a detailed accounting of costs and allocation to specific expenditure areas	Provides a more detailed accounting of actual costs; Provides significant detailed information; Breaks down into per-participant costs	Use may be restricted to specific program types; Requires detailed knowledge of needs before initiating the budget; May not include all costs because of accounting system used
Unit Budget	Used frequently in large organizations it groups costs by different organizational units. It may employ a different budget process within the unit.	Useful for looking at operational costs across the whole organization. It does not suggest all units are similar, rather shows where funds are being expended.	Provides a clear description of costs; Relatively simple to present and comprehend; Opens the budget process to multiple constituencies	Is not a stand alone budget system; Does not show budget detail or division operating costs; Requires top down policy and procedures setting
Increment / Decrement Budget	A traditional approach of adding a percentage to the existing budget without regard for need or importance.	Makes the budget process relatively simple addressing issues of increase with a static figure	Provides for hassle-free and predictable growth; Simplifies the budget process, requires minimal decision making	Provides no flexibility based on need or demand; Encourages status quo; Discourages creativity and flexibility
Running Budget	Budget that is developed and modified based on income sources and expenditure needs. Driven by income and expenses are expected to conform.	Allows organizations who don't have a stable source of income to modify their budget based on income sources. Provides flexibility to the budgeting process.	Provides day to day accounting system; Functions on a time-line fiscal chart; Tied to revenues and income	Supplemental budget process required for budget administration; Requires constant attention to budget process; Time consuming to establish

ensures that the budget conforms to the guidelines proposed by both the CEO and the legislative body and that it is linked to the department's strategic or long-range plans. The department BPO briefs each member of the organization who has contributed to the budget, coordinates closely with the department executive officer, and prepares the final budget document for submission to the legislative or policy body.

The Relationship of Strategic Planning to Budget Preparation

The budgeting process is intricately linked to strategic planning. An organization, during the process of development of the strategic plan, should align the budget with the strategic plan. Budget preparation decisions should be based upon following the strategic plan. Strategic planning is about achieving organizational futures. Linking the budget to strategic planning becomes a visible method of moving from planning to action. All budget decisions should focus on the organization's values, vision, mission, and action plan. A strategic plan is not intended to address all operational issues of the organization. Rather, the emphasis is upon those action items necessary to achieving the organization's vision. Strategic planning complements and enhances, but does not replace effective evaluation of day-to-day operations, special initiatives, capital projects, etc. Strategic planning is another budget preparation component that the BPO and budget manager must consider.

Budget Preparation Philosophies

How budget needs are estimated depends upon the type of preparation phi-

losophy adopted by the organization. An *open-ended budget* allows an organization to submit a budget that provides an optimal program of services. The open-ended budget is not hindered by restrictions on spending, but it does require decision makers to adjust the budget to meet the organization's dynamic fiscal capabilities. This adjustment is typically accomplished through reductions in expenditures. Open-ended budgeting is still done, but it has fallen into disfavor in an era of accountability and limited budget growth.

A *fixed ceiling budget* normally places a limit on the growth of a budget. A fixed ceiling budget assumes that previous budgets have been adequate and that minimal growth in allocated resources will continue to meet needs. Such budgets fail to take into account the changing needs of the organization. The format reacts to available funds, which suggests that either politics or an attitude of sharing proportionately among competing groups is an equitable way to assign budgets. A fixed ceiling budget is still a common approach for many organizations.

A budget based on *workload measurement and unit costing* seeks to devise units of work and to determine unit costs. This budget approach attempts to quantify work as performance and output. In sport, tourism and leisure service organizations, workload measurement budgets work best with repetitive types of activities.

An *increase/decrease analysis* is a form of fixed ceiling budget that depicts increases and decreases from the previous year's expenditure lines. An item-by-item control looks at each budget item and asks if it is essential, desirable, or justified. Alternative budget proposals ask staff members to prepare a basic budget supplemented by an outline for alternative budget levels. Alternative budgets provide rationales for different budget proposals and detailed budget information. Almost all budget preparations go through some form of alternative budget preparation, but rarely in a formally requested manner. Such an approach requires a considerable amount of time and effort on the part of the budget preparers and suggests little reason for the additional work.

Factorial estimating looks at past expenditures and then factors what it believes will be future expenditures. More specifically, it looks at operating and revenues in a detailed format over a period of years and attempts to estimate or forecast what future expenditures will be. The reliance upon historical data is appropriate for most sport, tourism, and leisure service organizations, but those organizations that rely wholly upon the past to predict the future will find themselves ill prepared to meet the demands and needs of their constituents or legislative body.

Historical analysis is an almost identical approach, except it typically leaves out personnel-related services. Multiple preparation philosophies are frequently used in a single budget. Historically based open-ended measurement or work measurement has been the most commonly used budgeting process in determining work program requirements. Personnel needs have used work measurement and historical analysis. An estimation of the cost of supplies, materials, and equipment usually relies upon historical analysis and some workload measurement. Equipment needs have used a fixed ceiling format as the primary method, although in some instances, open-ended budgeting has been used.

It is not uncommon for organizations to approach budgeting using multi-ple approaches. This allows the organization to work from different perspectives on a proposed budget. The use of multiple perspectives provides greater knowledge of the potential impact of budget decisions.

Preparing the Departmental Work Plan

The departmental work plan is an integral part of the budget preparation process. It identifies the work of the sport, tourism and leisure service organization for the planned fiscal year and then attempts to match the proposed budget with the desired work. Its preparation usually requires a series of trade-offs between what the organization would like to do and what it can realistically accomplish within the constraints of its potential budget. The department work plan involves at least three components: (1) ongoing functions of the leisure service organization, (2) new or proposed functions of the organization, and (3) special one-time or infrequently reoccurring functions of the organization.

Preparing an annual work plan requires in-depth knowledge of the organization's work processes and their relationship to both the vision and the mission of the organization. Delegating budget preparation and management to the lowest possible level in the organization assumes that those who do the work are best prepared to estimate its costs and effects. The delegation of budget preparation does not eliminate the need for constant oversight and justification at each step of the process. In an era of limited economic growth, it is appropriate for each service or program to participate in a continuous evaluation of how well it meets customer expectations, annual work plans, and the vision and mission of the organization.

To facilitate the process of budgeting for annual work plans, the sport, tourism, and leisure service organization should do the following:

- Conduct an annual review of each program or service and assess how each one agrees with the organization's vision and mission.
- Annually assess the effectiveness of each program and service in relation to the organization's goals and objectives, the standards established for the program or service, and customer satisfaction.
- Initiate a level-of-performance review to determine that the program or service meets agreed-upon levels of service or satisfaction.

Estimating Personnel Service Requirements

In most sport, tourism, and leisure service organizations, personnel costs are the single largest expenditure item. They will range from 50% to 90% of the organization's operating costs. Given this level of funding, the importance of determining personnel costs cannot be underestimated. In the budget process, it is important to determine the type, quantity, and quality of personnel needed to accomplish the work plan of the organization during the fiscal period.

Personnel costs are most frequently figured on a *fixed growth* as opposed to a fixed ceiling budget. An organization should take several approaches to determining personnel costs. First, it should determine the costs for full-time personnel. Since the bulk of these individuals are already on a fixed salary, the annual allowable percentage of growth is frequently determined by the legislative body. In government and nonprofits, it may be a fixed percentage of a salary base (e.g., cost-of-living raises will be 3.5% of base salary for the next fiscal year). This continues to be the most common type of approach to salary adjustments. The fixed growth may be based on anticipated available funds, government determined cost-of-living increases, inflation figures, or what the legislative body negotiates with the employees or their representatives.

Most full-time, salaried employees are compensated within a fixed or stepped salary range. Employees are hired at a negotiated salary within the established range. Every year the employee is promoted to the next salary level within the range. Table 4.4 illustrates the steps within salary ranges for different positions.

The salary ranges, or steps, as shown in Table 4.4, represent the increased salary that each employee will receive after a specified period of time with the organization. A person starting at step 1 of position code 87456 (program supervisor) will receive $32,653 in annual wages.

Table 4.4
Sample Annual Step Increase with Cost of Living Adjustment

Position Code	Position Title	Step 1	Step 2	Step 3	Step 4	Step 5
87456	Program Supervisor	$32,653	$35,069	$36,577	$38,150	$39,791
85543	Assistant Director	$53,365	$57,314	$59,779	$62,349	$65,030

Each review period, usually one year, the person can anticipate a salary increase to the next range. Step increases are frequently linked to performance measures and reviews. In addition, there may be annual cost-of-living increases that would affect each step. The salary steps in Table 4.4 are based on a 4.3% increase, from one step to the next (i.e., $32,653 * 1.043 = $34,057.08). However, governing bodies frequently include a cost-of-living increase to the base salary. In this example, the program supervisor at Step 1, when moving to Step 2, is authorized a 4.3% increase. Additionally, the governing body authorizes a 3.1% cost-of-living increase. The salary step plus the cost-of-living increase amounts to a 7.4% pay raise ($32,653 * 1.074 = $35,069.32) and this amount becomes the new step 2 base salary.

Cost-of-living increases are not automatically granted, but are awarded at the discretion of the governing body. At step six, the individual has achieved the highest pay possible in that position. Salaries for permanent part-time positions may be determined the same way, or they may be based on another approach. Seasonal or temporary part-time positions can be determined in any number of ways. For these positions, most organizations begin with a minimum wage approach and then value each position on the basis of its contribution to the organization, the prevailing wage for a similar position, and the availability of qualified individuals.

Staffing Issues

Determining staffing needs for programs is a function of each budget manager. Information pertaining to the number of personnel, the rate of pay, the length of time to be employed, and the justification for the position need

to be given to the BPO for inclusion in the budget. Tools that are used by BPOs and CEOs to determine staffing needs include reviewing staffing patterns and analyzing organization charts, tables of organization, or manning tables. Additionally, the BPO needs to look at workload trends in the organization. Leaders of organizations should be involved in some type of workload analysis that provides this information. Included in workload trends are new or amended legal requirements affecting the organization's programs and services, newly initiated policies or changes in existing policy regulations, planned changes in the organization, changes in systems and/or procedures, and approved workload consolidations. The CEO must attempt to balance workload demands with available personnel and match these demands with existing commitments. At the disposal of the CEO is his or her experience over a period of years with staffing patterns. This experience quotient, although not scientifically based, is an important component of the budgeting process. Finally, the CEO has to make certain assumptions about the future. These assumptions are based on existing facts, past history, knowledge of the organization and its members, political implications and realities, and stakeholder expectations.

Personnel costs are collated for all positions and placed in the department's operating budget. If the personnel costs are assigned to different funds within the organization, the positions are appropriately categorized. This process can become complicated, but when properly organized and cross-referenced, it becomes a clear and whole picture. In most organizations, there will be some salary savings every year. A salary savings occurs when one or more positions in the organization remain empty for any period of time. For example, a position paying $2,000 a month that is vacant for three months results in a $6,000 salary savings for the organization. Over a period of time, these vacancies can produce significant savings for the organization. In some cases, the BPO may know about these vacancies in advance; in other cases, they will occur during the fiscal year, and adjustments will have to be made in the operating budget. Most BPOs anticipate salary savings and figure them into the budget.

For some organizations, the cost of overtime pay is a significant issue. The Fair Labor Standards Act (FLSA) prescribes overtime rules for most organizations. Employees can be identified as exempt from overtime, depending on their position and responsibility, but most employees will more likely be affected by the FLSA overtime rules. Public organizations are particularly challenged by the overtime costs. In a northern community, for example, the parks and recreation department may be tasked to be part of the snow removal process—a responsibility whose cost is almost impossible to predict, but which will always involve overtime. Most organizations set aside a certain amount of the personnel costs for overtime. The organization must determine what is an acceptable level of overtime and how the organization will fund the overtime. In some cases, organizations have adjusted work hours to overcome their overtime costs.

Contractual Service Requirements

A service delivery option that has gained in popularity among sport, tourism, and recreation organizations in all sectors is the practice of contracting other agencies or businesses to do those functions that were traditionally done by the contracting organization. The justification is a belief (usually supported by evidence) that outside providers can, in certain situations, perform a service with better quality and/or greater efficiency. "Contracting out," is not seen as an admission of weakness, but as a positive step in serving clients and promoting business opportunity. California State Parks, for example, devotes a web page to "Doing Business with California State Parks" and lists over 50 different opportunities ranging from water testing services, to film and video services, to hotel/motel accommodations, to waste management. New York City, like many organizations, makes a number of concession opportunities available to the private and nonprofit sectors. The YMCA is an example of a nonprofit organization that operates public facilities under contract to communities. For example, Maplewood, Minnesota contracted with the YMCA to operate its aquatic facilities. In North Las Vegas, Nevada, the YMCA has operated a multi-generation center since 2011. Agreements with nonprofits are becoming more common as public agencies look for ways to reduce operating costs.

A growing operations trend in public, nonprofit, and private organizations is the use of limited contractual services, also known as public/private partnerships or agreements. The growth of contractual services is also based on the belief that some functions can be done more effectively and efficiently at a lower cost by an outside vendor. Portland Parks and Recreation Department (Oregon) describes its openness to such partnerships by encouraging public/private agreements.

Businesses, nonprofit organizations, and individuals are invited to form public-private agreements to carry out revenue-generating programs or capital-related activities supporting Portland Parks & Recreation's goals. Effective public-private agreements have the potential for not only mobilizing additional resources for park and recreation programs citywide, but also promoting greater effectiveness of those programs—helping us sustain a healthy park and recreation system.

Many organizations have some form of contractual arrangement with outside vendors, even if it is only for maintenance the office copy machines. The level and extent of contractual management is not typically an issue in the budget process. At some policy level, the decision (and action) to become involved in contractual management has already been made. If the organization has not made the decision about contracting for services, then the budget preparation process may

Case Study
Texas State Park System Leased Concessions Opportunities

Concessions are a significant element in the Texas State Park System. State park concessions offer economic benefits in many smaller communities. They also generate revenue to offset the cost of operating Texas State Parks.

Typical concessions are marinas, recreation equipment rentals, food service operations, equestrian facilities, park stores, and other accommodations. A concession may be as simple as vending machines or as complex as a resort development at Ray Roberts Lake or an entire park, like Longhorn Cavern State Park.

The purpose of offering a concession program is to seek public/private partnerships and assistance, where appropriate, and to provide quality services, programs, and facilities that enhance the enjoyment and provide convenience and recreational experiences for state park visitors.

Our goals are:

–Develop and maintain concession facilities and services that contribute to high quality experiences for park visitors

–Seek new opportunities to improve and provide services, programs, and facilities to park visitors through concessions

–Park visitor services and accommodations in the following categories may be operated by a concessionaire under contractual arrangements:

• Food and merchandise sales
• Equipment rentals for recreational use
• Merchandise vending machines
• Marine supplies and services
• Horse livery
• Transportation
• Automotive supplies and services
• Fishing piers and fishing marinas
• Resort developments

Source: https://tpwd.texas.gov/state-parks/jobs/park-concessions

be used to make such a determination. Issues that need to be resolved include the following:

- comparative costs between the sport, tourism, and leisure service organization accomplishing the task versus a commercial contractor
- presence of qualified contractor personnel
- actual cost
- impact upon the organization's productivity
- quality of work

Materials, Supplies, and Equipment Costs

Materials and supplies comprise the second-costliest item in most operating budgets. Budget managers need to determine the type, quantity, and quality of material required to carry out the annual work plans. Organizations will take into account issues such as present inventories, cost, patterns in changing use or provision of services, and new programs and services. The organization usually begins with an assessment of what was purchased the previous year and whether it was sufficient to accomplish the tasks. Program reports, year-end reports, and inventories should provide some of this information. Proposed work plans are compared with the previous year's work plans to determine changes in anticipated needs. If standards have been established for programs or services, or if they exist and are modified, they may affect the need for materials and supplies.

Projected inventories assist in providing another picture of material and supply needs. Many organizations have adopted a just-in-time delivery process in which the supplier provides storage and delivers on call. For example, one park district decided that it needed 30,000 pounds of seed for the entire year. In previous years, it had purchased seed on three separate occasions. Consolidating into a single purchase and requiring the supplier to maintain the inventory reduced the cost significantly and eliminated the need for long-term storage requirements. The purchase was negotiated so that payment was made only when seed was delivered. Thirty thousand pounds was the guaranteed purchase at a guaranteed price.

Where purchasing departments are nonexistent, it is incumbent upon the sport, tourism and leisure service organization to participate in well-formulated purchasing processes. The establishment of *standing purchase orders* with local vendors is a common strategy for maintenance operations. Larger purchases are typically bid to a number of potential vendors. A set of specifications is established for each purchase item and used as a guide for the vendor to make a bid. Careful development of the specifications is essential, as well as an effort to ensure that bias is removed from the purchasing process. There is rarely a requirement that an organization take the low bid, but when not taking the low bid, the organization must demonstrate that the higher bid more closely conforms to the advertised specifications. At what level the organization must go in order to bid is typically determined by statute and also by the legislative/policy body.

Equipment purchases include items that have a longer life and contribute to the operation of the organization. They can include items such as fitness equipment, pitching machines, computers, lawn mowers, trucks, and cars. In almost every situation, the equipment has a specific life span, after which it will need to be replaced. In preparing the equipment portion of the budget, the sport, tourism and leisure service organization needs to ensure that there is an inventory of all equipment. The inventory should include date of purchase, classification code of the equipment, description of the item, purchase price, its current location, current condition (which may require an annual inspection), and life expectancy. For some pieces of equipment, the BPO may desire to establish a replacement schedule. A replacement schedule allows the BPO to look forward and anticipate major equipment costs for the organization. Some organizations set aside money every year for replacement of equipment. These reserved funds are usually kept in a special capital replacement fund/account. This strategy reduces the drain on the operating budget for major purchases that all take place in one fiscal year. Equally important is the spreading of major purchases over several years, rather than trying to make all purchases in a single year.

Reviewing Budget Estimates at the Departmental Level

While the CEO must ultimately accept responsibility for the final budget document, it is the formal and informal processes that make up the submitted document. Throughout the process, there is a continuous flow of information up and down the organization, exchanges of detailed data, analyses of decisions regarding the budget, etc. Each budget manager should meet with the BPO and the CEO and brief them on their section of the budget document. The CEO should provide a completed budget presentation for the sport, tourism and leisure service organization's budget managers and then answer questions. This final review assures that all of the issues associated with the budget's preparation have been discussed and the document is ready to be submitted to the legislative or policy-setting body.

Summary

Budgeting is an essential management tool in any sport, tourism and leisure service organization and requires an understanding of how budgets work, of basic budgeting processes, and of how managers use budgets. The budget cycle, budget calendar, and budget guidelines drive the budgeting process for sport, tourism, and leisure service organization administrators. A knowledge of funds and how they operate contributes to the ability of managers to allocate appropriate resources. Budget formats are prescribed by the legislative or policy body and determine how they choose to look at budgets. Corresponding budget preparation philosophies suggest an approach to budgeting ranging from fixed ceiling to alternative budget proposals. The 18-month to two-year planning cycle for any budget allows a sport, tourism, and leisure service organization to plan, approve, implement, and close a budget. The knowledge of estimating budget costs increases with experience, but knowing how to prepare an activity budget is often the foundation for all budget processes in sport, tourism and leisure service organizations.

Additional Resources

https://www.portlandoregon.gov/parks/46379

https://www.parks.ca.gov/?page_id=22313

https://www.lasvegasymca.org/about-the-y/y-history

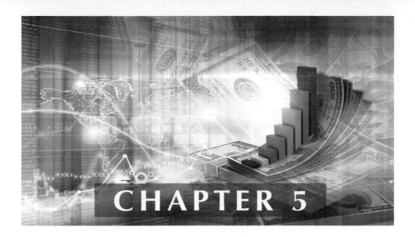

CHAPTER 5

Budget Formats

Introduction

Budget preparation is, at a minimum, a two-stage process. Establishing budget guidelines and determining the budget format are essential tasks. There are many budget formats that an organization can select. Each sport, tourism, or leisure service organization must determine the format that is appropriate for its needs. A commercial or nonprofit organization may select a format that meets its unique needs, but the format for public organizations is more likely dictated by legislation. A board of directors or a legislative/policy board may establish a different format consistent with its own needs, and a large organization may specify the use of a variety budget formats, each with a different purpose and linked by a unit budget. This chapter looks at the most common budget formats that sport, tourism, and leisure service organizations use.

Common Budget Formats

Budgets can be presented in a variety of formats, but the choice is typically dependent upon the organization CEO's preference of how a budget should be organized. The purpose of budgeting is to secure financial control and to achieve the goals, mission, and vision for the organization. Additionally, managerial productivity is seen as an important outcome of budgeting. The type of approach adopted by a sport, tourism, or leisure service organization is a reflection of how the legislative or policy body best feels the organization should achieve its goals. Different types of budget formats reflect an emphasis upon different goals. For example, an object classification or line item budget focuses on financial control. Program and performance budgets focus on goal attainment. Zero-based budgeting and planning-programming budgeting systems focus on managerial productivity. Performance budgets focus on employee, program, and organizational performance measures. The CEO and the BPO should determine the level of detail that is needed for any budget format. Six of the most common operating budget formats are presented in this chapter. They are representative of formats found in most sport, tourism, and leisure service organizations.

Object Classification and Line Item Budgets

The object classification and line item budgets are the most common of all budget formats used by sport, tourism, and leisure service organizations. Both styles of budgets, for example, rely on a coding system for all revenue and expenditure items. In this section, primary emphasis is given to the object classification budget, although the same principles can be used for a line item budget. An object classification or a line item budget organizes budgets into predetermined categories. Each line in the budget reflects either an expenditure or a class of expenditures. For example, "personnel costs" becomes a class with sub-classifications. Sub-classifications might include types of personnel (program, maintenance, support, full-time, and part-time). "Benefit costs" is another class that can be subdivided into accounts, such as medical, retirement fund, and uniforms. The emphasis in the object classification budget is on input rather than measurement. Conformance and compliance with an established budget is paramount to understanding how the funds are being used or collected. Construction of an object classification budget involves four steps, but before initiating the budget

construction, specific information must be gathered. The data to be gathered were addressed in Chapter 4 and are partially repeated here. In an object classification budget, the organization commonly uses a fixed ceiling approach to allocation. Preparation items include the following:

1. budget letter with guidelines from the legislative authority
2. approved budget growth allowance (usually a percent of the current budget)
3. list of classification codes
4. personnel salary ranges and steps
5. specific or unusual budget request issues
6. budget forms

Items 1, 2, 4, and 5 will be common to most budget formats.

Step 1: Collect All Budget Data

Begin by collecting all budget data from the organization's budget managers. The assignment of budget data collection should be delegated to the lowest possible level. Budget managers should complete as much of the budget process themselves for familiarity purposes. The BPO will ultimately check all information provided.

Step 2: Identify Appropriate Classification Codes for Each Budget Item

The classification codes and budget forms will be unique to the object classification budget. The list of lines or classification codes is given to the BPO and budget managers who must ensure that each item in the budget conforms to the existing codes. The list of codes can be many pages long and will have definitions to assist the budget manager as he or she attempts to determine which item fits within a particular code. Examples of expenditure classification codes and definitions appear in Table 5.1.

Step 3: Place Items in Detailed Sub-classifications (Object Codes)

Assignment of expenditure and revenue items to classification object codes, as depicted in Table 5.1, is followed

Table 5.1
Example Object Classification Codes and Definitions

100	<u>Personnel</u> <u>Services</u> - Expenditures for direct personnel services including wages, benefits, overtime, special benefits, and the like. Includes full-time, part-time, and seasonal employees.
200	<u>Contractual</u> <u>Services</u> - Services involving work performance by non-organization employees through a contract or agreement. The work may include the contractor to provide equipment and commodities.
230	<u>Printing</u> <u>Services</u> - Expenses related to printing, copying, reproduction, binding, publications, advertising and the like.
240	<u>Utilities</u> - Charges for heat, water, electricity, telephone, cable or satellite television, network connections, 2-way radio, and so forth.
250	<u>Repairs</u> - All repairs for fixed structures. Includes building repair, but does not include repairs to vehicles, equipment, and expandable items.
300	<u>Commodities</u>
310	<u>Materials</u> - Items, more permanent in nature, that may be combined or converted for other uses. Includes lumber, concrete, concrete blocks, paint, and other building materials.
320	<u>Supplies</u> - A commodity consumed, impaired or worn out in an expectedly short period of time. Includes such items as paper, crafts supplies, food, clothing, fuel, oil, grass seed, fertilizer, and so forth.
400	<u>Encumbered</u> <u>Obligations</u> - Fixed expenses and/or binding contracts created from previous obligations of the legislative authority. Included in this category could be temporary loans, interest on city's debt, grants and subsidies, court ordered payments, and the like..
500	<u>Existing</u> <u>Charges</u> - Provided at the option of legislative authority. It could include costs of insurance, licenses, rent, leases, and the like.
600	<u>Debt</u> <u>Payment</u> - Includes the amount of annual payment for reduction on debt incurred by the legislative authority.

by placing the same items into more detailed expenditure and revenue object codes (Table 5.2). Recall that the purpose of the object classification budget is to provide financial control. Placing each expenditure and revenue item into a detailed sub-classification allows the CEO and the BPO to have a clear and detailed understanding of the total budget and where the money is going to be spent. It allows multi-year tracking of revenues

and expenditures for comparative and evaluative purposes. The advantage of this type of a budget format lies in the CEO's ability to be aware of subtle, as well as major, shifts in the budget.

The amount of detail desired determines how many object codes the organization will utilize. An organization that is not concerned about budget detail may have few object codes, while an organization that is trying to gain

Table 5.2
Example Classification Codes by Object (Partial Listing)

100 - <u>Personnel</u>	252 - Repairs to Buidings / Structures
110 - Salaries, Regular	253 - Repairs to Playgrounds,
120 - Salaries, Temporary	Equipment and Services
130 - Salaries, Seasonal	300 - <u>Commodities</u>
140 - Salaries, Permanent Part Time	310 - *Materials*
200 - <u>Services, Contractual</u>	311 - Masonry
210 - *Communications*	312 - Road Materials
211 - Postage	313 - Lumber
212 - Telephone	314 - Paint
213 - FedEx, UPS, Freight	315 - Sand
214 - Internet Communications	316 - Other Materials
215 - In State Travel	330 - *Supplies*
216 - Out of State Travel	321 - Office Supplies
220 - *Subsistence, Care & Support*	322 - Program Supplies
221 - Storage & care of vehicles	323 - Sport Supplies
222 - Per Diem - In State	324 - Craft Supplies
230 - <u>Printing Services</u>	325 - Aquatic Supplies
231 - Printing	326 - Food Supplies
232 - Photocopying	327 - Clothing & Dry Goods
233 - Wordprocessing	328 - Chemicals, All Kinds
234 - Photography	400 - <u>Encumbered Obligations</u>
235 - Web Page Design/Maintenance	410 - *Rent*
236 - Marketing / Advertising	411 - Buildings & Spaces
237 - Publication of Notices	412 - Equipment & Vehicles
238 - Blueprints / Plans / RFPs	420 - *Insurance*
240 - <u>Utilities</u>	500 - <u>Existing Charges</u>
241 - Natural Gas Utilities	510 - Interest on Debt
242 - Propane	520 - Pensions & Retirement
243 - Electrical Utilities, Outdoor	530 - Grants & Subsidies
244 - Electrical Utilities, Indoor	540 - Taxes
245 - Water Utilities	600 - <u>Debt Payment</u>
246 - Sewer Service	610 - Serial Bonds
247 - Telephone Service	620 - General Obligation Bonds
248 - Network Connections	630 - Revenue Bonds
250 - <u>Repairs</u>	640 - Sinking Fund Installments
251 - Repairs to Equipment	650 - Other Debt Payment

control of its expenditures may require very detailed coding. One park and recreation director noted that almost 50% of the department's expenditures were coded as "miscellaneous." Upon investigation, it became obvious that no one had previously shown a concern about tracking expenditures. When it was explained to the organization's members that the goal was to gain a better understanding of expenditures, the director refused to accept miscellaneous classifications, and expenditure control and knowledge of expenditures increased significantly. The object classification codes shown in Tables 5.1 and 5.2 are illustrative extracts from much larger documents.

Figure 5.1 illustrates how an object classification code is used. In this case, the first two numbers represent the department, such as the parks and recreation or the convention center. The middle four numbers represent the expenditure classification code (Table 5.2), which describes where the money was spent. This can also be a revenue object code. The last four digits represent the program area (e.g., sports, recreation centers, marketing, communication, office administration) and specific programs. This might include the sport program area and its programs of softball, volleyball, and flag football. Codes can allow highly detailed analyses of budgets.

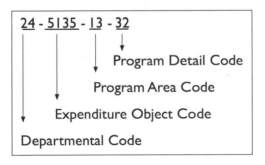

Figure 5.1. Object Classification Code

The code in Figure 5.1 could represent the Guest Activity Department [24] purchasing art supplies [5135] for the arts program's [13] pottery classes [32]. Expenditures identified down to the program detail provide budget managers with a clear picture of costs of programs and allow managers to make fiscal decisions based on relevant information. The object classification budget can function simultaneously with other budget formats.

Step 4: Organize the Budget Information

The main effort at this stage involves collating the collected budget information, checking and verifying budget requests, organizing data for a budget review, making recommendations regarding budget allocations, and presenting the budget to the legislative body for approval.

Table 5.3 illustrates a traditional object classification budget for an aquatics program. The budget is combined with all other activity budgets in the agency to provide a total budget picture for the legislative body. The budget provided to the legislative body would provide the level of detail seen in Table 5.3, and a summary table representing all of the budget areas as depicted in Table 5.4.

The budget request is presented showing (1) the previous fiscal year actual, (2) the current fiscal year approved, and (3) the proposed fiscal year request (Tables 5.3 and 5.4). The terms that are used to present each fiscal year are important. In the case of Tables 5.3 and 5.4, the *last year actual* represents the expenditures for that fiscal year. The fiscal year is complete, and all of the expenditures have been reported and recorded. The current fiscal year

Table 5.3
Partial Object Classification/Line Item Budget

Object Code	Description	Last Year Actual	This Year Projected	Next Year Requested
100	Personnel			
110	Salaries, Permanent Full-Time	$35,242	$37,568	$38,556
120	Salaries, Temporary	$2,500	$1,850	$3,240
130	Salaries, Part-Time	$67,561	$72,558	$75,042
200	Services: Contractual			
220	Subsistence & Support			
221	Storage & care of vehicles	$250	$325	$380
328	Chemicals, pool	$2,785	$3,200	$3,540
322	Program supplies	$986	$1,100	$1,250
	Concession Supplies			
326	Snack Bar Supplies	$2,250	$2,685	$3,100
328	Cleaning Supplies (Chemicals)	$250	$250	$285
252	Repair concession counter	$0	$0	$2,500
	Other Supplies			
322	First Aid Kits	$250	$310	$365
323	Sports Awards - Patches	$185	$200	$225
235	Flotation Devices	$450	$250	$520
240	Utilities			
241	Natural Gas	$1,100	$1,250	$1,400
244	Electricity	$1,150	$1,500	$1,850
247	Telephone	$1,200	$1,300	$1,400
248	Internet Connection	$75	$100	$115
420	Insurance			
421	Fire & Comprehensive	$850	$1,000	$1,200
422	Liability	$4,500	$6,500	$7,200
230	Printing Services			
236	Marketing	$35,000	$42,000	$51,000
235	Web Site Design	$2,500	$1,500	$3,200
231	Printing, Brochures	$12,000	$15,000	$18,000
	Total	$171,084	$190,446	$214,368

Table 5.4

Summary Budget Data

Object Code	Description	Previous Year Actual	Current Year Projected	Next Year Requested
100	Personnel	$102,893	$110,126	$114,314
200	Services, Contractual	$1,072	$4,100	$4,500
	Utilities	$1,072	$1,164	$1,425
	Insurance	$3,625	$3,871	$4,125
	Marketing	$14,343	$16,250	$17,500
300	Supplies & Equipment	$8,747	$9,954	$12,336
	Total	$131,752	$145,465	$154,200

approved indicates the budget that is in process and is called *this year projected*. The legislative body has approved the budget, but because the fiscal year is not complete, there is only an estimate of what the actual budget will look like at the conclusion of the fiscal year. This picture of the budget is incomplete, but has been reported on the basis of anticipated revenues and expenditures. The proposed fiscal year is called *next year requested*. At this point, the legislative body has not approved the proposed budget. Until it is approved, it remains a requested budget.

The object classification budget is the most common of all budget types. It is malleable enough to be used with other budget formats. This flexibility allows the sport, tourism, or leisure service organization to maintain fiscal control and simultaneously administer the budget in other formats in order to accomplish other objectives. Almost all other budget formats use the object classification budget as a foundation for the creation of more complex budget styles.

Program Budget

Program budgeting is also called the program planning budgeting system (PPBS). Traditional budgeting formats focus on input (personnel, program, and capital costs), but program budgeting focuses on outputs (end results, goals, and objectives). The emphasis of program budgeting is upon effectiveness rather than efficiency or spending. This emphasis represents a major shift in the way budgets have historically been constructed. The major advantage of the program budget is its ability to cross unit boundaries when budgeting for a program with expenditures from more than one department. Program budgeting is not used much at the federal government level, but is used widely at the state and municipal levels of government, and by nonprofit agencies. The high data needs of this budgeting system and the relative complexity of large organizations has been suggested as a reason for the lack of utilization of PPBS in places like federal government agencies.

A program budget takes expenditures and breaks them down into viewable units according to the service provided. For example, the object classification budget looks at the entire budget, but not at programs. It provides no understanding of how or why funds are to be expended. The program budget provides more information to the budget manager and others who have a desire to know how the allocated funds will be spent. The budget is subdivided into program areas, and each program area is reported as a separate part of the budget. For program managers, this separation provides greater authority and accountability. Their decisions are reflected in their management of their portion of the budget. Figure 5.2 shows how a program budget format might be organized. A program budget is organized to provide details to the program manager, the administrators, and the legislative/policy body.

The department represents the level of budget authority and responsibility. At this level, the department or division refines the organization's vision, mission, and major goals to fit programs. The program areas are aimed at specific goals, or in the example of many sport, tourism, and leisure service organizations, program-specific areas (or populations). Programs are designed to meet more specific population needs; they are also referred to as support activities. They

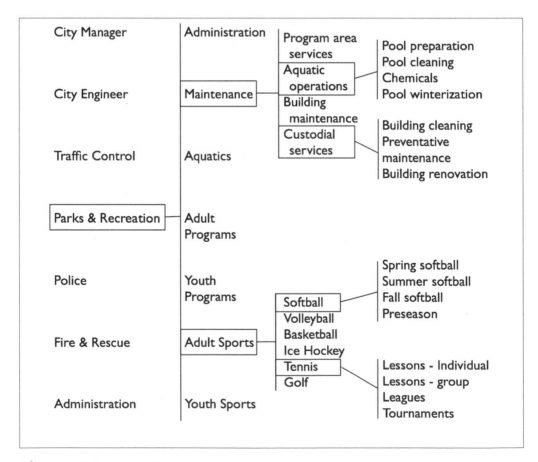

Figure 5.2. Example Structure of a Program Budget

emphasize the importance of focusing on who is to benefit from the service or program. Program elements represent the basis that budget units use to achieve the goals and objectives of the organization. Consistent with the budgeting process is the development of goals and objectives at each level of the structure. Examples of goals and objectives developed for the adult sports tennis program in Figure 5.2 are represented in Figure 5.3.

The development of program budgeting has necessitated the rethinking of how budgets are administered. Moving decision-making and budget administration down to the lowest levels of the organization introduced a new set of concepts and budget terms, such as *cost centers*. Cost centers comprise an independent entity embracing all of the costs of activities and items necessary to achieve a distinct and measurable outcome. Operating funds for the cost center may come from several divisions or departments. When expenditures are made, they are charged back to the parent budget authority, but the cost center identification remains consistent. Assuming softball is a cost center, the maintenance division will fund softball field maintenance and preparation and charge it back to adult sports. In an object classification budget, field maintenance and preparation would only appear as an expenditure that's not necessarily tied to a program area. In a program budget, with softball as a cost center, the cost of maintenance and preparation is linked to both the program area and the maintenance division. The maintenance manager now knows how much is being spent overall and how much is being spent just for softball.

Department of Parks and Recreation
  Goal: To provide recreational services and opportunities for leisure experiences
        for all members of the community.

Program Area: Adult Sports
  Goal: To provide opportunities for adults to participate in life-time sports
        promoting physical and mental well-being.

Program: Tennis
  Goal: To increase the opportunity for members of the community to be exposed
        and to participate in tennis programs.
  Objective: Provide opportunities for individual lessons.
            Provide opportunities for group lessons.
            Provide leagues for individual and team participation.
            Provide tournaments for local, regional, and state level participation.

Program Element: Individual Lessons
  Goal: To provide opportunities for individuals to improve their tennis game
        through individualized instruction.
  Output Measures: Number of individuals participating in lessons
                   Number of individuals returning from previous sessions/years
                   Effectiveness of lessons as measured by participant satisfaction
                   survey
                   Cost-efffectiveness of program

Figure 5.3. Program Budget Goals and Objectives for Figure 5.2

For the budget manager who may have previously budgeted only for staff and program supplies, he or she now has a clear picture of the total cost of the program, including salaries, supplies, maintenance, marketing, and administration.

A new concept called *responsibility centers* (also known as budget decision points) has also been introduced. The term indicates a focus on budget analysis and decision making. A responsibility center manager knows each program budget's cross-functional boundaries within and between divisions and departments. Program managers with cost center responsibilities make decisions regarding budget allocations within the context of their authority, and negotiate with other responsibility center managers for additional resources. For example, if the budget manager for softball determines that maintenance costs need to be increased substantially, he or she cannot arbitrarily make that decision. Rather, the cost center budget manager must discuss the issue with the functional area budget manager. In this case, the adult sports supervisor will discuss the issue with the maintenance superintendent.

Step 1: Goals and Objectives

Step 1 assumes the organization is already organized around program areas of functions, as illustrated in Figure 5.3. This suggests that program managers and functional area budget managers are already talking to one another. The sport, tourism, or leisure service organization develops goals and objectives for the fiscal year that can be a continuation from previous years, updated, modified, or completely new for each fiscal year. Program managers develop goals and objectives for each level of the program budget, down to program detail. Desired outcomes are determined in advance, as well as decisions about methods of measurement.

Step 2: Provide Detailed Narrative for Each Program

Program areas were identified in step 1. In step 2, the program manager will identify those features of the program that meet specific goals and objectives. The program manager further explains how and why each is important. The narrative relates to the program's goals and objectives.

Step 3: Determine Expenditures and Revenue for the Program

Using the processes discussed regarding the preparation of a simple activity budget (see Chapter 3), the budget is adjusted to a program budget format. In those areas where measurements are defined, the expenditures will be tied to specific objectives.

Table 5.5 illustrates a completed aquatics program budget. Presenting revenue plans is accomplished in the same way. However, revenues are not necessarily tied to objectives. The budget presented in Table 5.5 depicts a program budget with objectives, a narrative, measurement criteria, and income and expenditure expectations. Although each sport, tourism, and leisure service organization will have its own format for developing a program budget, each will follow a similar pattern. The components remain remarkably similar, with an emphasis on outcomes rather than inputs.

Performance Budget

A performance budget is often referred to as a measurement of efficiency.

Table 5.5
Example Program Budget

			2018 Actual	2019 Projected	2020 Proposed
Program: Aquatics					
Program Description: The aquatics program is designed to provide recreational opportunities, competitive opportunities, and learn-to-swim lessons to residents.					
Performance Objectives: 1. Provide open swim opportunities for all members of the community. 2. Increase the number of program offerings by 5% over the previous year. 3. Achieve a 90% positive satisfaction rating from participants in all programs.					
Measurement	Program	Objective	2018 Actual	2019 Projected	2020 Proposed
Demand					
Estimated Participants	Open Swim	1	38,146	45,000	47,600
	Other Swim	1	9,877	10,000	10,500
	Learn-to-Swim	1	2,300	2,600	2,800
Estimated Programs		2	30	45	47
Workload					
Actual Registrations	Open Swim	1	38,166	45,000	47,600
	Other Swim	1	9,877	10,000	10,500
	Learn-to-Swim	1	2,300	2,600	2,800
Actual Programs		2	30	45	47
Actual Participation		2	50,353	57,645	60,947
Total Community Population			110,000	110,000	110,000
Productivity					
Average cost per participant			$2.67	$2.51	$2.52
Average cost per participation			$2.67	$2.51	$2.52
Effectiveness					
Program participation increase/decrease over previous year			0.00%	14.48%	5.73%
Program offerings increase/decrease over previous year			0.00%	50.0%	4.44%
Participant percentage positive rating			88.00%	88.00%	90.00%
Percent Total Population Served			45.78%	52.40%	55.41%
Narrative					
The aquatics program serves a variety of populations in the community, including people with disabilities, adults, seniors, and pre-school and school-age youth.					
Resources					
Expenditure categories	Personnel		$102,893	$110,126	$115,200
	Operations/Maintenance and Supplies		$13,590	$15,038	$16,800
	Insurance		$3,488	$3,600	$3,800
	Marketing		$14,354	$16,200	$18,000
		SUBTOTAL	$134,325	$144,964	$153,800
Revenues	General		$15,600	$15,000	$16,000
	Fees & Charges		$105,314	$109,964	$115,000
	Donations & Grants		$13,368	$20,000	$25,000
		SUBTOTAL	$134,282	$144,964	$156,000

It is most frequently used with recurring routine or recurring operations, where measurements can be readily developed and applied. Performance budgeting became popular with municipal governments in the early 1950s and remains in use today. It fits well into operations where repetition and measurement can be made easily, such as certain repetitive maintenance functions (e.g., mowing, grounds maintenance, and custodial work). One of the benefits of a performance budget is its ability to provide managers with performance-cost data. Although the development of measurement data is beyond the scope of this book, it requires an assessment of what work needs to be accomplished, what equipment is available to do the work, and capabilities of employees to accomplish the task. It requires a constant assessment and monitoring of the measurement performance standards by managers.

Step 1: Identify Those Components of the Budget that Fit a Performance Format

The budget preparation officer must determine which of the organization's operations are most conducive to a performance budget format. These operations should meet the following criteria:

- It should be possible for the work to be quantified into measurable work units
- It should be possible for the quality of the provided service or activity to be measured
- The performance should be able to hold constant

Examples of work that can be easily quantified include mowing, tree planting, fertilizing, ball diamond preparation, and most grounds maintenance activities, construction activities, and some custodial work.

Step 2: Establish Work Units

For each activity that will be measured, work units must be established. This is accomplished by measuring current work levels, benchmarking work activities against the same work accomplished by similar organizations, and looking at standards established by various measurement organizations. In the early stages of establishing standards, flexibility is important until an achievable and acceptable standard is determined. Work units are normally measured in performance per hour, although they can be established in other ways. Examples of measurements include square feet per item, cubic yards, acres, sales per advertising campaign, revenue per available room (RevPAR), etc. A grass-mowing crew using hand mowers may have a work unit established as .75 acres per hour. The same crew using gang mowers may have a standard of 4.5 acres per hour.

Step 3: Determine the Cost per Work Unit to Be Measured

The cost per work unit is based on a number of variables, which include the task to be completed, the capabilities of the employees, the cost of expendable supplies and special equipment, the depreciation of equipment, and travel time and distance. The BPO looks at all of the variables that affect the work unit and establishes a cost standard. For a mowing crew that travels throughout the city, the cost standard would include travel time between sites, salaries of the mowing crew, cost of gasoline for travel and mowing equipment, maintenance costs of equipment, actual time spent on site mowing, and other associated costs of the task.

For illustration purposes, assume that an 18-acre park has 10 acres of open area suitable for a gang mower; four acres that require hand mowing with a 42-inch mower; and two acres that call for 22-inch hand mowers. Two acres are not mowed. The mowing crew takes an average of 2.5 hours to accomplish the task. The cost of personnel is $35.00 an hour and other costs are figured at $13.00 per hour, with an additional 30 minutes assigned for travel. Three people work on the mowing crew. After a period of assessment and evaluation, the following standards are established:

- Gang mowing at 8 acres per hour
- 42-inch hand mowing at 2.2 acres per hour.
- 22-inch hand mowing at .75 acres per hour

By these standards, 1.25 hours are needed for gang mowing and 1.8 hours for hand mowing with the 42-inch mower. Based on budget projections (expenditures for mowing), only 2.5 hours (average) have been allocated for mowing and there is insufficient time or money available to accomplish all of the tasks. Either the standard, the time available for the work, or the equipment must be modified.

Step 4: Determine the Frequency with which Work Must be Completed

Determining costs is, in part, a decision on how frequently particular work needs to be completed. Frequency of recurring tasks and of annual tasks is based on need and the level of quality assigned to a particular task. Using the mowing example, the standard for cutting is that the grass will be cut when it reaches six inches in height. In a normal year, that would be every 10 days from late April through mid-October. If, however, it rains more than normal, the grass will grow more quickly, and mowing may occur every eight days instead of every ten. This legitimate frequency change will require a budget adjustment. It will also require a workload adjustment, as the mowing crew will not be able to accomplish other tasks that may have been assigned to them. Just the opposite would occur in a low-rain year, when mowing might be needed as infrequently as every three weeks. More than likely, the mowing crew's responsibilities would change, and they might have to water new trees and turf areas to preserve them through a drought. At best, the budget manager must work on what he or she believes will occur. In those activities not affected by weather, the budget planning can be more accurate but the budget manager must still recognize that things will not always go as planned.

Step 5: Organize Budget

When all of the performance budget steps are completed, the budget manager or BPO compiles the budget. Table 5.6 depicts a sample format for a performance budget.

New Directions in Performance Budgets

In recent years, public agencies have made major advances in quantifying outcomes. While performance budgeting follows the same process previously described, it is also linked to strategic

Table 5.6
Performance Budget Format

Activity	Work Unit	Cost per Work Unit	Number of Work Units	Frequency	Number of Times	Total Cost
Softball diamond preparation	per diamond	$9.45	18	daily	98	$16,669.90
Gang mowing	per acre	$4.45	800	10 days	12	$42,720.00
Hand mowing	per acre	$7.25	120	10 days	12	$10,440.00
Tree planting	per tree	$12.85	1200	once a year	1	$15,420.00
Pool cleaning	per pool	$32.50	3	7 days	18	$1,755.00
Trash pickup	per day	$26.50	2	daily	275	$14,575.00
Sign installation	per sign	$21.50	40	as required	1	$860.00
Total						$102,439.80

planning. One of the key elements of a performance budget is its collection of adequate performance data and, while this collection is routinely done in the private sector, it is an approach that is relatively new to the public sector. Results have been less than convincing to many budget managers, but processes continue to be refined. The key difference in performance-based budgeting is the asking of a different set of questions. In traditional object classification budgeting, budget managers ask what it will take to complete a particular task. In performance budgeting, the first question asked is, "What is the outcome to be achieved?" The outcomes become the basis for performance measures.

Performance budgeting focuses on results from budget expenditures. Where a line item budget shows what is allocated for a particular function, such as cleaning park restrooms, a performance budget depicts what each dollar spent will achieve, such as park user satisfaction with the cleanliness of park restrooms. It could include residents served, trees planted, water use reduction in gallons saved, sport teams served, special events provided, places for relaxation, and so forth.

Running Budget

A running budget has become more common among nonprofit organizations and businesses, as they attempt to rapidly adjust budgets to changing revenue streams. The running budget is more of a way of managing expenditures than it is of constructing a budget. The budget can be constructed in any format, but decisions about expenditures are made on a scheduled basis throughout the fiscal year. If revenues exceed expectations, the budget can be adjusted to reflect the increased revenue. If revenues decline, the budget can be reduced to accommodate the decreased income. There are some distinct disadvantages to this type of budget. First, budget managers never know from day to day exactly what their budget will be. Second, good decision-making is hampered when the focus of decisions appears to be on revenue rather than on needs. Third, budget managers may be encouraged to make big purchases early to ensure that their major items are secured. This can lead to a mind-set in the organization that is not conducive to stability or growth.

On the positive side, a running budget allows an organization that experiences negative financial growth to be responsive to that situation by appropriately reducing costs. In addition, the organization does not extend itself beyond its capabilities and also recognizes a responsibility to its legislative body and to its constituents by not incurring debt. This type of budget is most often seen in organizations experiencing or anticipating significant declines in funds that are available for the operating budget.

Step 1: Construct the Operating Budget

Any budget format can be used, whether it is an object classification, line item, program, or performance budget. The principles for construction are similar to those for any of the other budget formats. As just noted, the change comes in the administration of the budget. When the budget preparation is complete, it is submitted to the legislative body for review, modification, and ultimate adoption.

Step 2: Determine Frequency of Budget Reporting

The benefit of the running budget is that it helps the organization to always know the status of its expenditures and revenues and to make adjustments in authorized expenditures. Adjusting expenditures at different times during the fiscal year allows the organization to adjust

its budget when revenues are uncertain. Adjustments can occur on a daily, weekly, bi-weekly, monthly, or quarterly basis. The decision of frequency will be determined largely by the anticipated variance in revenues and how often revenues are received. A historical analysis provides a great deal of information for making this decision. If it is a membership-based organization, and membership dues are received on a scheduled basis, anticipated revenues might be predetermined. If, for example, dues statements are sent out quarterly, then the organization can project on a quarterly basis its progress toward achieving its revenue goals. Under these circumstances, it may only be necessary to do a budget adjustment on a quarterly basis.

Step 3: Establish Spending Limits

Establishing spending limits is a common practice of BPOs as they attempt to lighten the impact of concentrated spending by the organization. In a running budget, it is particularly important. Each part of the organization will need to negotiate levels of spending in any given time period. For example, arbitrarily allowing the different parts of the organization to spend only one-fourth of their budget per quarter does not take into account the special needs of the different parts of the organization. The administrative branch might easily spend one-fourth of its budget each quarter, but the convention division might spend 60%

Case Study
A Bicycle Shop Uses a Running Budget

Many commercial enterprises in the sport, tourism, and leisure services arena are small to medium size and may be geographically dependent. Bicycle shops are such a case. In 2015 there were approximately 4,000 bicycle shops (specialty bicycle retailers) in the United States and in excess of 66 million bicyclists. Creating an

Case Study (cont.)

operating budget for an existing bicycle shop and using a running budget allows the owner to remain focused on budgets and expenditures. Table 5.7, below (Belle's Bicycle Shop) depicts a budget report 5 months into their fiscal year. The report would be for May, since most commercial enterprises run on a January to December fiscal year. This report could easily be produced by their bookkeeper using commercially available basic accounting software like QuickBooks. Recognize that, depending on where the bicycle shop is located, they will not likely spend exactly 8.3% (1/12th) of their budget each month or generate an equal amount of revenue. Like most commercial enterprises, bicycle shops have peak seasons —Christmas, late spring, early summer, and back to school (September). Bicycle sales tend to follow those peak seasons. Bicycle maintenance, by contrast, tends to flow more evenly over the entire year, with a slight decline between Thanksgiving and New Year's Day. The running budget allows the owners to determine when it is the best time to make major purchases, allows them to lower inventory during non-peak seasons, and anticipates when the repair and maintenance operations will carry the primary burden for revenue generation.

Table 5.7
Sample Report for Use with Running Budgets

Belle's Bicycle Shop Running Budget - 5 Month Report

	BUDGET	ACTUAL TO DATE	UNDER/OVER
INCOME			
OPERATING INCOME			
Bicycle Sales	$ 76,000.00	$ 42,500.00	$ (33,500.00)
Merchandise for sale	$ 20,000.00	$ 10,600.00	$ (9,400.00)
Bicycle Maintenance	$ 15,600.00	$ 8,580.00	$ (7,020.00)
Bicycle Repairs	$ 42,500.00	$ 26,350.00	$ (16,150.00)
TOTAL INCOME	**$ 154,100.00**	**$ 88,030.00**	**$ (66,070.00)**
PERCENT			**57.1%**
ANNUAL EXPENSES			
OPERATING EXPENSE			
Advertising	$ 3,800.00	$ 1,710.00	(2,090.00)
Depreciation	$ 400.00	$ 400.00	-
Dues & Subscriptions	$ 150.00	$ 150.00	-
Insurance	$ 1,100.00	$ 1,100.00	-
Interest Expense	$ 75.00	$ 75.00	-
Maintenance/Improvements	$ 500.00	$ 250.00	(250.00)
Taxes & Licenses	$ 450.00	$ 180.00	(270.00)
Telephone	$ 800.00	$ 400.00	(400.00)
Utiliites	$ 1,380.00	$ 690.00	(690.00)
Merchandise for sale	$ 82,327.00	$ 53,512.55	-
	$ 90,982.00	**$ 58,467.55**	
PAYROLL - Annual			
Payroll Expenses	$ 13,200.00	$ 5,280.00	(7,920.00)
Salaries & Wages	$ 26,400.00	$ 10,560.00	(15,840.00)
	$ 39,600.00	**$ 15,840.00**	
OFFICE			
Office Supplies	$ 350.00	150	(200.00)
Postage	$ 200.00	120	(80.00)
	$ 550.00	**$ 270.00**	
TOTAL	**$ 131,132.00**	**$ 74,577.55**	**56.9%**

of its budget in the second quarter and the other 40% over the next three quarters due to normal seasonal fluctuations. Creating an acceptable balance of spending across the different parts of the organization requires a thorough understanding of the budget process. Of necessity, it must be negotiated with the budget managers throughout the organization.

Step 4: Determine How Often the Budget Will be Adjusted

Making budget adjustments based on actual revenue and expenditures is the heart of the running budget process. Applying the same criteria discussed in step 2, the legislative/policy body must determine how often the budget will be adjusted. Typically, budget adjustments will be made in both the revenue and expenditure portions of the operating budget. A fiscal quarter (three months) is the most frequently accepted adjustment period; however, in a highly volatile budget situation, adjustments can be made more often. Historical and current information must be provided to the legislative body, along with recommendations for adjustment. A clear rationale should be made for the adjustment, along with a discussion of how the adjustments will affect programs, services, and outcomes.

Zero-Based Budgeting

A zero-based budget is so named because it assumes that the organization starts each fiscal year as if it doesn't have an existing budget. While this isn't entirely true, its purpose is to allow the sport, tourism, or leisure service organization to look at everything it does and value each activity's importance to the organization and its stakeholders. It allows the organization to look at all of its operations, activities, and functions and to justify each one. In doing so, it promotes the re-allocation of funds from lower priorities to higher priorities. The zero-based budget is an effort to be responsive to changing needs of the organization and of those it serves. This budget format is designed to facilitate competition among units and functions.

Assumptions of Zero-Based Budgeting

Several assumptions are made about an organization's capability to implement zero-based budgeting. First, it is assumed that the organization can clearly define its goals and objectives. This can be a somewhat daunting task that requires considerable attention at each level of the organization. Second, it is assumed that there is adequate budget preparation time. Zero-based budgeting is a time-consuming task. If the organization's members do not have time to contribute, then it should not be used. Third, it is assumed that there is a healthy relationship between units in the organization. There will be an impact upon the morale of the organization, due mostly to increased competition for available budget funds. Fourth, it is assumed that the budget can appropriately be based on internal needs. Zero-based budgeting is internally focused and does not always take into account external needs or requirements. Fifth, zero-based budgeting incurs a significant cost in terms of time, money, and effort as the initial transition is made. There will be ongoing costs for time and effort as the process progresses. First introduced in the 1970s, zero-based budgeting struggled for acceptance because the process was so ponderous and time consuming. Organizations simply could not operate day to day activities and simultaneously spend the hours required for data collection, data analysis, and reporting of data to create a new budget. In today's connected and data driven world, the term "big data" is embraced and software and analysis methodologies can do in hours what before took weeks and months. Some have suggested that it may be time to rethink and more positively embrace zero-based budgeting.

Step 1: Defining Goals and Objectives and Decision Units

Program and budget goals and objectives are established and decision units are defined at the program/service level. The development of measurable goals and objectives is based on outcomes and user/customer-defined expectations. Great care must be taken in developing these goals so that effective measurement can occur. Goals are developed at multiple levels and assumed to be part of a top-down process. The organization's goals are developed at the CEO level jointly with the legislative or policy body. These goals become the guiding or overarching goals of the organization. All other goals and objectives developed need to be consistent with these corporate goals. Ultimate measurement of the effectiveness and appropriateness of programs and services will be based on these goals. At each descending level, goals are developed to provide direction and to ensure consistency.

A *decision unit* is a point at which budget and programming decisions are made—ideally, at the lowest reasonable level in the organization. In aquatics, for instance, the decision unit may not be the whole aquatics program, but rather, could be one of its program divisions

such as learn-to-swim, swim club, adult lessons, and youth lessons. At a later analysis level, these could be combined or remain separate. Budget requests should not be based on previously experienced levels of expenditures. To do so reduces the effectiveness and purpose of zero-based budgeting.

Table 5.8 depicts an example decision unit worksheet without the fiscal information. The decision units do not need to be consistent with the organizational structure, but frequently are. In a YMCA, for example, the initial decision unit would likely be at the program manager level. If, however, a program manager has responsibility for multiple program areas, then the decision unit could be modified. It would seem logical that, wherever possible, the decision unit and organizational structure are consistent.

Step 2: Decision Assessment and Analysis

Step 2 involves analyzing and assessing each decision unit within the framework as a *decision package*. The decision package becomes the building block of zero-based budgeting. The decision package is a cluster of decision units related to the accomplishment of the unit's goals and objectives. As the budget process moves up the organization, decision packages can be grouped according to commonality of objectives. This grouping could result in decision units not remaining within the structure of the organization. Managers at the program delivery level must look at alternative means of achieving objectives, as well as determining appropriate levels of service and use of resources. Zero-based budgeting is meant to encourage managers to focus their energies on

Table 5.8
Decision Unit Worksheet Example

Program Area: Learn-to-Swim	Division: Aquatics	Fiscal Year: 2009
Level of services currently provided	Justification for current / expanded level of service	Funding Recommendations
• Lessons offered throughout the year with an emphasis on summer months • Lessons offered for beginners through advanced swimmers • Lessons offered to pre-school through seniors and people with disabilities • Summer services offered at 11 community pools 3 times a week and 4 time each day offered • Other seasons offered at 3 indoor pools after school for youth, during the day for seniors and people with disabilities and evening for adults • Currently meet Red Cross learn-to-swim guidelines	The learn-to-swim program has been offered for over 40 years by the department. Each year more than 5,000 youth and adults are served by the program. It represents the only community-wide program provided. The school district does not provide a program and the YMCA caters to a smaller number of individuals, all members. The program has consistently been revenue positive (paid for itself and generated a profit) in the aquatics division.	It is recommended funding be retained at the current levels. Any reduction in funding would result in a degradation of the program and it has high community support and visibility. It has consistently received high marks from those who participate. In some cases families are in their 3rd generation of participation in swim programs. Revenue levels could be increased if fees are increased. A study to determine the impact of a fee increase is recommended.

those activities that are perceived as most critical to the organization's mission and vision. Activities that do not directly contribute to the vision and mission are either eliminated or receive reduced levels of funding. Such decisions encourage managers to set up levels of service and to seek alternative funding.

Included in the decision process are variables such as workload, performance measures, cost-benefit associated with each level of service, revenue, and expenditures. Each decision package can receive one of four responses:

- increased resources
- commitment to maintain current resources
- reduced resources
- elimination of resources

Additionally, decision makers are given alternatives to accomplish each decision unit. The alternatives allow decision makers to determine the most appropriate approaches for the delivery and level of services.

Step 3: Ranking Decision Packages

Once all of the data have been generated, the ranking of decision packages occurs at predetermined levels. Decisions are based on consistency with the organization's goals and objectives, determined cost-effectiveness, how well each decision package meets the needs of the users, availability of funds, and any predetermined policy guidelines. Rankings of decision units are made and funds are allocated to the decision units. Once funds are allocated to decision units, they are returned to the appropriate organizational level for budget action. If a decision unit does not receive the level of funding necessary for sustaining it, the program manager will already have created alternatives for funding at reduced or increased levels, either for different delivery approaches, or for no funding at all. The decision process will put such alternative approaches into action.

Step 4: Budget Request Formulated

The budget format may be any of the budget formats previously discussed. It is submitted through normal processes to the budget preparation officer and the CEO for final submission to the policy or legislative body.

Advantages and Disadvantages of Zero-Based Budgeting

There are several advantages to using a zero-based budgeting approach. First, in zero-based budgeting, all programs start out on equal footing at the beginning of the process—no single program is favored over another. Programs, services, and functions all have the same opportunity to receive funding. Second, budget decision makers will find that more detailed information is generated than it is with other budget formats. When implemented properly, there is a systematic and well-conceived allocation process. Third, the goals of the organization and its individual and collective activities are under constant review and prioritization. For this reason, individuals who work in this format are more actively engaged in goal setting, goal attainment, and goal negotiation. Fourth, this budget format provides service level options where none may have existed before. It requires that program managers look at alternative program and service delivery methods and at what level each program or service should or could be delivered. Finally, it has been suggested

that zero-based budgeting eliminates waste in the organization by eliminating or reducing funding for programs that are not meeting the needs of the organization or its clientele.

A number of disadvantages have been suggested for zero-based budgeting. Most significant among the reported disadvantages is that it has not lived up to its promises. In instance after instance, there were high levels of budget pre-activity as individuals and groups attempted to influence the decision-making (sometimes with high levels of success). The results provided outcomes similar to the pre-zero-based budgeting format and also there appeared to be no perceptible change in the decision-making process or quality. The second major disadvantage of zero-based budgeting concerns information overload. Decision-making is ultimately top-down in zero-based budgeting, and everything generated at the lower levels is designed to aid the decision maker. Under zero-based budgeting, one state governor found himself with 11,000 decision packages—far more than any management expert would recommend and more than can be effectively dealt with by any one individual.

Modified Zero-Based Budgeting

While zero-based budgeting as a single budget format for an organization has fallen out of favor, it remains in use in a modified form as a supplemental format in many organizations. For example, in Phoenix, Arizona, city departments submit an estimate (called the base) of the costs associated with providing their current levels of service for the following year. City budget and research staff review the base budget submissions to ensure that only that funding necessary for current service levels is included in the department's base. The review is called a "technical review" because of its non-programmatic line item-by-item review of a department's budget. A department's base funding may differ from its current-year funding for a variety of reasons. For example, an increase or a decrease in utilities would be reflected in the base.

In addition to base budget submissions, departments submit 5 to 10% of their following year's base budget for potential elimination. These submissions are called "base reductions," and they represent the department's lowest-priority activities. At the same time, departments are also asked to submit any requests for new, restored, or expanded programs, which are called "supplemental budget requests." The base reductions and supplemental requests include all costs associated with a specific program or service, such as the cost of operating a new swimming pool. Costs for pool operation would include those associated with personnel, chemicals, building maintenance, supplies, and utilities.

When the base reductions and supplemental requests are submitted, they are ranked according to the department's priorities. The department's ranking indicates whether it would be possible to make a base reduction in order to add a new program. The ranking also indicates which supplemental programs and base reductions are most critical to the department.

Summary

Budget formats allow sport, tourism, and leisure service organization managers and administrators to view a budget from a particular perspective. These formats may be combined for differing purposes. The object classification budget is the most common of all budget formats for sport, tourism, and leisure service organizations. Other common and effective budget formats include the program budget, the performance budget, the running budget, and the zero-based budget.

Additional Resources

https://www.entrepreneur.com/businessideas/bicycle-repair-service

https://trektravel.com/2015/04/lessonsfrom-owning-a-bike-shop/

https://nbda.com/how-to/want-to-start-a-bike-shop-pg70.htm

https://drive.google.com/drive/u/1/folders/1O4MmUI2-hrrqegHKt5P0B-vXZuJk20rZ2

https://www.mckinsey.com/businessfunctions/operations/our-insights/why-zero-based-budgeting-makes-sense-again

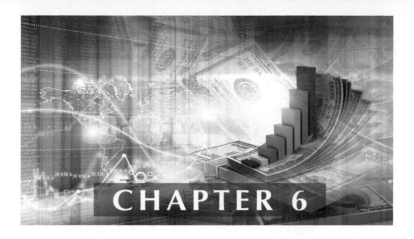

Budget Presentations

Introduction

Budget preparation essentially ends with required presentations to authorized decision makers. Decision makers are policy or legislative bodies that may include board members, city council members, the owner of the company, key stakeholders, a board of directors, or members of the organization. All agencies must, at some point, make budget presentations. There is no standardized format for creating a budget presentation and each organization may approach budget presentations differently. It could include a simple overview of proposed revenues and expenditures or a more complex description of program areas, projected revenues and expenditures, and a linkage with the organizational goals and vision.

Purposes of Budget Presentations

Budget presentations have many purposes, but ultimately, the primary purpose of the presentation is to inform decision-makers and facilitate a discussion and decision for the proposed operating and capital budgets. Beyond an informative role, budget presentations serve several additional purposes. A budget presentation is the culmination of the budget preparation period and suggests to those receiving it a completion. Second, the presentation provides an overview of the proposed budget with sufficient detail to determine sources and amounts of revenue and proposed expenditures. It frequently allows for a historical perspective when the budget presentation includes comparisons with previous years' budgets.

The budget presentation is seen as an introduction to the detailed printed budget that can be as long as 300 or more pages or as short as five pages in length. In public and nonprofit organizations, as well as in commercial business enterprises, the budget presentation is frequently made in conjunction with the delivery of the budget document. Most organizations operate with goals and objectives and/or performance measures. Effective budget presentations link financial recommendations to organizational goals and objectives and performance measures. Budgets are a reflection of trends that impact an organization's need to deliver products and services in a specific area. Chicago (IL) Park District states in their fiscal year (FY) 2018 budget document that the key goals of the budget include the following (Chicago Park District, 2017):

- Additional designated Special Recreation sites to meet the increasing demand for programming and pilot programs for adaptive sports, cultural and social opportunities in various communities
- New aquatic programs, including triathlon training and advanced skill adult fitness
- Increased outdoor and environmental education programs through the Nature Play Space Initiative
- Advancing the Building on Burnham initiative by growing natural area acreage toward our goal of 2,020 acres by 2020

Budgets are tools used by organizations to maintain and strengthen existing operations and to create new or expanded resources in communities and organizations. In times of recession, budgets will reflect how reduced resources are allocated and identify services that are either reduced or eliminated. In the Naperville, Illinois Park District budget, three capital projects were highlighted in the proposed budget document (Naperville Park District, 2018):

- Frontier Sports Complex Improvements (Phase III) ($600,000)
- Southwest Community Park Design ($92,000)
- Playground Renovations ($930,820)

In the preceding example, the three emphasis areas involve capital improvement funds (discussed in Chapter 16). Naperville Park District's use of strategic and master plans to identify and justify budget recommendations is typical of public organizations. Reference to strategic plans, master plans, and long-range budget plans are integral to budget development and presentation. In addition, the use of these documents strengthens decision-makers' and stakeholders' understanding of relationships between the operating and capital budgets and the intended agency outcomes.

The Written Budget Document

The foundation of any budget presentation is the proposed budget. It contains the proposed operating, revenue, and capital budgets for the organization. Revenue and operating budgets are combined as a single budget, with the capital budget as a separate document. The two budgets are frequently discussed at separate budget presentations. Budget documents, for mid-sized and large communities may be hundreds of pages in length. The 2018 Naperville Park District budget document was 208 pages in length. A municipal park and recreation agency, which is part of a larger city or county government will typically have their budget included in the city/county budget. For a separate agency, such as a smaller park district, nonprofit sports program, youth-serving organization, or a private event management company, their budget document may be considerably smaller. The larger and more complex the organization, the larger the budget document. Almost all organizations utilize a standardized budget format (Chapter 5), and this standardization allows for consistency in reporting processes and for comparison between budgets.

The budget document is organized around the operating and capital budget. Typically, the document has an introductory letter from the chief executive officer (CEO) presenting the budget and providing a transmittal letter or an executive summary style letter. It is written to the governing body, such as a city council, park board, board of trustees, or owner. The next items in the budget document are included at the discretion of the CEO. These can include, but are not limited to the following.

Reader Guide

The reader guide prefaces and highlights each section of the budget document. The Elmhurst Park District, for example, has 10 sections including a transmittal letter, budget summary and district profile, operating budget, capital budget, revenue analysis, and glossary (Elmhurst Park District, 2018).

Vision, Mission, and Goals

This section provides the core direction-setting documents and measures for the organization. Most agencies link their budgets to these documents. Stakeholders are demanding increased budget

accountability, and so alignment with the vision, mission, and goals is essential.

Budget Philosophy

The budget philosophy provides the decision-maker with the fundamental commitments associated with the budgeting process. For example, the Forest Preserves of Cook County (FPDCC), IL (2018) identified among their budget philosophies the commitment to (1) "Restoring ecological health and protecting the diversity of plants and animals that depend on the preserves, (2) providing well-maintained buildings, trails and other facilities, and making them accessible to all county residents, (3) increasing outreach to underserved communities and expanding educational and recreational opportunities for all residents, and (4) managing with excellence, transparency, and sound financial practice."

Current Challenges

This section presents issues or concerns with which the organization is presently dealing. In most instances, these are major issues, areas of focus, or new initiatives that were introduced with the previous year's budget. FPDCC stated their current challenges (2018) as "(1) Restoration work, a core part of the FPDCC's mission, has historically been funded with reserve funds. The district currently spends about $3.9 million per year on restoration and land management; this work will be incorporated into the district's annual Construction and Development budget without further reliance on reserve funds, and (2) cost of living adjustments included in collective bargaining agreements and increasing health care costs represent an increase of approximately $1.6 million in 2018.

Significant or Proposed Changes

This identifies shifts in the organization's funding priorities. This section alerts readers to changes that impact the overall budget. In some instances, the changes may signal a major realignment of expenditure or income priorities. More often new projects, expansion or contraction of existing projects, shifting funding from one project or program to another, and elimination of programs, are included in this area. The changes are presented separately for the operating and capital budget. FPDCC identified a $5.5 million gap in the FY2018 budget that it is closing through both cost-reducing measures and revenue-generating efforts.

Future Issues and Concerns and Trend Analysis

This area demonstrates an awareness of potential new funding commitments or reduction in funding sources. Trend analysis allows the organization to identify future issues and concerns that will positively or negatively impact the organization and its operating budget. Budget presentations focus on these issues and alert decision makers to potential issues. FPDCC, as an example, identified 70 partners in the development and launching of a collaborative network implementing the District's Next Century Conservation Plan (2018). The plan includes scenarios and strategies to make Cook County a national leader in urban conservation.

Organizational Chart

The organizational chart provides the decision maker with an overview of the organizations operational structure. It offers decision-makers a view of the

organization and an awareness of where funds are allocated in order to make more informed judgments.

Revenue Summary

The revenue summary provides a written description of the revenue sources, the level of revenue anticipated from each, historical presentation of revenue services, potential or anticipated shifts in revenue, and projections for the next fiscal year. The revenue summary provides an overview for decision makers and helps the CEO focus the discussion. In addition to a traditional revenue summary FPCC provides a two-page "revenue glossary" identifying all revenue facilities in the system and the type of revenue collected and projected. It includes contract/concession services to outside vendors, partnerships, and internal revenue.

Expenditure Summary

The expenditure summary has the same function as the revenue summary, except it focuses on expenditures.

Budget Detail

This is usually the last item in the budget document and includes the entire budget. Detailed budget items are grouped into budget classifications. It is the largest section of the budget package. The budget detail gives the particulars of each component in the organization. For example, a sport facility might have its operating budget divided into personnel, multiple program operations (such as special events, sport specific events, rentals), maintenance operations to include specific and general, and so forth.

Presenting the Budget

The budget presentation is crafted by the CEO and chief finance officer (CFO). It follows the structure of the written budget document emphasizing key issues of the sport, tourism, or leisure service organization's budget as well as providing a community-wide perspective. A budget presentation can take 10 minutes to several hours, based on organizational traditions, complexity and size of the budget, expectations of the board, or the desire of the CEO. In more complex organizations, the CEO may require each division or department to provide a budget presentation. The presentation is designed for delivery to the governing body with opportunity for questions, input, and recommendations. Budget presentations can be divided into multiple meetings if the budget is overly complex. This can occur when the approving body wants budget detail and selects specific sections of the budget to look at separately, such as revenue, expenditures, and operations.

There are no standardized formats for budget presentations. Grand Rapids, Michigan Parks and Recreation Department FY2018 budget presentation focused on five areas (City of Grand Rapids, 2018): Capital projects financed by millage, operational efficiency, recreation program growth, park maintenance ideology shift, and tree planting and long-term care. Their proposed operating budget of $5.8 million was presented using 50 visual aids (PowerPoint slides). The overview included an initial link to the organization's strategic plan, FY2018 initiatives, detailed description of proposed budget allocations, specific information on how funds will be allocated within specific budget areas, statistical facts about the parks and recreation system, progress toward meeting performance measures, programs, and planned and completed capital projects. The presentation was organized to orient decision-makers to the organization, critical issues, successes, plans for the future, and positive impact on the community, and to reflect what the CEO identified as being consistent with the organization's vision and mission. The budget summary was divided into operational areas including recreation, forestry, park maintenance, golf course, and cemetery operating budgets, capital budgeting, and funding sources. Grand Rapids Parks and Recreation is a department of the city government and its budget presentation was a component of a larger budget presentation comprising many city divisions and departments.

Elmhurst Park District is an independent governmental agency with separate taxing power. Its FY2018 $21 million budget took 29 slides to present and included budget philosophy, major goals, focus points, budget capability, a five-year financial forecast, the proposed budget, fund balances, and department presentations (Elmhurst Park District, 2018). The parks and planning department's budget presentation provided detail on capital projects such as playground replacements, paving and parking lots, athletic field establishment and renovation, and vehicle and equipment replacement. The recreation and facilities department focused on the delivery of programs and services and divided the budget presentation into delivery areas including recreation programs, indoor swim center, museum, racquet and fitness club, tennis club, and golf operations for three golf courses. For each area, the presentation included usage statistics, and relevant information about program participation, revenues, evaluations, and expenditures.

Principles of Effective Presentations

The budget presentation is typically made with standard presentation software, such as Microsoft's PowerPoint application, Prezi online presentation application, Apple's Keynote application, or Google Slides (online). Any presentation software should be reviewed for its ability to effectively structure and deliver a presentation. The easier it is to create and operate the presentation, the more likely it is that the presentation will meet the objectives. Below are some guidelines to assist CEOs, budget directors, and program managers when utilizing visual aids in presenting budget information. Remember, the presentation software should compliment, not detract from the focus on the budget.

First, know the audience. Most individuals, including board members and stakeholders, will not readily understand some of the terminology used by the staff. When making assumptions about what listeners know, it is better to provide more rather than less explanation. For example, the term CIP, meaning capital improvement program, can also mean catalog in production, classification of instructional programs, center for international policy, center for instructional performance, center for institutional planning, and so on. It is not necessary to provide a description of the terminology on the presentation screen, but it is always safest to avoid the use of acronyms.

Second, ask "What do I want the final presentation to look like?" Begin with the end in mind and look at the presentation as a set of building blocks that, when organized, create a broad level of understanding. In other words, the whole is more powerful than the parts, but the whole cannot exist without the parts. When the presenter becomes engrossed with the parts more than the structure, then the whole presentation is weakened. Presentations should be outlined in advance. Too often budget presentations are organized in sections that are independent of one another and the final product looks disjointed and fails to engage the viewer. When a presentation is poorly organized, the decision-makers are left at a disadvantage, trying to determine what is more important and what is less important. Decision-makers and public or stakeholder audiences are key to the development of a presentation. Two separate presentations are recommended. Public and stakeholder audiences have general and specific concerns. Almost always it revolves around, "What's in it for me (or my group)?" Decision-makers have a broader scope of understanding of the organization and its needs while stakeholder audiences may focus on details that primarily impact their interests. Smoothly guiding the viewers to proposed alternatives or solutions allows for better decision-making. A visual presentation does not stand alone, but is dependent upon a well-prepared oral presentation. It can be supplemented with handouts that highlight the key points of the proposed budget.

Third, what is the internal structure of the presentation? There are some general guides that should be used in making any presentation. The font size and type should be easy to read from a distance. As a general rule, the font size should not be smaller than 30 point. There are two primary styles of typography. Serif fonts are considered to be more readable on the printed page while sans-serif fonts are considered to be more legible on monitors or projection screens. A sans-serif typography is depicted in Figure 6.1. Common sans-serif fonts used for presentations include Arial, Avenir, Trebuchet, Tahoma, Gill Sans, and Verdana.

Parks and Recreation Budget Presentation

Fiscal Year 2020

Figure 6.1. Example of a Clear Font to Use in Visual Presentations

It is effective and useful to utilize graphics and photographs. Research suggests that retention is improved by 50% when graphics are used, and only 10% when bullet points are exclusively used. The principle of keeping it simple should be maintained in the use of graphics. The graphic should support the text and presentation. A good rule of thumb is to determine if the graphic can stand without the text. If so, then consider either eliminating the text or reducing it considerably. Too many presentations include whole paragraphs of information with the presenter reading the information to the listener. Figure 6.2 provides an example of a graphic element that focuses on simplicity in its design.

Presenters should avoid using busy backgrounds in presentation slides. The effective use of photos as a background to the text is difficult to achieve and too often the background diminishes impact of the text (Figure 6.3).

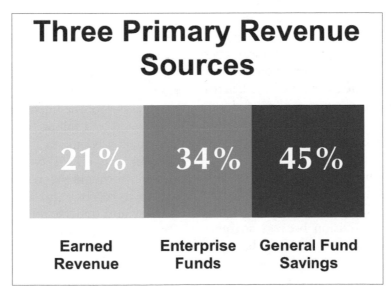

Figure 6.2. Sample Image with a Simple Message.

Figure 6.3. Example of a Slide with a Distracting or Confusing Background.

If the text is difficult for the listeners to read, then they won't read it. They may even disengage from the presentation.

Avoid putting too much information on a single slide. Information overload reduces the attentiveness of the listener. It is better to use two or three slides on a topic than to cram it into a single slide. Figure 6.4 shows a slide that is guilty of information overload.

In Figure 6.4, the text is informative and deemed important by the organization, but the viewer experiences fatigue or confusion because so much information is presented in one blast. The result is disassociation with the slide and loss of intended communication.

Using background sounds and audio clips to highlight slides, a variety of different slide transitions, and multiple text builds is tempting, but it can be very distracting to the audience. The slide transition and text structure should remain consistent and simple throughout the presentation. A single, simple-to-read font may appear boring, but it is much easier for the intended audience to understand and follow the presentation. Individual letters or graphics flying all over the screen only confuse the viewer. It should be remembered that the focus of any presentation is the delivery and understanding of a budget, not a demonstration of the presentation software's flexibility.

The presentation of graphs and tables should be done carefully, with the viewer in mind. Most individuals cannot process multiple sources of conflicting data. For example, a chart that shows many crossing lines is much more difficult to

Some Common Rules for Graphics and Tables

- Keep the form of a chart consistent across the presentation.
- Bar charts should always begin a zero.
- Don't blow apart pie charts (separating the chart). It makes it difficult for the viewer to put it back together.
- The National Institute of Health reports that as many as 8 percent of men and 0.5% of women with Northern European ancestry have the common form of red-green color blindness.
- Use Vischeck.com to review your graphics for color deficiency.
- Don't use more than six colors in a single table or graph and be consistent across all pages.
- It is actually easier for viewers to use a grayscale to create perceptual ordering. Focus on black and gray scales.
- A grayscale with perceptual ordering (black to light gray) that is consistent is more easily read. There has to be a perceptive differentiation in the grayscale.
- If you are using colors, use universal colors—red, blue, green, yellow, etc.—are more easily recognizable and make it easier to see differences between colors.
- The intent of a graphic or table is to supplement the text and enhance understanding.
- Test all of your graphics on an audience who is NOT familiar with the topic.

Figure 6.4. An Example of a Presentation Slide that Includes Too Much Text.

follow than a bar chart depicting data more simply. It is difficult for the brain to conceptualize more than three or four data points simultaneously. Figure 6.5 shows a slide with multiple data points. The scale depicts differences between the data, but the table is not self-explanatory. It leaves the viewer confused about the data because they cannot make sense of them. The presenter would need to spend considerable time explaining the data and likely they would still not be understood.

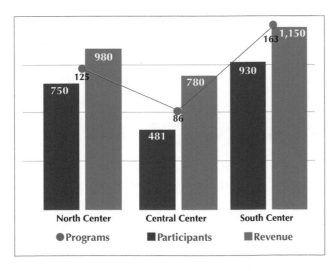

Figure 6.5. Example of a Presentation Slide with Too Many Data Points.

Figure 6.6 is a historical treatment of the a city's share of property tax over a 23-year period. The line graph depicts a data point for each year supplemented by a corresponding value label that reports the actual percentage. The graph is simple, the title is reflective of the content, and the reader can visually track the decline in the city's share of property tax. The graph is both descriptive and expressive. The only problem with this representation is the size of the font. The text is so small that it would be difficult to read from a distance.

The use of tables and pie charts is very common, as is the use of colors and legends that show what the colors depict (see above for rules on developing and using graphics). Carefully label tables and charts and, where appropriate, elements within the graphs. Creativity is generally a valued attribute, but it is best to stay away from 3-D charts and animated graphics. Studies show that 3-D effects reduce comprehension. Individuals struggle to put an exploded chart back together. If people have to work too hard to understand your presentation they will stop listening. Tables and charts should be kept simple, as demonstrated in Figures 6.6 and 6.7. The latter shows two effective ways that the same data can be displayed; a column chart and a pie chart. Pie charts are graphically pleasing, but individuals have more difficulty determining value differences in pie charts than in column or bar charts.

Note the use of within-graphic text rather than a legend, and the actual percentages that are presented on the pie chart so that viewers do not need to guess.

Figure 6.6. Example of a Good Presentation Slide with Font Size Problem.

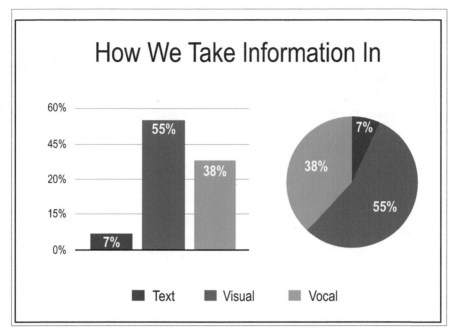

Figure 6.7. Presentation of Data Using a Column Chart and a Pie Chart

Presentation Tips

Here are some final tips for presentations. The first is practice, practice, practice! Rehearse the presentation in the presence of individuals who you have asked to challenge the presentation. Rehearse it in front of a mirror and look at the performance. Record it and critique the recording. Be critical and watch for personal idiosyncrasies, such as scratching your nose, that might detract from the presentation.

During a presentation it may be important to have the audience focus on the speaker rather than on the screen. Punctuate the visual presentation with dark screens, and then return to the graphic or text slide when appropriate. In some software packages, the dark screen feature is referred to as the "B" key. When you press the "B" key on the keyboard it blanks out the presentation.

Decide who will control the visual presentation. With modern remote control capabilities it is easy to control the presentation while you talk. If you find that to be a personal distraction, then have someone else control the presentation. Make sure that this person rehearses with you. A constant "Next slide please" distracts from the presentation and suggests that you are unprepared. You should be prepared to do it both ways, just in case your assistant is not available.

Do not present in the dark. Keep the lights on. Projectors have sufficient illumination to project in a well-lit room. Do not use a podium unless mandated. Most individuals do not perform their best when trapped behind a podium. Know the material well enough to walk away from the podium and remove the barrier between the speaker and the audience.

Make eye contact. Listeners want to know that the speaker is interested in them. Eye contact gives the speaker hints about audience attention, questions, concerns, and acknowledgment. Finally, don't be afraid to show passion for the cause (the budget) that is being promoted.

Summary

The budget document may be a simple overview of proposed revenues and expenditures or a more complex description of program areas, projected revenues and expenditures, and a linkage with the organizational goals and vision. Budget presentations may have many purposes, but ultimately, the primary purpose of the presentation is to inform decision makers and facilitate a discussion and decision for the proposed operating and capital budgets. The use of best practices in presentations will enhance the delivery and reception of a budget presentation.

References

Chicago Park District. (2017). Capital Improvement Plan. Retrieved from https://assets.chicagoparkdistrict.com/s3fs-public/documents/page/2017-2021_Capital_Improvement_Plan_11.2016.pdf

City of Grand Rapids, MI. (2018). Budget Office. Retrieved from https://www.grandrapidsmi.gov/Government/Departments/Budget-Office?BestBetMatch=parks%20and%20recreation%20department%20budget%20presentation|d13b95b2-5146-4b00-9e3e-a80c73739a64|4f05f368-ecaa-4a93-b749-7ad6c4867c1f|en-US

Elmhurst Park District. (2018). 2018 Budget. Retrieved from https://www.epd.org/sites/default/files/pdf/2018%20Budget%20Presentation%20FINAL%20With%20Page%20Links%20for%20GFOA.pdf

Forest Preserve District of Cook County, Illinois. (2018). Executive Budget Recommendation. Retrieved from http://fpdcc.com/downloads/FP-CC-2018-Budget-Recommendation.pdf

Naperville Park District. (2018). 2018 Budget. Retrieved from https://www.napervilleparks.org/files/2018Fiscal-YearBudget.pdf

SECTION C

Accounting and Reporting

Communicating the results of financial management activities is facilitated by a variety of standard reporting formats of guiding principles. The two chapters in this section discuss and describe reports that focus on completed or in-progress financial actions, as well as reports that provide information to assist in guiding future actions. Management of revenue includes accounting for all income received by the sport, tourism, and leisure service organization. In addition to personal integrity, the financial manager needs skills in bookkeeping, accounting, and financial reporting in order to deal with another very important management concern—that of accounting for revenues and expenditures . This section is not intended to serve as an all-encompassing treatment of the very complex world of business accounting, but it does provide an introduction to and overview of the most commonly used accounting and reporting tools, along with a discussion of the basic principles and generally accepted accounting practices.

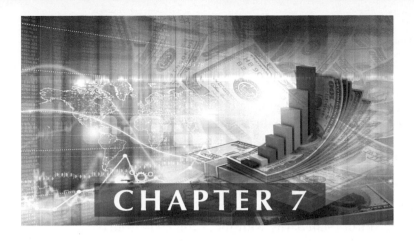

CHAPTER 7

Financial Status Reports

Introduction

One of the most important factors that, from a financial management perspective, separates successful sport, leisure service, and tourism enterprises from those that fail is the system of keeping records and reporting financial activity. The system of keeping financial records is called *accounting*, and its purpose is to allow the sport, leisure service, and tourism manager to find and easily understand information about the history of transactions and about the current financial condition of the organization. This chapter presents the basic principles of accounting and explores their use in reporting important findings to the financial manager. There could be as many ways in which financial information is recorded and organized, records are managed, and reports are summarized and interpreted as there are people who need the information. Highly customized accounting systems might meet the very specific needs of financial managers and decision-makers, as well as help to keep confidential information as cryptic as possible, but therein lies their weakness. If a highly customized accounting system is so unique that it is understood only by the user, others who may need specific financial information in order to regulate or cooperate with the organization may find it difficult or impossible to do so. This may result in penalties and/or loss of opportunity. For example, imagine a taxpayer tossing out the tax department's forms and submitting her annual tax return using a different method of reporting that she developed to match her shoebox filing system. Not a good idea! Imagine asking the bank for a business loan and providing a financial report that uses budget classifications, record systems, and report formats that are completely incompatible with those of the potential lending institution. Also not a good idea!

There is a need for order in business, and that need is probably nowhere greater than in the area of financial management.

The established order for recording and reporting financial information in sport, leisure service, and tourism organizations is based on Generally Accepted Accounting Principles (GAAP). These principles are described in publications by such recognized organizations as the Financial Accounting Standards Board or are derived from familiarity with the professional body of knowledge and prevalent practices. It is important to note that the principles and practices discussed in this chapter are "generally accepted," not "universally applied."

Accounting and reporting systems provide for measurement and analysis of the current state of financial affairs, recent financial activity, accountability and control, and operational efficiency.

Stock and Flow

In developing an understanding of and appreciation for accounting, it is important to differentiate between the concepts of stock and flow. *Stock* refers to the financial resources available to the sport, tourism, and leisure service organization at a given point in time. It is a measure of what the organization owns and what it owes. Stock information is used by financial managers to report on and to make decisions based on the current financial condition of the organization. To use a sports analogy, stock information is the score at a

particular point in an athletic contest. At the beginning of the game, both teams have 0 points of stock. At the end of the game, the home team may have 45 points and the triumphant visiting team may have 52 points. Obviously, coaches' decisions made when the stock (score) is 0-0 at the start of the contest will be very different from those made when the clock is about to run out and the stock (score) is 50-43.

Flow refers to the movement (increase or decrease) of financial resources during a certain period of time. Reports of flow focus on the net change (loss or gain) in resources, but also provide information about the nature and extent of financial activity that brought about the eventual loss or gain. In the sports analogy, flow is the activity between the start of the game and the final buzzer. The official score sheet, coaches' comments, and newspaper articles describing the game are forms of flow reports. They describe how the game moved from a score of 0-0 to a score of 45-52. Measuring and reporting flow helps managers to know how the organization moved from one stock position to another. Financial managers use balance sheets to report point-in-time (stock) conditions, while the income statement (also called a profit and loss statement or an operating statement) is used to report on financial activity (flow) between two points in time. An example of stock and flow is depicted in Figure 7.1.

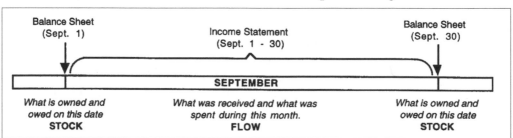

Figure 7.1. The Relationship of Balance Sheets and Income Statements in Detailing Stock and Flow

Other standard reports also help to describe the financial status of an organization. In addition to balance sheets and income statements, commonly utilized reports include retained earnings reports, petty cash reconciliation statements, budget statements, project reports, and daily RevPAR reports.

The Balance Sheet

What the organization owns and what it owes at a given point in time are recorded on the balance sheet (see Figure 7.2). Things that are owned are referred to as *assets* and are detailed on the left side of the balance sheet. Assets may be tangible items or properties, such as cash, equipment, inventories, buildings, land, etc., or they may be valuable intangible items, such as trademarks, names, or patents. Furthermore, assets may be classified as "current" (i.e., something that is or can be converted into cash within one year) or "fixed" (i.e., something that cannot readily be converted into cash). Assets are economic resources that are owned or controlled by the organization and that may benefit future operations.

Figure 7.2. Placement of Information on the Balance Sheet

What the organization owes are called *liabilities* and are recorded on the right side of the balance sheet. Liabilities include short-term (current) and long-term financial obligations or commitments to staff, contractors, lenders, suppliers, etc. The current value of investment made by the owner(s) is also a liability in the sense that it is a financial resource that is owed to the owner(s). The value of the owners' investment in the organization is more commonly termed *equity*. Both liabilities and equity appear on the right side of the balance sheet and are equal in combined value to that of the assets. Remember, the left side of the balance sheet is equal to (i.e., balances) the right side.

The simple equation that describes the balance sheet is:

Assets = Liabilities + Equity

Figures 7.3 and 7.4 are sample balance sheets for Natalie's Quilting Center. One describes the financial condition of the quilting center on February 1, and the other describes the conditions on February 29.

Notice on the balance sheets the current asset item called "accounts receivable." This item includes all amounts that the organization expects to receive in the near future due to services actually rendered or goods actually sold to customers. For example, the quilting center may have issued an invoice to a customer and is waiting for a $250 check as compensation for tutoring services recently provided. The accounts receivable category differs from cash in that the former represents money due but not yet received; and it differs from inventory in that the latter is the value of goods or service-related goods that the organization holds but has not yet exchanged for currency.

Figure 7.3. Sample Balance Sheet (February 1, 2017)

Figure 7.4. Sample Balance Sheet (February 29, 2017)

On the right side of the balance sheets shown there is a liability category identified as "accounts payable." This short-term liability item presents the value of all goods or services received by the organization and for which payment is imminently due. For example, the pile of utility bills on the director's desk represents some of the ongoing or regular payable accounts.

The Income Statement (a.k.a. Profit/Loss Statement)

Financial transactions that occur during a specified period of time (a fiscal period) are summarized in a document called the income statement. A typical income statement (illustrated in Figure 7.5) reports all expenditures and all income during the business period and identifies the difference between the two totals as either a profit or a loss. Revenue and expenditure categories used in the income statement mirror the income and expenditure categories used in the

organization's formal budget document.

It is natural to expect that the net revenue or net loss shown on the income statement would be evident in the difference between the balance statements prepared for the first and last days of the period of financial activity. That is, it seems that the $44,700 equity shown on February 1 (Figure 7.3) should increase by the $1,320 profit realized in the following 29 days (Figure 7.4). While it may occasionally be so, such a clear relationship is rarely this discernible. The reason it is not is that the balance sheet contains some information that reflects future financial activity. Note that the balance sheet in Figure 7.3 lists accounts receivable and accounts payable. Each of these items, respectively, indicates expected in-flows and out-flows of cash during the period covered by the next income statement (Figure 7.5). The balance sheet for the end of the reporting period, however, may have different asset, liability, and equity amounts, simply because those amounts will include

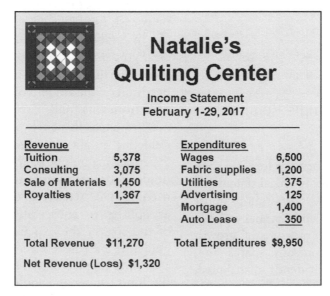

Figure 7.5. Sample Income Statement (February 1-29, 2017)

expected receivables and payables for the period immediately after (see Figure 7.4). The February 29 balance sheet is based on the stock described on the February 1 balance sheet, the flow described in the February 1–29 income statement, and additional economic activity for which there are new accounts receivable and payable.

Retained Earnings Report

When an enterprise has had a profitable period of operation, the profits can stay with the company and add to the owners' equity total. Or, at the discretion of the directors, some or all of the profits can be paid out to owners as dividends. That portion which is not paid out and, therefore, builds the equity is referred to as retained earnings. The simple Retained Earnings Report (see example in Figure 7.6) identifies net income (profit), dividends disbursed, and the earnings that are retained as equity.

Patriot's Village Amusement Park	
Statement of Retained Earnings for year ending December 31, 2017.	
Net Income for FY 2017	$1,756,890
Less Dividends declared and paid FY 2017	$800,000
Retained Earnings 31 December 2017	$956,890

Figure 7.6. Sample Retained Earnings Report

The Retained Earnings Report is one of only four primary financial statements that publicly traded corporations must publish quarterly and annually. They serve as a reliable measure of growth in the value of company shares and, if coupled with dividends distributed, indicate the profitability of the enterprise.

Internal Control

Most large sport, tourism, or leisure service organizations employ trained accountants and bookkeepers to control financial operations, accounting, and reporting. These people will record transactions, pay bills, deposit funds, and maintain accounts. They will also help the sport, tourism, or leisure service administrator to establish a petty cash fund and thereby reduce some potential organizational barriers to efficient program management.

Petty Cash

Most expenses of the sport, tourism, and leisure service organization are paid by check, but sometimes it is impossible or inefficient to draw a check to make a payment. For example, on-street parking or postage stamps may cost so little that the expense of writing the check would exceed the cost of the item. Furthermore, it would be very difficult to find a parking meter that accepts checks! To help the organization deal with small expenses, a petty cash fund may be established.

In establishing the petty cash fund, clear guidelines or rules regarding its use must be articulated. One guideline might be a limit on the amount of expenses to be paid from this fund. Expenses in excess of $20 are usually paid by check. Another guideline might describe the types of expenses that may be paid with petty cash funds. Petty cash funds are not typically used to pay recurring expenses, such as utilities or subscriptions, regardless of the size of the expense. Yet another guideline or rule concerning the petty cash fund might concern management of the fund, someone should be appointed as custodian of the fund and held responsible for its proper management.

The petty cash fund is created by the treasurer upon writing a check to the custodian or manager of the fund for a fairly small amount of money, usually $50–$100. The check is recorded. The fund manager cashes the check and places the cash in a petty cash secured envelope or cash box. Authorized persons within the organization may then claim funds in advance or as reimbursement for minor (petty) expenditures. Petty cash funds are issued after the claimant submits a petty cash voucher (with attached receipts where possible). Pads of blank petty cash vouchers like the one shown in Figure 7.7 can be purchased at most stationery or office supply stores. After the claimant has been paid, the petty cash voucher is kept in the petty cash box.

Figure 7.7. Sample Petty Cash Voucher

The money in the box and the face value of all the vouchers in the box should always add up to the original amount of cash issued to establish the fund. When the money in the petty cash box is almost spent, the vouchers and receipts are submitted like any other invoice, and a check for the total value of the vouchers is issued to the fund manager. The check is cashed and the money returned to the petty cash box in order to bring its total back to the level of funds originally established.

It is important to note that petty cash is not a budget line. It is a means of payment only. Any expense that is paid using petty cash is charged to the appropriate budget account. Periodically, the fund manager should prepare a petty cash reconciliation statement. This simple form (shown in Figure 7.8) helps the manager to monitor the fund and anticipate cash replenishment needs.

Figure 7.8. Sample Petty Cash Reconciliation Statement

The petty cash fund offers convenience, but because of that convenience, it also has the potential to be abused. Great care should be taken to manage the petty cash fund according to established principles and practices of accounting.

Efficiency Reporting

There are many kinds of reports that can be generated by accountants and bookkeepers. Three of the most useful for financial managers in sport, tourism, and leisure service organizations are described below. They are *budget statements, the project report, the daily operations report,* and the *RevPAR report.*

The Budget Statement

The sport, tourism, or leisure service organization budget is a revenue and spending plan for a period of time, usually a year. The goal of the financial manager is to ensure that revenues reach the expected level and that expenses do not exceed the projected amounts. This two-pronged goal is referred to as "staying within the budget," and the realization of this goal must be a priority for the financial manager. The budget statement is a useful tool that allows the manager to review the financial activity of the organization with respect to the budget. The sample budget statement shown in Figure 7.9 lists key budget classes and the amount of money projected as revenue or expenditure for that class. As of the date listed at the top of the budget statement, the actual receipts and expenditures are reported, along with any commitments for revenue or expenditures that have been made. The budget statement also shows the portion (percentage) of each budget item that has been received or spent and reports the remaining balance.

In the preceding example, 50% of the budget period has elapsed, but less than 50% of the revenues have been received and less than 50% of the expenditures have been made. Noticeably, several expenditure items are at or near 75%, and a major revenue category is at 33%. Is this disparity an early warning of budget

PINE CREEK RESORT
Recreation Services Department
Budget Statement

June 30, 2017 (50% of budget period)

	Budget	Actual	Committed	%	Balance
REVENUE					
Guest Service Assessment	120,000	60,000	0	50.0	60,000
Bike Rentals	18,000	5,920	0	32.9	12,080
Supply Fees	2,000	831	0	41.6	1,169
Total Revenue	140,000	66,751	0	47.7	73,249
EXPENSES					
Personnel	108,000	42,000	2,000	40.7	64,000
Equipment Maintenance	9,000	6,850	0	76.1	2,150
Program Supplies	1,500	988	0	65.9	512
Transportation	4,500	2,123	1,200	73.8	1,177
Promotion	2,000	1,112	400	75.6	488
Administration	12,000	5,857	0	48.8	6,143
Contingency/Enterprise	3,000	800	500	43.3	1,700
Total Expenses	140,000	59,730	4,100	45.6	76,170

Figure 7.9. Sample Budget Statement

problems? Not necessarily. The budget statement only tells the manager how much of the budget has been received or spent at a particular point in the fiscal period. It does not indicate how much of the revenue should be received or how much of the expenses should have been paid at that time. The manager must use his or her knowledge of seasonal and other fluctuations in demand and cost in interpreting the budget statement and making judgments about how well the organization's finances are being managed.

Project/Event Report

In addition to the budget statement, many sport, tourism, and leisure service managers find the project report to be particularly useful. This report compares projected and actual revenues and expenditures for specific programs or events and includes commentary that helps future organizers of the program/event to understand what contributed to the financial success or failure of the project. A sample project report is shown in Figure 7.10.

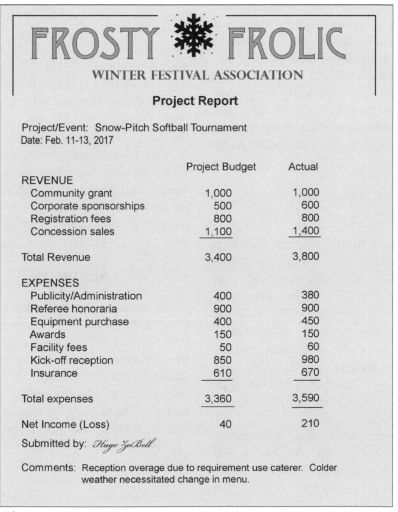

FROSTY ❄ FROLIC
WINTER FESTIVAL ASSOCIATION

Project Report

Project/Event: Snow-Pitch Softball Tournament
Date: Feb. 11-13, 2017

	Project Budget	Actual
REVENUE		
Community grant	1,000	1,000
Corporate sponsorships	500	600
Registration fees	800	800
Concession sales	1,100	1,400
Total Revenue	3,400	3,800
EXPENSES		
Publicity/Administration	400	380
Referee honoraria	900	900
Equipment purchase	400	450
Awards	150	150
Facility fees	50	60
Kick-off reception	850	980
Insurance	610	670
Total expenses	3,360	3,590
Net Income (Loss)	40	210

Submitted by: *Hugo ZoBell*

Comments: Reception overage due to requirement use caterer. Colder weather necessitated change in menu.

Figure 7.10. Sample Project Report

The project report is a document that helps organizers of future events. It is rarely used in financial audit situations or for legal or highly technical documentation. For these reasons, the project report should be accurate and, more importantly, easily read and understood.

Daily Operations Report

In hospitality settings such as hotels or resorts, a frequently used report is the Daily Operations Report. Similar reports may also be used in other sport, tourism, and leisure service enterprises. This report is usually prepared at the end of the business day by the hotel's night auditor and includes a summary of the business conducted that day. The Daily Operations Report is used by the general manager and by other department heads as they review operating statistics and cash exchanges at each of the hotel's profit centers.

RevPAR (Revenue Per Available Room)

Managers in the tourism industry, particularly those with hotel or resort management responsibilities, rely on the RevPAR report as an important measure of performance. The RevPAR report provides a single metric (also found in the daily operations report), which is a function of both room rates and occupancy. RevPAR is calculated by multiplying the average daily room rate times the occupancy rate.

For example, if the Cummorah Resort and Lodge has 300 rooms that sell for an average of $210 per night, and an average occupancy rate of 74%, then RevPAR is calculated as follows:

$$\text{RevPAR} = \text{Average Daily Rate} \times \text{Occupancy Rate}$$

$$\text{RevPAR} = \$210 \times .74 = \$155.40$$

RevPAR is usually expressed and discussed as an annual average, but it can also be calculated and used to measure performance over a shorter period of time, such as a season, a month, week, or even a day. The period to which the RevPAR value pertains should be clearly stated on the report.

Financial managers look for changes in RevPAR. A rising RevPAR indicates that either occupancy is increasing, or average room rates are up (or a combination of both). RevPAR is also used as a ratio for comparisons with other properties. Finally, it is important to remember that RevPAR is not the only measure of financial health in the hospitality sector. It evaluates the strength of only one revenue stream, and should be used in conjunction with other budget statements and activity reports for profit centers such as restaurants, golf courses, casinos, spas, meeting services, etc.

Summary

In order to effectively and efficiently manage the financial resources of a sport, tourism, or leisure service organization, the manager must have a basic understanding of accounting principles and practices. By following generally accepted accounting principles, reports that are meaningful, timely, and accurate can be prepared for use in executive decision making. The report or financial statement that indicates the single-point-in-time condition of the organization is the balance sheet. The income statement

LAKE HOLIDAY LODGE - DAILY BUSINESS REPORT				DATE			
		MTD			YTD		
PARTICULARS	TODAY	Actual	Budgeted	Last Year	Actual	Budgeted	Last Year
STATISTICS							
ROOM AVAILABLE							
ROOM OCCUPIED (W/O COMP + HOUSE USE)							
COMPLIMENTARY							
HOUSE USE ROOMS							
ROOM OCCUPIED (WITH COMP + HOUSE USE)							
OCCUPANCY % (W/O COMP + HOUSE USE)							
OCCUPANCY % (WITH COMP + HOUSE USE)							
ARR (W/O COMP + HOUSE USE)							
ARR (WITH COMP + HOUSE USE)							
REVPAR							
REVPAR (W/O COMP)							
NO OF GUESTS							
% OF DOUBLE OCCUPANCY							
ROOM REVENUE							
TRANSIENT							
GROUP - Business							
GROUP - Leisure							
Other							
TOTAL ROOM INCOME							
F & B OUTLETS (ALL SALES)							
POOLSIDE CAFE							
ISAAC'S RESTAURANT							
BANQUET							
IN ROOM DINING							
MINI BAR							
LOBBY LOUNGE							
OTHER INCOME							
TOTAL F&B OUTLET INCOME							
OTHER DEPARTMENTS							
TELEPHONE and INTERNET							
BUSINESS CENTER							
SPA & HEALTH CLUB							
TOTAL OTHER DEP. INCOME							
GRAND TOTAL HOTEL REVENUE							

Figure 7.11. Sample Form for a Hotel Daily Operations Report

(also called the profit and loss statement, statement of receipts and disbursement, or operating statement) details financial activity between two dates for which balance sheets are prepared. Where available, trained accountants and bookkeepers help to prepare financial reports. Sport, tourism, and leisure service administrators may, however, be responsible for maintaining and being accountable for a petty cash fund. Rules governing the use of the petty cash fund should be understood and followed by all users. A particularly useful report that helps the sport, tourism, or leisure service manager to be aware of the state of the budget is the budget statement. This report shows how much of each budget category has been received or spent at a particular point in the fiscal period. For specific programs, projects, or events, the project report is a common form of reporting on the financial outcomes of the project. The daily operations report has general applicability but is used, along with the more specific RevPAR report as an important efficiency monitoring device in the tourism industry for measuring the success of crucial hotel and resort operations.

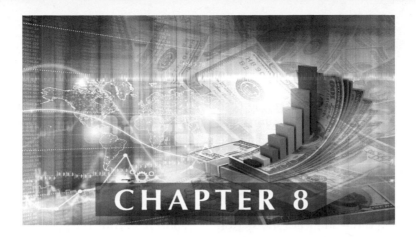

Planning Reports

Introduction

Financial reports, especially those discussed in the preceding chapter, typically identify financial activity that is current or concluded. They reflect what has happened and what the financial state of the organization is at the time of the report. If it can be assumed that the past points to the future, then most reports will also help in corporate planning activities. It should be noted that the utility of any financial report that is used for planning purposes is only as good as are the underlying assumptions about future conditions and any estimates about future demand, supply, costs and revenue. Two reports that are used widely in evaluating future success and preparing for future financial conditions are the *cash flow analysis report* and the *ratio analysis report*.

Cash Flow Analysis

In the normal course of business activity, a company receives cash and spends cash. Obviously, a successful enterprise must receive at least as much cash as it spends. However, there may times when the necessary outflow of cash exceeds its concurrent inflow. The inverse can also be true. The financial manager needs to analyze the timing of revenue production and expenditures to be sure that cash is available when it is needed and that excess cash is not in a non-productive state.

Seasonal operations or businesses that experience wide swings in demand are organizations that require careful management of cash flows. A summer camp operation, for example, incurs many expenses in the early spring as facilities are readied, staff members are hired, advertising begins, and supplies are ordered and received. Campers, however, do not register and pay their fees until early summer. Observing cash flows, it seems that the organization has a serious shortfall in the spring and a cash surplus in the summer. Cash flow analysis allows the manager to predict how much operating cash needs to be held over from the previous year or borrowed for a short term in order to meet early season obligations. It also helps the manager to know how much of the surplus summer cash is profit or surplus in the total annual budget.

Figure 8.1 is a sample cash flow analysis report. It considers revenues and expenditures on a quarterly basis, but such an analysis can also be done for both shorter and longer fiscal periods. For each fiscal period, the projected cash inflows are compared to expected cash expenditures. If the net cash flow is positive (i.e. greater than zero), the organization is able to pay all its bills. Such is the case in the first quarter. If the quarterly net cash flow is negative (2nd quarter), bills can be paid using the balance carried forward from previous fiscal periods and shown as the cumulative net cash flow. If the cumulative net cash flow is also negative (3rd quarter) bills cannot be paid unless additional cash is found. At this point, the cash flow analysis report is alerting the manager to the need to reduce the operating deficit and/or to borrow cash to stay in operation until the net cash flow is positive and the loan can be repaid. In the example shown in Figure 8.1, the manager should borrow $1,400 sometime in the 3rd quarter but plan to repay it in the 4th quarter from the large ($18,050) projected surplus. The cash flow analysis would then be revised to show an additional inflow of $1,400 as cash from loans during the 3rd quarter, and an additional $1,400 as a debt service/retirement expenditure in the 4th quarter. The revised cumulative net cash flow in the 4th quarter will be

	1st Quarter	2nd Quarter	3rd Quarter	4th Quarter
Cash inflow				
Beginning cash balance	$11,000			
Cash from sales	$23,500	$19,800	$17,000	$34,000
Cash from investments	$3,000	$3,000	$3,000	$3,000
Other cash			$500	
Total inflow	$37,500	$22,800	$20,500	$37,000
Cash expenditures				
Operating expenses	$18,900	$26,000	$24,000	$14,650
Capital purchases				
Debt service and retirement	$4,300	$4,300	$4,300	$4,300
Other expenses		$400		
Total expenditures	$23,200	$30,700	$28,300	$18,950
Quarterly Net Cash Flow	$14,300	-$7,900	-$7,800	$18,050
Cumulative Net Cash Flow	$14,300	$6,400	-$1,400	$16,650

Figure 8.1. Sample Cash Flow Report

the beginning cash balance in the first quarter of the succeeding year.

Cash flow analysis facilitates planning for the use of cash. When adjustments are made to the cash flow analysis report to reflect planned cash flow management, the report effectively becomes a cash flow budget and is a valuable guide to the manager of financial resources.

Ratio Analysis

Ratios are quantitative indicators of financial strength and operating success. The figures used in calculating ratios come from financial statements (or projections) like the balance sheet and income statement. Different readers of financial reports will focus on the ratios that interest them most. For example, lenders will be most concerned with ratios that indicate the degree of risk associated with extending credit to the sports, tourism, or leisure service organization, and potential equity investors will be more concerned with return-on-investment indicators. Not surprisingly, there are many ratios that could be calculated and reported. Those that are of greatest utility in planning for a sports, tourism, and leisure service enterprise are briefly described here. Ratios of four general types are discussed. *Liquidity ratios* (also called solvency ratios) indicate the ability of a sports, tourism, or leisure business to meet its short-term obligations. *Activity ratios* (also called efficiency ratios) are quantitative indicators of the ability of the business to expediently and efficiently exchange its products for financial resources. *Profitability ratios* show how successful the business has been during a certain period of time (usually a year) in terms of investment returns. *Debt/Coverage/Leverage ratios* measure the long-term solvency of the business.

Examples of the commonly used ratios are as follows:

Liquidity Ratios

Quick Ratio: Used to estimate the ability of a business to meet its short-term financial obligations without selling off its inventory.

Quick = (Current Assets-Inventories)/ Current Liabilities

Current Ratio: Used to estimate the ability of a business to meet its short-term financial obligations (assuming ability to dispose of inventory at full value). It is sometimes called the banker's ratio.

Current = Current Assets/Current Liabilities

Debt-to-Net Worth Ratio: Used to compare the total financial obligations of the business to the investment of its owners. This is used by lenders as a measure of risk involved in extending credit to the business.

Debt-to-Net Worth = Current and Long-Term Liabilities/Net Worth

Current Liability-to-Net Worth Ratio: Another measure of the short-term risk associated with lending to the business.

Current Liability-to-Net Worth = Current Liabilities/Net Worth

Current Liability to Inventory Ratio: Used to estimate the ability of a business to meet its short-term financial obligations without disposing of its assets (other than inventory).

$$\text{Current Liability to Inventory} =$$
$$\text{Current Liability/Inventory}$$

Activity Ratios

Average Collection Period: This is not a ratio, but is often included in the ratio analysis. It shows the average time (in days) to receive payment for products delivered.

$$\text{Avg. Coll. Period} = (\text{Accounts Receivables/Sales}) \times 365 \text{ days}$$

Sales-to-Inventory Ratio: Used to indicate the inventory turnover rate. Low numbers may indicate an overstock situation.

$$\text{Sales-to-Inventory} = \text{Cost of Goods Sold/Average Inventory}$$

Assets-to-Sales Ratio: This ratio is used in determinations of how well the assets are being utilized.

$$\text{Assets-to-Sales} = \text{Total Assets/Total Sales}$$

Profitability Ratios

Return on Sales: This ratio is used only when comparing with similar businesses or with performance over a period of time. It indicates ability to generate profits from sales.

$$\text{Return on Sales} = \text{Net Income/Net Sales}$$

Return on Assets: Sometimes called the productive ratio, this index is useful for comparisons with other enterprises and with gauging the effectiveness of asset utilization.

$$\text{Return on Assets} = \text{Net Profit after Taxes/Total Assets}$$

Return on Net Worth: This ratio measures the ultimate profitability of the enterprise from the perspective of stockholders/owners. It indicates ability to earn adequate profits and should be higher than conservative (safe) investment rates.

$$\text{Return on Net Worth} = \text{Net Profits after Taxes/Equity}$$

Debt/Coverage/Leverage Ratios

Equity Ratio: This ratio indicates the extent of the owner's investment in the enterprise.

$$\text{Equity Ratio} = \text{Equity/Total Assets}$$

Debt-to-Total Asset Ratio: This ratio indicates the extent of the enterprise's borrowing.

$$\text{Debt-to-Total Asset Ratio} = \text{Total Liabilities/Total Assets}$$

The calculated ratios are instructive in themselves, but they also provide very specific information that allows the financial manager to compare the current or expected financial condition of the enterprise with others in a similar class of ventures. In ratio analysis, comparisons are made between the enterprise in question and the class of businesses represented by an appropriate Standard Industrial Code (SIC). Unfortunately, but understandably, not all sport, tourism, and leisure enterprises fit neatly into existing SICs. This means that ratio analysis can only provide a comparison between the proposed enterprise and others in an industrial classification that is judged to most closely resemble it. Table 8.1 lists most of the sport, tourism, and leisure service–related SICs used in the United States since 1997.

In reviewing the list presented in Table 8.1, the difficulty in classifying an enterprise such as a resort-based recreation program becomes readily apparent. Should it be included in SIC#7011 (Hotels and Motels), where lodging and other major business activities strongly influence ratios, or might it more appropriately be included in SIC#7997 (Membership Clubs) because being a guest at the resort is, in fact, like having membership privileges in the exclusive resort recreation club setting? Perhaps the fitness orientation of the program makes it best suited to SIC#7991 (Fitness Facilities), or SIC#7999 (Miscellaneous Amusement and Recreation). This system of classification has been used in the United States, Canada, and Mexico since 1997, and is called the North American Industrial Classification System (NAICS).

Once the appropriate comparative industrial classification has been selected, a variety of publications can be referred to in order to find the industry standard for each ratio. The most popular publications of this type are the following:

- Robert Morris and Associates' Annual Statement Studies.
- Dun and Bradstreet's Industry Norms and Key Business Ratios.
- Leo Troy's Almanac of Business and Industrial Financial Ratios.

Table 8.1
Sample Enterprises from Selected North American Industrial Classifications (U.S. Census Bureau, 1998)

4511 Sporting Goods, Hobby and Music Instr. sport goods stores, hobby, toy, game stores, music instruction, sewing and needlework stores. **4512 Book, Periodical, and Music Stores** book stores, recorded music stores **4811 Sched. Air Transport.** Passenger transport by air **4821 Rail Transport.** **4871-9 Scenic and Sightseeing Transport** land, water, and other transport **5121 Motion Picture and Video Industries** production, distribution, and exhibition **5141 Information Services** libraries **5322 Consumer Goods - Rental** video tape and discs	**5615 Travel Arrange.** Travel agencies, tour operators, convention and visitor bureaus **7111 Performing Arts** dance companies, musical groups, theater companies **7112 Spectator Sports** sports teams and clubs, racetracks **7113 Arts, sports Promoters** with facilities and without **7114 Agents and Managers** for artists and for athletes **7115 Independent Artists** writers and performers **7121 Museums, Historical Sites and Similar Inst.** Museums, historical sites, zoos, nature parks, etc.	**7131 Amusement Parks and Arcades** theme parks and amusement arcades **7132 Gambling** casinos **7139 Other Amusement and Recreation** golf/country clubs, skiing facilities, marinas, fitness/ rec. sports, bowling centers, other recreation **7211 Traveler Accommodation** hotels, motels, and casino hotels **7212 RV Parks/Camps** RV campgrounds and RV camps **7213 Rooming and Boarding Houses** **7221 Full Service Restaurants** **7222 Limited Service Restaurants** **7223 Special Food Services** **7224 Drinking Places (alcoholic beverages)**

- The Financial Survey of Canadian Business Performance.

Ratios reported in these publications are often given for businesses that differ in sales output, asset value, or place within the range of reported ratio values. These reports recognize that, although they may reside in the same industrial classification, businesses vary greatly in their productivity, efficiency, and profitability. Fortunately, some publications list ratios and other important financial data for similar enterprises across a wide range of sizes (as measured by sales volume or by value of assets). For example, the Leo Troy publication identifies operating costs (including salaries, advertising, interest, taxes, etc.) and income (including sales, interest, rent, and royalties) for SIC#7131 - Amusement, Gambling and Recreation Industries, as well as ratios for businesses with less than $500,00 in assets, $500,00-$1,000,000 in assets, and so on. In SIC#7131, the current and quick ratios for businesses with less than $500,000 in assets are 1.1 and 0.7 respectively. For larger businesses in the same SIC, the comparable ratios are 1.6 and 1.2. This emphasizes the need to conduct a ratio analysis using the industry norms for the type and size of business that most closely matches the one being proposed in the business plan.

Reporting the results of the ratio analysis is simply a matter of tabulating the calculated ratios for the enterprise and for the comparative industrial class, as well as providing commentary to explain major differences between those ratio figures.

In reviewing the industry standards, it may seem that the statistics given are an indication of "what should be." In fact, they are merely measures of "what is."

HomeFun Recreational Services

Ratio Analysis

Current Ratio = 2.0
Industry Standard = 1.2

Our ratio is much higher than the industry because we do not need to maintain large i and our short term obligations are incurr of service delivery. By policy, we maint reserve equivalent to 3 months operating

Debt to Equity Ratio = .83
Industry Standard = .87

Consistent with industry standard.

Return on Sales Ratio = .05
Industry Standard = .07

Our lower ratio reflects temporary inef normal at start-up. Three year plan pro ... s ratio ... ore ...

Figure 8.2. Sample Format for reporting the results of a ratio analysis

They reflect the current conditions of the entire industrial class and are therefore very useful benchmarks. However, a particular enterprise at a particular stage of its development may have quite different ratios, and what is most important is that the manager of that enterprise understands what the ratios and the comparisons are saying about how the business operates or will operate.

Table 8.2 displays selected ratios for three SIC classes of sport, tourism, and leisure service business. Again, these are indicators of how things were, not necessarily how things should have been.

How Financial Reports Relate to Each Other

Whether for indicating present status, activity, or potential, financial reports are essential tools in business operation and planning. In this and the preceding chapter, several report types were described and illustrated. Each emphasizes different information and presents it in a way that addresses particular questions. Some reports answer the question "What

Table 8.2

Comparison of Selected Ratios Reported by Dun and Bradstreet for Three Types of Sport, Leisure Service, and Tourism Industries

	SIC#7991 Physical Fitness Facilities	SIC#7011 Hotels, Motels	SIC#7992 Public Golf Courses
Liquidity (solvency):			
Quick (times)	0.9	0.7	0.4
Current (times)	1.0	1.0	1.0
Total Liability to Net Worth (%)	562.5	162.3	110.7
Current Liability to Net Worth (%)	17.5	32.1	33.9
Activity (efficiency):			
Average Collection Period (days)	12.1	9.5	1.8
Sales to Inventory (times)	129.2	82.1	35.4
Assets to Sales (%)	112.2	158.7	116.6
Profitability:			
Return on Sales (%)	5.2	4.6	1.1
Return on Assets (%)	5.2	2.7	1.7
Return on Net Worth (%)	12.5	8.1	2.9

happened?" and others answer the question "What is the current situation?" Reports discussed in this chapter respond to questions such as "What are our future needs? And "How does our performance compare to that of other successful enterprises?"

While answering different questions, financial reports are not independent of each other. For example, petty cash accounting is reflected in the balance sheet and income statement. Information contained in the balance sheet is also used in compiling the income statement and appears again in the ratio analysis. Project reports display the same details that are included in the summative budget report, and are directly related to figures reported in the balance sheet and income statement. Data from the income statement are used in the statement of retained earnings, and common information is used in the balance sheet and the cash flow statement. Figure 8.3 diagrams the data sharing relationship between some of the most common financial reports.

Summary

Financial accounting not only tells the story of what has occurred and what is now the financial situation. Accounting also allows for planning and evaluation aided by informative and accurate reports about future conditions and relative efficiency. Cash flow analysis and ratio analysis are important management activities that use reports of past and current financial positions extrapolated into the future or compared with relevant standards. Reports that facilitate planning and evaluation are based on data contained in stock and flow reports such as the balance sheet, income statement, and retained earnings report. They also use data contained in program or function specific reports such as budget statements, project reports, daily operations reports, RevPAR analysis, cash flow analysis, and ratio analysis.

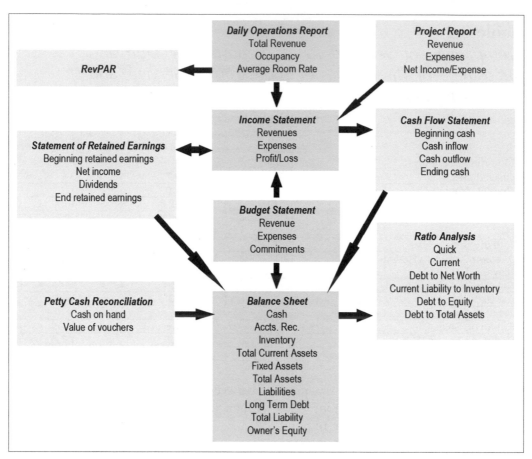

Figure 8.3. Illustration of the Relationship between Selected Financial Reports

SECTION D

Revenue Generation

The next six chapters of this book explore the need and opportunities for generating revenue in support of the sport, tourism, and leisure service enterprise. Income provides for expenditure, and expenditure is required for business activity. Chapter 9 identifies several major sources of revenue for organizations in the public, private nonprofit, and commercial sectors. It presents a detailed discussion of compulsory income and introduces other sources, including earned income. Pricing is an important consideration in generating earned income, and is discussed in Chapter 10. Pricing principles and strategies are presented, and the impacts of price and price adjustment on consumer behavior are described. Revenue management (also known as yield management) takes the pricing discussion further with direct application to the tourism industry. Revenue management is the topic of Chapter 11. Gratuitous income is discussed in Chapters 12 and 13, and the process of grantseeking is carefully detailed. Because grants are usually awarded by foundations or other philanthropic organizations, this section of the book includes an exploration of philanthropy and fundraising. In the sport industry, sponsorship is a particularly important source of revenue and it is discussed in Chapter 14.

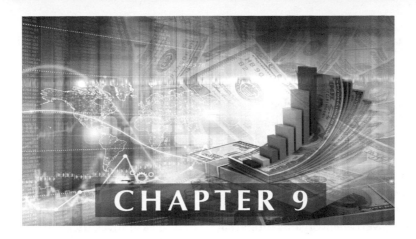

CHAPTER 9

Revenue Sources

Introduction

Income is essential to all sport, tourism, and leisure service organizations. Without income, these organizations would not be able to function. Regardless of whether it is a private fitness center, a nonprofit sport stadium, or a state park system, each uses similar, and yet different, sources of income. The different types of sport, tourism, and leisure service organizations rely on different types of income in different ways, and in some cases, their sources of income will be unique. Initially, this chapter will discuss the types of income common to the three sectors: commercial, private nonprofit, and public. Governments have different ways to secure income, and the methods of achieving it may vary on a state-by-state level. This uniqueness of government sources will receive particular attention.

Types of Income Sources

There are multiple sources of income available to any organization. In this section, five of the most common types of income will be discussed. They are compulsory income, gratuitous income, earned income, investment income, and contractual receipts. While these are the most commonly accepted terms, not all organizations use the same terminology. For example, the National Association of State Park Directors (a nonprofit organization) uses revenues appropriated, revenues unappropriated, general funds, dedicated funds, and federal funds to describe sources of income for the various state park systems (McLean, 1996). The meanings are similar, but this example of a different classification system emphasizes the point that while there is a general acceptance among terms, they are not universal. Table 9.1 illustrates the five most common sources of income for sport, tourism, and leisure service organizations and identifies the level of importance each source has to the sectors. It also emphasizes the uniqueness of compulsory income to the public sector and the relative importance of earned income to all three sectors.

Compulsory income consists of funds secured by government organizations that are generated through taxes, licensing, or some other sort of government-instituted income source that requires all or specific individuals or organizations within a legislative jurisdiction to contribute.

Gratuitous income is received without expectation of a return. Sources for gratuitous income include grants, bequests, gifts, and blind and open sponsorships. In each case, the giver typically does not receive a direct benefit or compensation for the gift. Much of what is discussed in Chapters 12 (Grantseeking) and 13 (Philanthropy and Fund-raising) is considered to be gratuitous income.

Earned income consists of cash resources generated from fees and charges instituted by the sport, tourism, or leisure service organization. These can include program fees, charges for use of areas and facilities, income from sales of supplies, equipment, gift shops, entrance fees, admission fees, rental fees, and user fees. Fiscal investments that earn interest are also considered earned income.

Investment income includes new money generated from investment in the form of interest, dividends, and capital appreciation. Investment income is the result of investing a fixed amount of dollars (principal) in such a way as to generate new money. The increase in wealth is the investment income available to sport, tourism, and leisure service organizations.

Contractual receipts are revenues generated from legal agreements with other organizations. Agreements can include the management of resources, rental of facilities, rental of equipment,

Table 9.1
Income Sources and Their Level of Importance to the Three Sectors

Sector / Income	Compulsory Income	Gratuitous Income	Earned Income	Investment Income	Contractual Receipts
Commercial Sector	None	Minimal	Major source of income for operations	Key source of income for some business enterprises	Can be a major source of income dependent upon scope of enterprise
Nonprofit Sector	May have some impact when tied to public funded, but limited	Essential and major source of income	In some types of nonprofits becoming a major source of income	Limited based on organization's capability to secure gratuitous income and invest the income	Growing importance through partnerships
Public Sector	Essential source of income	Growing importance as an income source	Essential source of income	Limited source of income, but frequently used	Growing source of income among some agencies

management of special operations such as golf courses or marinas, concession operations, tennis centers, zoos, stadiums, gift shops, or other types of enterprises. They can also include arrangements generally referred to as privatization, a practice of contracting out for the delivery of a specific service.

Compulsory Income Sources

Compulsory income includes cash and non-cash sources collected through the taxing and regulatory powers at different government levels as prescribed by state and federal law. Government sources of income have changed dramatically for sport, tourism, and leisure service organizations since 1978, when California voters passed Proposition 13 (a landmark initiative that cut property taxes by almost 50%) (California Tax Data 1979). Prior to that, public agencies gained the vast majority of their income from the general fund, which was primarily supported through property tax revenues. Since 1978, governments across the United States have responded to voter demands for lower taxes with sometimes massive tax cuts. In some cases these have been prompted by voter-initiated propositions, as in California, Oregon, and Massachusetts (Lindsey, 1978). In other states, the legislatures responded to what they saw as a growing trend. Even the federal government has not been immune to the trend, as the president and Congress have sometimes competed with each other over who could appear to cut taxes more. The declining availability of general fund dollars has required public sport, tourism, and leisure service organizations at all levels to rethink how they secure and use income.

Taxes continue to represent the largest single source of income to government. There are several different types of taxes, including real property tax, personal property tax, excise tax, use tax, income tax, local option tax, special assessment tax, and impact tax. Each has a specific purpose and is discussed in the next two sections.

Types of State and Municipal Taxes

Real property taxes. Real property taxes are assessed in all 50 states and their subordinate jurisdictions (counties, cities, municipalities, etc.). Jurisdictions can set the tax at the local level in compliance with state law. Real property is defined as land and whatever is developed or erected or growing on the land. This includes subsurface features such as oil or mineral deposits. Tax assessors (see Chapter 2) are appointed at the local level and have primary responsibility for determining the value of the property.

In 1962, real property taxes represented 69% of the total local government tax revenue (Fisher, 2002). By 1999, that portion had shrunk to 44% of the tax revenue. In 2015, real property taxes were 30% of all local tax revenues (Urban Institute, 2015). Other types of taxes increased over the same period and became a larger part of the mix of revenues available to sport, tourism, and park and recreation organizations. In spite of the recent changes in compulsory income sources, property taxes continue to be a significant source of revenue for local governments. Table 9.2 depicts the various sources of general revenue received by state and local governments in 2014.

Table 9.2

Percentage of State and Local Government General Revenues from Selected Sources

Source	% of State tax revenue	% of Local tax revenue
Transfers*	31.7	36.3
Sales Taxes	23.7	6.9
Property Taxes	-	29.8
Charges and Miscellaneous	18.5	22.6
Individual Income Taxes	17.9	2.0
Corporate Income Taxes	2. 7	-
Other Taxes	5.6	2.4

* Transfers are revenues from other governments to support specific programs and activities provided on their behalf. Most of that money (96 percent) comes from federal income taxes.

Transfers are revenues from other governments to support specific programs and activities provided on their behalf. Most of that money (96%) comes from federal income taxes.

Municipal governments are, by law, allowed to establish different tax rates for different classifications of property. Decisions about the levels at which different properties are taxed are made by the local legislative body. Personal homes, undeveloped land, businesses, and farm property are typically taxed at different levels. Permanent tax-exempt status may be granted to certain types of land uses, such as governments, school districts, and religious and charitable organizations. A tax abatement, which is an exemption from paying taxes, can be granted to an organization for a specified period of time. Tax abatements are generally granted as an incentive to firms considering moving to a particular region.

Determining the value of real property is based on an estimation of its taxable worth or assessed value. Assessed value is different from market value. In many states, assessed value is slightly lower than fair market value. Fair market value is that at which a home may be valued for sale, whereas its assessed value for taxation purposes may be as much as 20% to 30% lower. For example, a home with a fair market value of $240,000, which is assessed at 85% of the fair market value, would have an assessed value of $204,000.

Each potential jurisdiction with real property taxing powers has a tax base. The tax base is the total assessed value of all taxable property in a community. Assessed values of communities will differ considerably and are difficult to compare within a state and almost impossible for comparison between states.

Tax rates are based on revenue needs of the government and the value of the tax base. To understand how tax rates are determined, consider the following illustration. A government decides that it needs $3 million from taxes to pay for its operations in the upcoming fiscal year. This decision is made after the public agency has completed its budgeting process and identified what portion of its operating budget needs to come from real property taxes. For example:

Total amount needed to operate:
$3,650,000

Subtract revenue (from user fees,
grants, permits, etc.): $650,000

Equals revenue (to be collected from
taxes): $3,000,000

The tax rate is then determined by
dividing the property tax requirements
($4 million) by the assessed valuation.
Note that assessed valuation does not
include all real property within the
jurisdiction because some organizations
or groups have a tax abatement. When
the tax abatement property is removed
from the total assessed value, what
remains is a net assessed value (tax base).
For example:

Total assessed valuation of the
community: $450,000,000

Subtract tax-exempt property:
$10,500,000

Equals net assessed valuation:
$439,500,000

The tax rate is based on net assessed
valuation. If this community requires
$4 million from taxes to operate, the
following formula is used, and the
example tax rate is calculated:

Required Taxes/Net Assessed
Valuation = Tax Rate

$3,000,000/$439,500,000 = .0068

There are three ways in which tax
rates can be expressed: (1) as a percent of
the value of property; (2) as a mill rate; or
(3) as mills. The tax rate from preceding
illustration would be expressed in the
three alternatives as:

Tax Rate Expression

Percent Tax Rate	0.68%
Mill rate	0.0068
Mills	6.8

The relationship between "Percent
Tax Rate" and the "Mill Rate" is obvious.
The 0.68% means 0.68 per hundred,
which is 0.68/100, which equals .0068.
A "mill," on the other hand, is equal
to 1/1000 of the assessed property
value. The net assessed property value
is $439,500,000, which means that the
value of 1 mill is $439,500,000/1,000,
which equals $439,500. How many mills
(valued at $439,500) does it take to make
the $3,000,000 to be collected from taxes?
It takes 6.8. ($3,000,000/$439,500 = 6.8)
Figure 9.1 shows the conversion factors
for the three tax rate expressions.

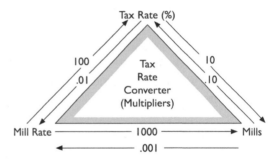

Figure 9.1. Conversion Factors
for Three Expressions of the Real
Property Tax Rate

Knowing the tax rate, the owner of
a property can calculate the property tax
that is owed. If the owner of a home with
an assessed value of $240,000 is subject
to the tax rate used in the above example,
the tax bill will be $1,632. This amount is
calculated as follows:

A. Applying the 0.68% Tax Rate

(% Tax Rate/100) x Assessed Value =
Property Tax
(0.68/100) x $240,000 = $1,632

B. Applying the 0.0068 Mill Rate

Mill Rate x Assessed Value =
Property Tax
0.0068 x $240,000 = $1,632

C. Charging 9.1 Mills

Mills x (Assessed Value/1000) =
Property Tax
6.8 x ($240,000/1,000) = $1,632

The property tax system is based on the idea that the more a person owns, the more that person should pay. The methods of tax calculation previously illustrated follow the principle that a property owner's contribution to the tax revenue total should be proportionate to his or her share of the value of the taxable property in the community.

Other types of taxes. *Personal property taxes* are allowed in most states. Taxing of personal property occurs in three common forms: (1) household tangible property (e.g., automobiles, recreational vehicles, and sport transportation devices); (2) business tangible property (e.g., inventory, business fixtures, furniture, equipment, and machinery); and (3) intangibles (e.g., stocks and bonds). In 27 states, a personal vehicle tax (ranging, in 2017, from 0.1% in Louisiana to 4.77% in Rhode Island) is charged, resulting in billions of dollars in local and state tax revenue.

Sales tax is administered at the state level, but there may be provisions for additional local sales taxes. In 2017, only five states (Alaska, Delaware, Montana, New Hampshire, and Oregon) did not have a state-wide sales tax. Where applied, state sales tax rates varied from 2.9% (Colorado) to 7.5% (California). Thirty eight states also allow the imposition of local sales tax. In those states, the combined state/local sales tax can be as high as 9.45% (Tennessee) or as low as 4.35% (Hawaii). In some states, a portion of the tax may, by legislation, be reserved for state and local sport, tourism, or leisure service functions. Sales tax is applied to a broad range of goods and is determined by state legislatures.

A *use tax* is imposed in some states on individuals who purchase items outside of their state of residence and who do not pay any state sales tax on those otherwise taxable items. The use tax is designed to replace uncollected sales taxes for items purchased outside of the taxing jurisdiction. Use tax is gaining popularity in some jurisdictions and is increasingly important in a time when online purchasing is so common.

Excise tax is imposed on the sale of specific goods, such as gasoline, cigarettes, and alcoholic beverages, and specific services, such as those provided by hotels and motels (sometimes called a lodging tax), restaurants, and auto rental agencies. These taxes may be levied at the state or local level. Excise taxes, which are authorized at the state level and collected at either the state or local level, are never popular with those who have to pay.

Income taxes are administered at the municipal, state, and federal levels. There are two types of income taxes—personal and corporate. Residents of all states are subject to federal income taxes. Personal income taxes are present in 43 states. State personal income taxes are typically levied on individuals who reside in the state and/or who earned income in the state.

Corporate income taxes are prescribed by state law and administered at the state and/or the municipal level.

Local option taxes are applied at the local level, but legislatively enabled at the state level. One of the most popular local option taxes is a local sales tax that is added to the state sales tax. There is enabling legislation for some type of local option tax in every state. Supporters of local option sales taxes argue that the taxes allow local governments (city and county) to diversify their revenue bases. They also argue that this form of taxation allows geographically large areas to provide programs and services from local funds rather than by tapping state resources. Local meals taxes or hotel/motel taxes are also a common form of the local option tax. These very specific taxes were initially focused on convention and travel destination localities, but have become much more widespread. Local option taxes are used for a wide variety of purposes. In most cases, the enabling legislation is very specific about the use of these taxes, while in other instances, the legislation can provide for almost unrestricted use of the funds collected.

Other Sources of Compulsory Income

Special assessment taxes are enabled at the state level and administered at multiple levels. Most often, however, they are administered at the local level. These types of taxes focus on a specific geographical area, such as the downtown or a particular residential neighborhood. Consequently, the taxes collected may be spent only in the source neighborhood. They may be used for improvements in a particular area, for land purchases, or for salaries of staff that maintain an area. The introduction and elimination of special

assessment taxes is generally agreed upon by those who will be taxed.

Dedication ordinances and regulations are available to local governments and are typically instituted by county and city councils within guidelines established by state legislatures. When dedication ordinances and regulations were initiated, they required developers of neighborhoods to set aside a portion of the land for park and recreation use. While this was commendable, all too often the land set aside was not acceptable for park and recreation use, but was land the developer could not use. Local governments quickly began to look at alternatives to land dedication. In some instances, they tightened up local ordinances and became more specific in the type of land they deemed acceptable. In other instances, they began to accept money in lieu of land dedication. The money generally had to be used to improve or add to existing property or to purchase new property for parks and recreation. One common use was to purchase greenbelts linking the community and its parks together.

The imposition of impact taxes is another method of recovering development costs, and has been in use for over 40 years. Impact taxes are intended to require developers and new home owners to help pay for public improvements that may be needed as a result of new construction. It is argued that existing city residents should not have to pay for the development of new home and commercial sites, but that the cost should be borne, at least in part, by those who will benefit most directly from the development. Impact taxes are most frequently used for infrastructure costs such as streets, utilities, schools, and other essential services. Sport, tourism, and leisure service organizations have successfully argued in a number of communities that they are an essential service and, therefore, eligible recipients of funds collected as impact taxes.

Licenses and permits. Licenses and permits are a relatively small source of income for sport, tourism, and leisure service organizations. A license is an authorization to act or to engage in an activity. Probably the most common example is a driver's license or a fishing license. Licenses in sport, tourism, and park and recreation organizations are frequently granted for the distribution or sale of a particular product. For example, the National Football League entered into an exclusive agreement with Pepsi, guaranteeing exclusive rights to the sale of its products in NFL stadiums.

A permit is an authorization for a person to engage in a particular activity—not necessarily recreational—or to use a facility or equipment. A common permit is a building permit issued by a local jurisdiction. In sport, tourism, and leisure service organizations, a permit might be issued for the serving and consumption of alcoholic beverages at a public facility, for the rental of a facility, or for the use of a significant natural resource. Usually, permits are good for a shorter period of time than licenses.

Federal Government Sources

The federal government has long been a source of revenue for state and local governments. Funds collected by the federal government and redistributed to state governments are called transfer payments. In 1980, the federal government made transfer payments worth $91 billion. By 2010, that amount had risen to $608 billion, and in 2018, it was $728 billion (Dilger, 2018). The greatest share of transfer payment money is used for public welfare, but other programs, such as highways, education, health and hospitals, and housing and community development have also received significant amounts. Historically, sport, tourism, and leisure service organizations are well served by transfer payments and federal government programs. However, federal government fiscal support for state and local sport, tourism, and leisure service organizations has been on the decline in recent years. For example, state parks received $34 million in 2015 from federal sources, but that is a major reduction from the $630 million they received just three decades earlier (Beitsch, 2016).

Some of the legislation and programs under which the federal government transfers funds to states and local jurisdictions include the Land and Water Conservation Fund (LWCF), the National Recreational Trails Fund Act (1990), the National Highway System, Intermodal Surface Transportation Efficiency Act (ISTEA), highway safety programs, scenic highway programs, and metropolitan planning. Each program has provided varying levels of funding to sport, tourism, and leisure service organizations. The LWCF has been in place for more than 50 years. During its early years, it provided significant levels of revenue to state and local governments. Beginning in the mid-1980s, levels of funding declined to the point where it now provides minimal funding at the state and local levels. The National Recreational Trails Fund Act has received limited funding since its adoption. It is set up so that 30% of the funds go to motorized trails, 30% to nonmotorized trails, and 40% to multipurpose trails. The money can be spent on maintenance, as well as on construction of trails. The National Highway System provides a potential source of money for trail development next to any National Highway System highway (excluding the interstate system). The ISTEA has been the steadiest federal government source of income for public sport, tourism, and leisure service organizations in recent years. As with other transportation sources, ISTEA focuses wholly on trail development and maintenance.

Gratuitous Income

Gratuitous income receives significant attention in Chapters 12 and 13. Grants are an important source of potential income for sport, tourism, and leisure service organizations. In 2016, $59.2 billion in grants were awarded from public and private grant sources, and it is estimated that sport, tourism, and leisure service organizations received almost $1.8 billion (3.2%) of that total (Giving USA, 2017).

Fund-raising is an organized process of seeking out gifts to support leisure service organization and capital improvements. The growth of fund-raising and support organizations for sport, tourism, and leisure service organizations has been dramatic over the last two decades. Many community park and recreation agencies have created their own foundations or sport promotion corporations that are financially supported by a companion foundation or a corporation through its own philanthropic mechanism. Corporate support is highly valued, but it should be noted that almost 70% of contributions to foundations come from individual donors. Grant-seeking and fund-raising are intertwined, and entrepreneurial sport, tourism, and leisure service organizations look to both of them as important elements of their income structure.

Earned Income

Earned income consists of cash resources generated from fees, as well as charges assessed by the sport, tourism, and leisure service organization. Types of fees can include program fees; charges for use of equipment, areas, and facilities; income from sales of supplies; gift shop and pro-shop revenues; entrance fees; admission fees; rental fees; and user fees. Fiscal investments that earn interest are also considered earned income. In recent years, the greatest growth in revenues for sport, tourism, and leisure service organizations has been from earned income. For most tourism and sport organizations, earned income is the primary source of operational funds, and the emerging emphasis on earned income has helped to reshape public leisure service organization management over the last 30 years. As a result of this emphasis, management has become more entrepreneurial and business focused. Even charitable nonprofit organizations report that as much as 75% of their operating budgets can come from program service revenues.

Earned income is derived primarily from fees and charges. The Government Finance Officers' Association, suggesting a technical difference between fees and charges, agrees that in most cases, the terms "fees" and "charges" are used interchangeably (GFOA, 1998). A fee may be imposed as a result of a public need to regulate activities, safety, or other protective measures. Fees constitute the purchase of a privilege or an authorization and are applied to services rendered, such as an inspection or the issuance of a building permit. In sport, tourism, and leisure service organizations, the term "fees" has come to be associated with the delivery of programs and services.

Examples of major classifications of earned income include entrance and admission fees, rental fees, user or program fees, sales revenue, and special fees. Entrance and admission fees are charged for entrance to any public or private sport or leisure facility, movie theater, art museum, children's museum, monument, historical building, etc. Income from fees may be used to cover the cost of operations, but in some cases, it may also be intended to provide additional revenue for such needs as debt retirement and capital improvement funding.

Rental fees are charged for the exclusive use of a tangible property, such as a Santa suit, park pavilion, sport equipment, sport complex, picnic equipment, game equipment, public address system, stroller, lawn chairs, paddle boats, coin telescopes, cabin, lodge, resort room, horse, camping equipment, bicycles, and golf clubs. The list of potential rental revenue sources can be very long indeed. Revenue from rental fees may be used to recover the cost of the purchase and replacement of the rental item(s), storage and handling, or maintenance and cleaning. Sport, tourism, and leisure service organizations may also use rental fees to offset operational costs in other areas, provide renters with additional recreation opportunities, and/or contribute to profits.

User and program fees are defined as charges made for the use of a facility or for participation in an activity, program, or service. The fee may be used for capital development, debt retirement, maintenance operations, and operation of the facility or program. User and program fees could be charged for almost any type of program offering, such as figure skating classes, pottery classes, modern dance classes, tie-dyeing classes,

child care, etc. The 75-page brochure for one service organization that serves a community of 150,000 included (for a three-month period) over 900 programs with fees attached to them. In this instance, fees were different for residents and nonresidents, with the latter paying a higher rate. User fees can also be charged for the use of facilities and might, on the surface, appear to be just like rental fees. However, user fees grant access to facilities whereas rental fees usually grant exclusive use thereof.

Sales revenue comes from the sale of goods and services through gift shops, stores, concessions, restaurants, and similar types of operations. Many professional teams own apparel and souvenir shops located at the sport arena, local malls, and airports. Concession operations are becoming a major source of income for sport, tourism, and leisure service organizations. Sales activities are almost always implemented in conjunction with some other service operated by the sport, tourism, and leisure service organization. In a fitness center, for example, there may be a pro shop, a snack bar, and a full-service restaurant. In Tacoma, Washington, the city parks and recreation department contracts with an outside organization to operate a full-service restaurant on the recreational waterfront. Many golf courses have pro shops and restaurants as part of their operations. Museums have gift shops, restaurants, snack bars, and other revenue-generating amenities. State and national parks may accommodate grocery stores, gas stations, motels, and lodges. The purpose of sales activity is to provide a service to the user and to generate revenue for the organization.

Special fees are generally charged for providing some extraordinary service to consumers. In many cases, special fees might also be included in one of the previously identified fee types. Examples include lights for tennis courts, park security for special events, and use of portable stages, sound equipment, etc. In some communities, a fee is charged for after-dark use of facilities, such as night softball, where teams are charged a fee to recover the cost of lighting and additional maintenance. Other examples include fees charged for special camps (basketball, baseball, cheerleading, computer, etc.), equipment storage, and facility reservation privileges (group picnic shelters, for example).

Investment Income

Investment income represents those funds generated from the investment of currently available resources. Most public, nonprofit, and commercial enterprises are allowed to invest either all or portions of their available funds according to sound investment strategies. Some of the most common investment strategies and opportunities are municipal and corporate bonds, money market certificates, stock transactions, and mutual funds. The investment of any money is almost always made in consultation with an investment professional that has expertise in the public, nonprofit, or commercial sector. In some instances, especially with public agencies, the investment is for short periods of time (less than six months). Even investments over a short period of time allow the organization to realize additional income for its operations. Investment income reduces the need for other types of income, such as compulsory income. Such investments are usually made in opportunities that are "safe," in the sense that they are less strongly affected by major downturns or upturns in the stock market. Nonprofit organizations may use investment income as a major source of revenue for their operations. Many state park and recreation associations and universities have made investments in mutual funds, bonds, or other sources and then used the annual interest income to fund scholarships.

Contractual Receipts

Contractual receipts are revenues that are generated from legal agreements with other organizations. Income-generating agreements are entered into for the management of resources, rental of facilities, rental of equipment, and the management of special operations, such as golf courses, marinas, food concessions, tennis centers, zoos, stadiums, or gift shops. They can also include those varied operations collectively referred to as subjects of privatization—a concept that has become popular in the management of public organizations.

A *contract* is a term that describes a unit of trading for a financial or commodity future. Contract management requires proficiency in a set of business and fiscal management skills from both the contractor and the owner. In the early years of contract management, it was not uncommon for a public agency to unwisely "give away" potential for revenue from the contract and then provide inadequate oversight to contract compliance. In response, one city eventually canceled the private contract for its golf course operations after the facility regularly posted annual losses of over $500,000. The city managers determined that they could no longer justify using tax dollars to support golf operations with such major losses. In the first year after canceling the contract, the city discovered that the driving ranges actually had revenues of over $250,000 and expenses of only $40,000. Under the previous contract, all of the driving range profits had been going to the golf pro. In this case, the golf pro had done nothing wrong (according to the terms of the contract), but the city had failed to manage the contract closely enough to see how it was limiting the revenue potential and forcing the city to assume too much financial liability. Good contract management requires time and expertise.

Partnerships and Collaborations

Partnerships and collaborations are becoming more common approaches to generating income. The terms *partnership* and *collaboration* are frequently used interchangeably; however, they have very different meanings. Partnerships are formed through agreements between two or more parties with a mutual interest and common need. A partnership may be for a fixed or indeterminate length of time. The key to success in a partnership is for all parties to clearly understand and easily identify their needs. By contrast, in collaborative arrangements, different organizations may work together to achieve a common goal, but they do not entirely share the same vision, resources, or risks. The foundation of collaborations is the hope that, by working together, several organizations will have a better opportunity to resolve an issue than would a single organization. Sport, tourism, and leisure service organizations use both partnerships and collaborations, but partnerships are more likely to produce income.

A partnership results from a formal or informal agreement between two or more organizations to work together to provide a service or to fund a project.

Partnerships can include any combination of public, nonprofit, and commercial organizations. For example, a partnership may result from co-sponsorship of a 5K run by the public parks and recreation department, the YMCA, a women's shelter, a local bank, a sporting goods dealer, the convention and visitor bureau, and the local hospital. The parks and recreation department plans and jointly conducts the event with the YMCA; the hospital's marketing department develops brochures, logos, T-shirt designs; the convention and visitors bureau distributes advertising and sets up lodging and sightseeing opportunities for out-of-town participants; the bank and sporting goods store provide the awards to the runners and help pay for advertising costs; and the women's shelter receives the bulk of the revenues earmarked for its operations.

Each of the partners receives some benefit from the partnership. In the preceding example, the parks and recreation department, the YMCA, the hospital, the sporting goods store, the convention and visitor bureau, and the bank all received recognition for their efforts. The parks and recreation department, the convention and visitor bureau, and the YMCA were perceived as fulfilling their mission to serve the community. The bank, the hospital, and the sporting goods store succeeded in enhancing their image as socially responsible entities. The women's shelter received financial support, additional legitimization as a social service agency, and a positive image boost. Each participant received support, recognition, and a feeling of contribution that it might not have been able to secure independently.

Partnering is about working toward common goals and outcomes. It brings to the table unique resources from each organization that may be unavailable to the other organizations. It strengthens the assertion that "the whole is greater than the parts" and reinforces the concept of working together so that all partners can receive a positive return on their respective and collective investments. The return does not always need to be a financial benefit and could be an intangible benefit, such as image, goodwill, or legitimization.

Further examples of partnerships and the benefits of partnership can be found in numerous communities, such as Indianapolis, Indiana, and Naperville, Illinois. The Indianapolis Parks and Recreation Department worked with neighborhood community groups to formalize their involvement and leadership in local parks (Indy Parks, 2016). Community groups and local churches accepted a shared responsibility for maintenance and the general upkeep of the parks (mowing, trash removal, graffiti reporting, etc.). As partners, they received a stipend of either cash, special services, or availability of department resources to the church or neighborhood association. The work was done at a lower cost than department maintenance crews, and local involvement has resulted in a higher level of maintenance and lower levels of vandalism. In Naperville, Illinois, the city and park district (the park district is a separate taxing district) have partnered with the Riverwalk Foundation to develop and maintain a downtown riverwalk. In celebration of the city's sesquicentennial anniversary, volunteers developed the riverwalk, and since then, it has become a focal point of the community. Its covered bridges, fountains, landscaping, and distinctive shepherd's-crook light poles have become symbolic of Naperville's ties to its historic past as the oldest settlement in DuPage County. The city, the park

district, and a community foundation worked together to ensure the continued success. Fittingly, city hall and the park district headquarters are adjacent to the riverwalk, and the high school is within walking distance. Numerous major park and recreation facilities are linked to the riverwalk, and it continues to figure prominently in community festivals and special events, as well as provide one more feature to attract visitors to the area (Naperville. 2018).

Revenue Structure Plan

The amount of revenue that an organization needs, and the source of that revenue, is detailed in the revenue structure plan. The purpose of the revenue structure plan is to help the financial manager understand the organization's expenditure needs and potential sources of revenue. A revenue structure plan is typically prepared for each fiscal year. Commercial and nonprofit sport, tourism, and leisure service organizations might identify a small number of income sources, but the expenditures may be distributed across multiple divisions or profit centers. Conversely, public agencies might identify many different sources of income to cover expenses in a single leisure service enterprise. Figure 9.2 illustrates an example of the different types of revenue sources reported by state park agencies.

The revenue structure plan focuses attention on the need to strive for an acceptable balance of income sources. Table 9.3 shows how one municipality's income is derived. As might be expected, property taxes constitute the largest source of income for the municipality, and sales tax is the second largest source of revenue.

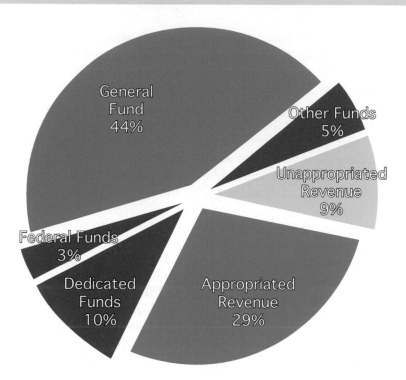

Figure 9.2. Example Revenue Structure Plan for State Parks

Table 9.3
Example of a Revenue Structure for a Municipality

Property Tax	Utility Tax	Sales Tax	Shared State Tax	Other Taxes	Licenses & Permits
16.7%	7.4%	15.2%	34.0%	5.0%	1.4%
$17,854,577	$7,906,570	$16,317,115	$36,420,521	$5,316,027	$1,448,228

Fines & Forfeitures	Investment Income	Inter-governmental services	Charges for Services	Other	Total
1.4%	3.0%	3.7%	3.3%	9.0%	100.0%
$1,551,597	$3,221,994	$3,976,524	$3,574,485	$9,602,968	$107,190,606

In today's changing fiscal environment, some public sport, tourism, and leisure service organizations are generating more than 50% of their income from non-tax sources. In this illustration, there are 11 sources of income for the municipality.

A private nonprofit or commercial sport, tourism, or leisure service organization's revenue structure would be different and would likely show a higher percentage that is derived from charges for services or other types of earned income.

It is important that any revenue structure plan be based on an established fiscal policy. That policy should articulate the revenue goals and describe, in general terms, how revenue should or may be generated. For example, Indy Parks developed its revenue structure model and identified two major funding categories: enterprise funding and underwriting (Table 9.4). The establishment of these two categories helped to further identify and classify revenue sources and place them on a service continuum with fair market pricing (where user fees cover full costs) at one extreme and city budgeting (where all costs are covered by tax revenues) at the other. Each program or service can be matched to a point on the continuum, depending on a variety of factors, such as need, ability to pay, community willingness to support, consistency with the mission of the city and the department, vision of the city and the department, consistency with the core principles of the organization, appropriate revenue sources for those programs, and services emphasized.

Developing the revenue structure plan as guided by fiscal policy maintains consistency and promotes efficient exploitation of revenue sources. Furthermore, following the fiscal policy ensures that revenue generation activities will be supported by policy makers.

Summary

Income generation is an important aspect of financial management in sport, tourism, and park and recreation organizations. The various revenue sources discussed in this chapter can provide the funds necessary to conduct programs, offer services, and maintain equipment and facilities. There are five types of income: compulsory income, gratuitous income, earned income, investment income, and contractual receipts. All of them provide different levels and types of funding for sport, tourism, and leisure service organizations. Not all sport, tourism, and leisure service organizations will secure income from the same sources. Understanding and awareness of income sources, along with the relating of that knowledge to policy directions, allow sport, tourism, and leisure service managers to more effectively meet the revenue demands of their organizations.

Table 9.4
Revenue Structure for Enterprise Funding for Indy Parks

Enterprise Funding	**Fair Market Price (fee covers total cost)**
	Fee Schedule (fee covers partial cost)
	Sponsorships (sponsor receives exposure as benefit)
Underwriting	**Self-Funding (funds shift from another internal budget)**
	Donor Base (corporate, individual giving, and grants)
	City Budget (compulsory income)

References

Beitsch, R. (2016). State parks find new ways to save, make money. PEW. Retrieved from https://www.pewtrusts.org/en/research-and-analysis/blogs/stateline/2016/04/14/state-parks-find-new-ways-to-save-make-money

California Tax Data. (1979). What is Proposition 13? Retrieved from https://www.californiataxdata.com/pdf/Prop13.pdf

Dilger, R. (2018). *Federal grants to state and local governments: A historical perspective.* Congressional Research Service. Retrieved from https://fas.org/sgp/crs/misc/R40638.pdf

Fisher, G. (2002). History of property taxes in the United States. EH.Net. Retrieved from http://eh.net/encyclopedia/history-of-property-taxes-in-the-united-states/

GFOA. (1998). *An introduction to treasury management practices.* Government Financial Officers Association. Retrieved from http://www.gfoa.org/sites/default/files/AnIntroduction-ToTreasuryManagementPractices.pdf

Giving USA. (2017). Total charitable donations rise to new height of $390.05 billion. Retrieved from https://givingusa.org/giving-usa-2017-total-charitable-donations-rise-to-new-high-of-390-05-billion/

Indy Parks and Recreation. (2016). Comprehensive Master Plan. Retrieved from http://www.planindyparks.com/pdf/indy-parks-comprehensive-master-plan-executive-summary.pdf

Lindsey, R. (1978). Many states move to limit spending. *New York Times.* Retrieved from https://www.nytimes.com/1978/06/26/archives/many-states-moving-to-limit-spending-coast-vote-spurs-efforts-to.html

McLean, D. (1996). A statistical report of America's state parks. National Association of State Park Directors. Retrieved from https://cuacs8.mck.ncsu.edu/naspd/research/rpafinance.html

Naperville Parks. (2018). Naperville Riverwalk. Retrieved from https://www.napervilleparks.org/facilities/riverwalk

Urban Institute. (2016). Property taxes. Retrieved from https://www.urban.org/policy-centers/cross-center-initiatives/state-local-finance-initiative/projects/state-and-local-backgrounders/property-taxes

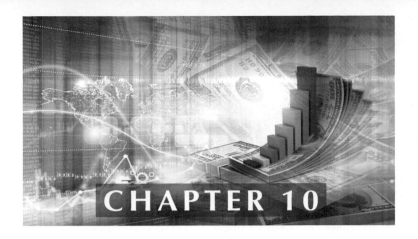

CHAPTER 10

Pricing

Introduction

One of the most challenging tasks associated with financial management in sport, tourism, and leisure service organizations is that of setting prices. In setting prices, the financial manager must be able to collect and appropriately analyze relevant data, make reasoned predictions about consumer behavior, and be creative in developing pricing strategies to help achieve the financial objectives of the organization. This chapter discusses the purposes of pricing in sport, tourism, and leisure service enterprises and explores the ways in which prices are established and adjusted. In addition, this chapter examines the effects of pricing on consumer behavior. Price quantifies the financial and other resources that a consumer of sport, tourism, and leisure services exchanges with the provider of those services. The nature, amount, and source of the resource that is exchanged

vary tremendously, but there will always be an exchange in the consumption process. Every service has a price, and every pricing strategy is designed to achieve particular purposes.

Purposes of Pricing

In most situations, pricing is used to recover the costs of production, but it can also be used to create new resources, establish value, influence behavior, and promote efficiency and equity.

Pricing to Recover Costs

Cost-recovery pricing is best illustrated by its application in public, private nonprofit, and commercial organizations. Though not exclusively, commercial organizations produce and deliver services on a for-profit basis, which means that the agency uses pricing to recover more resources from the consumer than were used in production and delivery. Organizations in the public and private nonprofit sectors typically price their services on a break-even basis (i.e., approximately the same amount of resources are recovered through pricing as are expended in production and delivery), and public sport, tourism, and leisure organizations frequently offer subsidized services which are priced in order to recover only a certain portion of their production and delivery costs.

Cost-recovery pricing assumes that the production costs are known and can be apportioned and assessed to a known number of consumers who are to pay the price. Production and delivery costs include fixed and variable costs, and the consumers (i.e., those who pay the price) may include non-users as well as direct users of the service. The method for calculating prices based on cost recovery will be described in detail later in this chapter.

Pricing to Create New Resources (Added Value Pricing)

Where pricing is used to recover more resources than constitute the cost of production and delivery, value is thereby added to the service, and new resources (profits) for the organization are created. The sport, tourism, and leisure service organization can retain those new resources to develop additional services, support other existing services, or maintain the support of investors by paying dividends or increasing the value of stock.

Pricing to Establish Value

While most people like to believe that "the best things in life are free," they also accept that, usually, "you get what you pay for." The latter assertion reinforces the suggestion that price is used as an indicator of the relative quality or value of a product. For example, a sporting event for which the admission price is $40 is expected to be much better than one that charges $2 at the gate; a $19 resort room is not likely to be as nice as a $200 room; a golf putter that sells for $15 is inferior to one that sells for $150; and so on. When the price for a particular sport, tourism, or leisure service is determined, the value of that service is established in the mind of the consumer. It is not unusual, therefore, to find sport, tourism, and leisure services that are priced well above the full cost-recovery level simply to establish and maintain a perceived level of value or quality.

Pricing to Influence Behavior

When consumers pay a price for a sport, tourism, and leisure service, they recognize that the service has value to them. The price is considered fair; otherwise, they would not have paid it. If, however, that fair price is increased because of failed performance or irresponsible behavior on the part of the consumer, the price may no longer be consistent with the value of the service. For example, $50 for 10 canoeing lessons may sound like a good price, but only if the student attends all 10 lessons. If he attends only one lesson, it is a very expensive lesson. In this case, the student is encouraged to attend all 10 lessons because of the price. He would not likely be so motivated if the price of all 10 lessons were only 49 cents. Similarly, the price of admission to a session of roller skating may seem reasonable, unless the skater violates safety or other rules of conduct and is ejected from the facility without a refund of the admission price.

The fear of having the experience reduced, but not the price, of having to pay the full admission price for readmission to the same session strongly influences the value-conscious skater to conduct himself according to the established standards. Many sport, tourism, and leisure service organizations use pricing to promote desired behaviors. Consider the following examples:

- Lower early registration fees are charged as an incentive to participants to sign up for programs early enough to give the agency adequate preparation time.
- Late fines or replacement fees are charged by libraries or movie rental stores to encourage users to return books and videos promptly and in good condition.
- Performance bonds are required of teams to make it seem too costly to withdraw from a tournament at the last moment.
- Care of facilities and equipment is promoted through the assessment of damage/cleaning deposits from groups renting recreational facilities and areas.
- Discounts are given for season tickets to promote regular attendance.
- Special prices are available for travelers who book their transportation or lodging on-line, thus avoiding the costly commissions that providers would normally pay to travel agents or other intermediaries.

Pricing to Promote Efficiency

The sport, tourism, and leisure service industry is subject to seasonal and other fluctuations in demand. There are times when the demand for certain services or products exceeds the supply, and there are times when the supply far exceeds the demand. Pricing is often used to shift the demand from peak periods to low periods and, thereby, promote efficiency. For example, the summertime demand for a commercial campground with 100 sites will normally exceed its capacity, but many sites will be empty during the spring and fall (especially on weekdays). If the campground operator added 50 new sites to accommodate the summer campers, he would be offering an inefficient solution, because the off-season surplus would then be even greater. A more efficient response might be to raise prices during the summer and lower them during other times. Some campers have flexibility in their vacation and travel plans and can be enticed, by the price differential, to camp during the off-season rather than during the busy summer months.

Bulk pricing, in the form of season passes or ticket blocks, can also promote efficiency by reducing the cost of selling individual tickets and reducing the uncertainty in estimating demand. Many amusement theme parks, for example, have abandoned the inefficient practice of selling individual tickets or coupons for attractions in favor of the all-inclusive admission price.

Efficiency can also be promoted through the use of *two-tiered pricing* structures. While some amusement parks, for example, have an all-inclusive admission price, others have the standard admission price that grants park guests access to most of the rides and services. However, an extra ticket or pass must be purchased to go on some of the more popular or thrilling rides, or to have guaranteed access to the ride regardless of how busy the park is.

Pricing to Promote Equity

Equity refers to fairness in the allocation of resources. Equity decisions are based on response to need and merit and, therefore, may result in unequal allocation of services. Pricing can be used to promote equity by redistributing the wealth of those who pay a higher price for a service to more needy or deserving people who would pay a lower price for the same service. For example, an adult may pay $5 to use a public swimming pool, while a child may pay only $2 for the same opportunity. This price structure is considered fair because children have fewer financial resources than adults, and because they need to develop aquatic safety skills and have available healthy recreation activities in their growing years. Pricing promotes equity by making the swimming pool more accessible to a needy or deserving market (the children) through fees that are made more affordable by the higher financial contribution of a more resourceful and less needy market (the adults).

The Appropriateness and Feasibility of Pricing

As stated earlier, every sport, tourism, or leisure service has a price. That price, however, may be or may include a non-monetary resource that the consumer is required to give up in exchange for the service. Only certain types of services can appropriately or feasibly be priced in direct monetary terms. In other words, charging a fee for a service is not always desirable or practical.

An example of a type of service for which it may not be desirable or practical to charge a user fee is a public service. Public services, such as neighborhood parks and playgrounds, trails, parades, and ecological reserves, are of value and benefit to a broadly defined community and, for that reason, have traditionally been supported by public funds (i.e., taxes) rather than user fees. The customary practice of having no direct user charges, coupled with the difficulty or inefficiency of limiting access for the purpose of charging admission, makes public services unlikely candidates for pricing.

A type of service for which pricing may be more appropriate and feasible is a merit service. Merit services are those that indirectly benefit the community, but are most beneficial to those who receive the service. Many of the facilities and programs provided by public recreation agencies qualify as merit services. For example, a minor soccer league is good for the community because it provides positive, wholesome outlets for the energy of young girls and boys. It also promotes many of the qualities of leadership and responsible citizenship.

Aside from benefiting the community indirectly, participation in the soccer league promotes the physical health of those who participate and also provides a great deal of personal enjoyment. Because of the benefit received by the community, it is appropriate for some community resources (e.g., playing fields built and maintained with tax dollars) to be used in support of the league. On the other hand, the individual participant benefits the most, so it is also considered appropriate and desirable for each boy or girl to pay a fee in order to play on a league team. Because player registration and game scheduling are required for the successful operation of the soccer league, it is feasible to charge a fee for individual participation.

Public, private nonprofit, and commercial sport, tourism, and leisure service organizations might also provide what are classified as private services. Though more common in commercial agencies, private services are those that are exclusive and that benefit only the individuals who use the service. It is, therefore, considered to be both desirable and feasible for the agency to charge a fee. Tennis lessons, dog grooming classes, weight training, movies, amusement parks, lake or ocean cruises, sky diving, river rafting, and professional sporting events are just a few of the thousands of private sport, tourism, and leisure services available to consumers. Participation in them is at the discretion of the consumer, and while they may be highly enjoyable and beneficial to the participant, their value to the general community is not readily apparent, so there is little reason for financial support of the services by anyone but the direct consumers.

It is important to recognize that a service is not inherently public, merit, or private. A weight-training facility at a particular university, for example, may be open to all students by virtue of the mandatory activity fee. Viewed as a benefit to all, it would be considered a public service in that campus community. Another university may provide access to its weight-training facilities only to those who pay the voluntary student activity fee. In recognition of the extended value of personal physical health to the university community, the university may subsidize the activity fee. In this case, the weight-training facility is a merit service. A third university, meanwhile, may determine that weight training benefits only the user of the facilities and that all costs of maintaining and operating a weight-training center need to be recovered from single usage or semester pass fees charged to individual users. The sometimes challenging task of classifying sport, tourism, and leisure facilities, programs, and activities as either public, merit, or private services is central to the debate about whether user fees should be charged.

The Nature of Price

Price, as a quantification of the resources exchanged by a consumer for a desired service, is usually expressed in monetary terms. The price of a hot summer afternoon at the swimming pool, for example, is said to be $3—the amount charged by the pool owner for admission to the facility. Likewise, the cost of taking a cruise might be $750—the cost of the cruise ship ticket. There are, however, other non-monetary elements of price that may play an equal or more important role in the decision about whether or not to purchase the service than the dollar amount displayed on the price tag. In addition to the monetary cost, the consumer of a sport, tourism, and leisure service will incur opportunity costs, psychological costs, and effort costs.

Monetary Price

The monetary price of a sport, tourism, or leisure program or event includes direct and indirect expenditures attributable to participation in that activity. Obviously, the registration or admission fee will be one part of the monetary price. Another part will be money that had to be paid for services that facilitate the individual's participation in the program. These facilitation costs include the following:

- **Transportation:** all the costs of getting to and from the activity, including fares, gasoline, maintenance, depreciation, and insurance.

- **Clothing and Equipment:** the costs of specialized clothing and/or equipment required for participation in the activity.
- **Proxy:** the costs of someone else fulfilling other obligations of the participant while he or she is engaged in the activity (e.g., expenses for child care, pet boarding, house sitting, employment substitution).
- **Refreshment/Sustenance:** the additional cost of purchasing meals or refreshments during the time of the activity.
- **Qualification:** the costs directly associated with making the individual eligible to participate in the activity (includes preparatory training and/or certification, medical clearance, membership fees, etc.).
- **Reference:** the costs of acquiring artifacts, such as souvenirs and photographs, that help the participant to later recall and describe the experience.

Opportunity Price

By participating in a sport, tourism, or leisure activity, an individual dedicates to that activity time and other resources that could have been utilized in alternate ways. The participant always pays the price for lost opportunity. Fathers who go out in the evening to play basketball with their co-workers give up the opportunity to spend that time with their families. College students who spend the weekend skiing lose the opportunity that those two days presented for rest, study, and preparation for an upcoming exam. Children who take piano lessons forfeit the opportunity to watch after-school cartoons on television. A recreational seamstress may spend carefully saved money to take a quilting class but, in so doing, lose the opportunity to buy a

new sewing machine. The opportunity cost of time can be measured in hours and minutes; the opportunity cost of lost wages or spent savings can be measured in dollars and cents; and the opportunity cost of not studying can be measured in grade points. There are, however, opportunity costs that defy quantification, such as family cohesiveness, spiritual health, a clear conscience, a sense of accomplishment, and so on. Though not always measurable, the opportunity price is perceivable by the consumer and is considered in the purchase/participation decision.

Psychological Price

Participants in sport, tourism, and leisure activities experience a certain amount of psychological stress. The stress may result from the uncertainty of a contest's outcome or the anxiety associated with performing at a level near the limits of the participant's capabilities. Other forms of stress manifest themselves as boredom, fear, or even embarrassment. All these conditions are a part of the psychological price of the activity. Participation may require the individual to step out of his or her personal comfort zone and place his or her self-esteem or social position at risk. By participating, the individual exchanges the psychological position of comfort for the expected stresses and anticipated outcomes, thereby paying the psychological price.

Effort Price

Sport, tourism, and leisure activities usually require substantial physical or mental exercise, and by so doing, exact a price of personal energy. Some programs may be too expensive for certain individuals—not because the monetary, opportunity, or psychological price is excessive, but because the prospective participant is "just not up to it."

Figure 10.1 presents a summary of the many costs that constitute the price for a man to spend his hot summer afternoon at the community swimming pool. It provides examples of the monetary, opportunity, psychological, and effort prices that the man must be willing to pay in order to go swimming.

Approaches to Establishing Price

One of the easiest ways to establish a price is to just pick a number and decide that it will be the dollar price for the service. This *arbitrary approach* ignores market conditions and requirements for cost recovery, and settles on a price with which the financial decision maker is most comfortable. For example, the director of a summer sport camp may decide to charge $20 just because $20 is a nice round number. Unfortunately, the positive simplicity of this approach is usually overshadowed by the negative ineffectiveness of such a strategy in meeting the financial goals of the organization.

Another relatively simple approach is to establish a price that is consistent with the price charged for the same or a similar service by a competing service provider. *Competitive pricing* can be an efficient and effective strategy if the competing provider has similar goals, production resources, costs, and market conditions. For example, the price for a recreational swimming session at a new YMCA Family Fitness Center may reasonably be set at the same amount as is charged for admission to the local public swimming pool because the costs of operation are comparable, the range of aquatic services is similar, the market is identical, and both agencies are pricing their services at the break-even level. If, however, the YMCA has a wave machine in the new pool and requires more lifeguards than the public recreation agency, then charging the same as the public agency would likely result in reduced profits or increased operating deficits.

A third approach to pricing sport and leisure services is to charge whatever the market is *willing to pay*. This *market pricing strategy* assumes that consumers are willing to pay at least the amount required by the organization for cost recovery and then seeks a higher amount

Product: Swimming

PRICE

$3 (admission), $25 (swimsuit), $2.50 (transportation), $2 (snack), opportunity to watch football game, opportunity to work overtime, enduring noisy kids, embarrassment due to uneven tan, embarrassment due to obviously poor physical condition, embarrassment due to limited swimming skills, risk due to poor swimming skills, physical fatigue, potential sunburn, emotional effort to drive to pool and find shaded parking stall, initial discomfort/shock of cold water, disfavor of spouse who wanted me to stay home and fix the dishwasher.

Figure 10.1. The Varied Elements of the Price Tag for Going Swimming that will optimize financial returns. Using the market pricing approach, a college athletic department with a nationally ranked basketball team may decide to charge non-student spectators $20 per game because that is the amount that these basketball fans have demonstrated a willingness to pay. These same fans, however, may only be willing to pay $5 per game if the basketball team goes for three seasons losing every game by as many as 50 points.

Finally, a *cost-recovery pricing strategy* is based on the principle of seeking a return from the consumers that represents a predetermined portion of the resources that are required to provide the sport, tourism, or leisure service to them. That portion may be less than, equal to, or greater than 100%, depending on the organization's financial objectives and how the service being priced is supposed to help achieve those objectives. Clearly, two pieces of information are essential before determining price based on cost recovery. The first is accurate information about the costs of providing the service, and the second is information about the extent to which the pricing strategy is expected to generate revenues equal to those costs. The latter item of *information is referred to as either the subsidization rate* or the *mark-up*.

Calculating Costs for Unit Pricing

In order to calculate the costs incurred in the provision of service to each consumer, the financial manager needs to know what the *fixed* and *variable* costs are, how much *contingency* is required, and how many consumers are likely to participate in the program or purchase the service at a given price. Estimating demand (i.e., the quantity desired at a given price) requires an understanding of the needs, interests, capabilities, constraints, and opportunities of the target market. Although demand will be discussed in detail in Chapter 18, it is appropriate here to emphasize that estimation of demand is an art founded in science and measurement. In other words, "knowing" how many people will participate in a sport, tourism, or leisure program requires an educated guess.

Contingency refers to being prepared for the unexpected. There is obvious wisdom in adding to the itemized costs of a product an amount that can be used if additional costs arise. How many contingencies should be built into the costs? Some managers are comfortable with only five percent of the costs being contingent, while other more cautious financial managers may want to have an amount as much as 15 percent of the itemized costs be available to deal with contingencies. For long-standing, established programs, or for programs requiring limited financial investment, the reduced risk would justify a relatively small contingency, but new, untried, or short-term programs, as well as those for which the consequences of financial failure are severe, should have a relatively high contingency built into their cost estimates.

Fixed and variable costs are the financial resources that are used in production and delivery of the sport, tourism, or leisure service. They can be itemized and are the basis of cost-recovery pricing. Fixed costs are those financial costs that the sport, tourism, or leisure service organization incurs, regardless of the status of the program. They are unavoidable, even if nobody registers for the program or attends the event.

Figure 10.2 identifies the fixed costs associated with the maintenance of a skating rink. If the facility is maintained as a rink, but nobody comes to skate, there will still be mortgage installments due and bills to be paid. There will still be a portion of the agency administrators' salaries that are actually rink-related costs, because maintaining the rink partly justifies the administrator's position. There will be the direct costs of installing and removing the ice surface at either end of the skating season. And even this unused and empty facility would require repairs and upkeep, as well as basic utility services.

Variable costs are those costs that result from the actual operation of the sport, tourism, or leisure service. The more the service operates, the greater the variable costs will be. Operating at full capacity, the skating rink lights would be on, the dressing rooms and spectator areas would be heated, showers would deliver thousands of gallons of hot water, floors would need cleaning, supervisory staff would be retained, and so on. The cost of operating the rink will vary depending on its use; hence, the term variable costs. Figure 10.2 also identifies the variable costs for the rink to operate for a seven-month skating season.

The actual cost of one unit of a product is calculated by applying the formula:

$$P=(F+V)/N$$

where P=the cost of a unit, F=the total fixed costs, V=the total variable costs, and N=the number of units expected to be sold.

Kotkawagan Ice Rink

COST SUMMARY

(October - April)

Fixed Costs

Capital costs	$4,300/month x 7 months	$30,100
Administration (overhead)	$375/month x 7 months	$2,625
Ice installation/removal		$2,000
Basic maintenance	$2,000/month x 7 months	$14,000
Basic utilities and service	$1,100.month x 7 months	$7,700
TOTAL FIXED COSTS		$56,425
HOURLY FIXED COSTS*		$25.08

Variable Costs

Utilities and maintenance	$11/hour x 2,250 hours	$24,750
Staff	$9/hour x 2,250	$20,250
TOTAL VARIABLE COSTS		$45,000
HOURLY VARIABLE COST*		$20
TOTAL COSTS		**$101,450**
HOURLY COST*		**$45.09**

*based on expected 2,250 hours of ice time sold

Figure 10.2. Sample Cost Summary for Ice Rink

Using the data from Figure 10.2, the recoverable hourly cost of operating the ice rink is calculated as follows:

$$P=(F+V)/N$$

$$P=(\$56,425 + \$45,000)/2,250 \text{ hours}$$

$$P=\$45.09/\text{hour}$$

To calculate the price that should be charged in order to recover all costs (i.e., break even), a revised formula that considers contingency may also be used. *Contingency costs* are the unforeseen costs or revenue shortfalls for which the host or sponsoring organization needs to be prepared. For example, if the price is based on an estimation that 10 people will participate and only nine actually do, then a contingency cost that was added to the price will at least partially cover the revenue shortage. Similarly, if a piece of equipment breaks down or additional materials need to be obtained after the program or event begins, then a contingency cost that was included in the price will help to pay for the unexpected expense. Contingency is added to the formula as a shared cost. The formula for calculating the price, with a built-in contingency, is:

$$P= (F+V+C)/N$$

where P = the average price per unit, and C = the total amount added as a contingency.

If the operator of the ice rink chooses to build a \$5,000 contingency into the pricing model, then the average price for one hour of ice time will be:

$$P = (F+V+C)/N$$

$$P = (\$56,425 + \$45,000 + \$5,000)/2,250 \text{ hours}$$

$$P = \$47.30/\text{hour}$$

Instead of using a fixed amount (\$5,000) as a contingency cost, the operator may use a percentage of costs. For example, the rink operator may decide to provide for 8% error in cost estimation. The average price for one hour of ice time would then be calculated as follows:

$$P = (1.08(F+V))/N$$

where 1.08 represents adding a 8% contingency factor or, in other words, using 108% of estimated costs.

$$P = (1.08(F+V))/N$$

$$P = (1.08(\$56,425 + \$45,000))/2,250 \text{ hours}$$

$$P = \$48.68/\text{hour}$$

Note that the per hour costs calculated in the preceding examples include all of the costs associated with providing the specific activity. This approach to cost quantification is referred to as *activity-based costing* (ABC) and is different from traditional approaches to accounting, which often ignore major fixed costs (e.g., capital, administrative overhead) and often do not relate costs to specific activities or program components.

The advantages of ABC over traditional cost measurement strategies include the following:

- ABC helps to identify manageable contributing factors to cost (thereby facilitating improvements to operational efficiency).

- ABC allows cost comparisons for the same activity provided by different units within the organization or for different market segments.
- ABC generates data for benchmarking and comparing the cost of an activity provided in-house or by contracting out.
- ABC tells the true story of cost and facilitates appropriate pricing based on cost recovery objectives.

Subsidization and Unit Pricing

Once the true cost has been determined, the next step in establishing the unit price for a particular consumer or target market is the application of a rate of subsidization. The rate of subsidization refers to how much of the unit cost is going to be recovered from sources other than the consumer. In the public sport, tourism, and leisure service organization, subsidization means using tax revenues to reduce or eliminate user fees for services. Private nonprofit and commercial sport, tourism, and leisure service organizations may subsidize some programs or services by using donated funds or the profits generated by another of their enterprises to reduce or eliminate the consumer's contribution to meeting the costs of the programs or services.

Using the profits of one program to reduce the price of another is called *cross-subsidization*. A common pricing strategy involves subsidizing different market segments at different levels. For example, the pricing strategy for the public skating rink could reflect a political decision to keep skating activities very affordable for special populations in the community while, at the same time, expecting commercial ventures to pay the full share (or more) of the costs of any public facilities or services that they use. The sample subsidization rates displayed in Table 10.1 demonstrate a commitment to youth recreation. Subsidization rates are used to convert the average per unit cost of a sport or leisure service to the final consumer price(s) for the product. The appropriate formula for calculating price is:

$$Pm=(1-Sm)P$$

where Pm=the price to be charged to a specific market (m) for one unit, and Sm=the subsidization rate applied to market m, and P is the cost of a unit.

Note that the subsidization rate can be as high as 100% (a free service) or as low as a minus percentage (a profit-generating service). A service that is "marked up" 30% is subsidized at -30% and priced at 130% of its cost.

The prices charged to various skating groups for one hour of ice time are shown in Table 10.1. The price for youth programs such as minor hockey, figure skating, and ringette (m1) are subsidized 35% and calculated as follows:

$$Pm1=(1-Sm_1)P$$

$$Pm_1=(1-.35)(*\$47.30/hour)$$

$$Pm_1=\$30.75/hour$$

* using the cost based on a $5,000 contingency

Table 10.1
Sample Subsidy Rates and Hourly Prices for Ice Rink Rental

User Group	Subsidy Rate	Price
Minor Hockey	35%	$30.75/hour
Figure Skating	35%	$30.75/hour
Ringette	35%	$30.75/hour
Public Skating	0%	$47.30/hour
Open Skate	100%	free
Gentlemen's Hockey	10%	$52.03
Junior A Hockey (practice)	-25%	$59.13/hour

The subsidization rate for the Junior A hockey club (m_2) is -25%, which means that the hourly cost will be marked up to establish a price for this user group. The formula given above can be used to calculate the price to be charged ($59.13/hour, which is 25% greater than the cost to be recovered).

$$Pm_2 = (1 - Sm_2)P$$

$$Pm_2 = (1 - (-25)(\$47.30/hour)$$

$$Pm_2 = (1.25)(\$47.30/hour)$$

$$Pm_2 = \$59.13/hour$$

Other Considerations in Establishing Price

While cost recovery is usually the most important consideration in establishing prices, there are other factors to keep in mind when determining how much to charge for a sport, tourism, or leisure service. The potential customers' willingness to pay the established price is certainly an important consideration, as is their sensitivity to price changes.

Willingness to Pay/The Going Rate

When cost-recovery goals are easily met because the calculated unit price is below an amount that all or most consumers are accustomed to paying or willing to pay, it may be appropriate (and, perhaps, necessary) to price the sport, tourism, or leisure service at a higher "going rate." Conversely, a service that costs more to produce than the consumers are willing to pay may also need to be priced at a going rate that results in a financial loss. In either case, the reasons for pricing at the going rate may be varied and may also include protection of perceived value, protection of consumer self-esteem, and promotion of competition.

A sport, tourism, or leisure service that is highly valued by consumers may not necessarily be costly to produce. However, if that low-cost service is priced too low, the potential appeal of and commitment to it may actually be diminished because of the commonly held belief that "you get what you pay for, and if it doesn't cost much, then it's probably not very good." Even if a private nonprofit organization's excellent fitness program incurs a cost of $10 per participant, it might be wise to charge around $30 per participant if that is what he or she is used to paying for services of similar value (i.e., perceived personal benefit) or for similar services offered by another provider. In this example, the consumers have indicated a willingness to pay $30 and thereby have implicitly suggested that a significantly lower price would probably generate doubts about the quality of the product. The $30 price tag helps to protect the perceived value of the service. The "problem" of what to do with the $20 profit that would be realized by this nonprofit organization may be quickly resolved if the organization also has a worthwhile program for which the production costs exceed the price that consumers are willing to pay. All the organization needs to do is to shift the profits of the former program to cover the losses of the latter. Clearly, consideration of the willingness of patrons to pay the going rate is important in pricing decisions, especially when the sport or leisure service organization uses cross-subsidization to achieve its financial objectives.

Consideration of the going rate in pricing decisions is also important for protecting the self-esteem of consumers. Generally, people like to feel that they have earned what they receive. When they receive benefits from a sport or leisure service, they feel better about themselves if they worked, sacrificed, or somehow paid a fair price for those benefits. Pricing decisions should allow for consumers to maintain or enhance their self-esteem in the knowledge that they will have "paid their dues." At the same time, pricing decisions should protect consumers' self-esteem by demonstrating sensitivity to the desire to believe that all basic needs and, perhaps, a few leisure wants are available and affordable to everyone. In other words, prices should

not make a consumer feel that it is impossible to satisfy perceived needs, but instead should make him or her feel that paying the price is an appropriate way to demonstrate deservedness of the benefits derived from consuming the sport, tourism, or leisure product.

Sometimes the going rate is used as a means to promote competition. For example, a state park agency may be able to provide serviced campsites at an average cost of $8 per night, but will choose to charge the going rate of $15 per night in order to help the neighboring commercial campground stay in business. The commercial campground also charges $15 per night, but its average campsite costs are $12. The state park is able to produce campsites at a lower cost because it does not pay off a mortgage on the land, does not pay local property taxes or sales and income taxes, and does not pay directly for marketing. In some respects, the state park has an unfair advantage and could exploit that through its pricing. The state park, however, cannot always satisfy the demand for camping, but is required to facilitate extensive use of the park. It needs the commercial campground to stay in business in order for the state park to continue to attract visitors and to avoid expanding the public campground to the detriment of protected natural areas. By establishing prices that are consistent with the going rate, regardless of production costs, the state park promotes competition and ensures adequate camping opportunities for overnight visitors.

It should be noted that the going rate for a particular service might vary according to product and market conditions. Products that are seasonal in their appeal will have a lower going rate in the off-season than during periods of high demand. Products oriented toward children or economically disadvantaged population segments also tend to have a lower going rate than those offered to adults and wealthier persons. There are several appropriate justifications for differential pricing that are based on willingness to pay and the going rate:

- **Customer characteristics.** Both the willingness to pay and the going rate may vary because of age limitations/opportunities, income, ability, intensity of consumption, etc.
- **Product levels.** Consumers are willing to pay more for advanced levels or elitist tourism, leisure, and sport opportunities and less for basic services.
- **Distribution.** Differential pricing may reflect the advantages of one service location or time over another. For example, concert tickets are priced according to the location of reserved seats, and rental fees for sports facilities are higher during prime-time hours.
- **Merit.** Prices and expectations of price differentials may reflect the historical contribution of the consumer to the product. For example, lower program registration fees for club or association members serve as recognition and expectation resulting from the earlier payment of membership. Bulk pricing (such as season passes and ticket packs) is also a practice based on recognition of the contribution and merit of the high-quantity/frequency customer.

Sensitivity to Changes in Price

The measure of price-induced demand fluctuations is called price elasticity of demand, and is discussed in Chapter 18. In that discussion, it will be emphasized that any change in price is going to have an impact of consumption and, most likely, on revenue. As a general rule, price increases should be avoided when dealing with an elastic market, but may be applied more liberally when dealing with a market or market segment that is relatively inelastic.

Adjusting Prices

It is natural to expect that a drop in sales or attendance will result from an increase in price. When a price increases, there will inevitably be a portion of the market that feels that the new price is too high, and therefore cannot or will not pay the higher amount. Some of those customers will need time to adjust to the new price and may eventually find the resources or the will to return and continue participating. Others will not be able to convince themselves that the higher price is worth paying, but could be convinced by the service provider. In doing so, the sport and leisure service provider is challenged with finding a way to adjust or redefine the consumer's reference price. Reference price is the amount that the consumer feels that the service might or should cost and is derived from the consumer's experience with similar services and/or from introductory information provided by the sport, tourism, and leisure service organization. The *reference price* for a youth soccer camp, for example, might be $40. Last year the consumer paid $45 for a basketball camp with a similar format, and her neighbor reported paying $38 to register his daughter in the children's soccer camp offered by the YMCA. Hence, $40 seems to be a reasonable expectation (reference price).

The sport, tourism, and leisure service organization only needs to adjust the soccer moms' reference price if it is significantly different from the objective price. The *objective price* is defined as the actual price charged for the service. For example, the registration fee for youth soccer may be $55. Expecting to pay $40 and then being presented with a bill for $55, the consumer would be inclined to consider the program to be a bit expensive. She may even consider it to be much too expensive. The words or expressions that a consumer uses to describe the difference between the reference price and the objective price are referred to as the *subjective price*. Essentially, the subjective price is how the consumer feels about the objective price, based on his or her reference price. The subjective price is a word or expression, not a number. Examples include the following: "expensive," "reasonable," "cheap," "bargain," "rip-off," "prohibitive," "a good deal."

There are several effective approaches to adjusting the consumer's reference price. One approach is to *inform the consumer of the actual costs* that the price is supposed to recover. For example, the soccer camp may cost the agency $65 per participant. Knowing this, the consumer would be inclined to adjust her reference price upward and recognize that the objective price ($55) is really a pretty good deal. A second approach to changing the consumer's reference price is to *emphasize the value or the benefits of the product to the consumer*. In the youth soccer camp example, the sponsoring agency could point out that

participation in the program provides the boy or girl with a wholesome, health-promoting way to spend time, a positive social environment, opportunities to experience success and failure (and help in learning how to deal with them), skill development, leadership experience, etc. Surely these benefits are worth at least $55! The third approach involves *comparing the cost of the service* with a similar service or activity offered elsewhere. The consumer could be informed that the price for the local soccer camp is $55, but that a similar program in a nearby community would cost $80. Furthermore, the soccer camp is $15 cheaper than both the basketball and volleyball camps offered by the same agency. The fourth approach to adjusting the reference price is to *enhance the image of the product* in the eyes of the consumer. In order to raise the reference price for the youth soccer camp, promotional emphasis could be placed on the success achieved by camp alumni or on the international reputation of the camp director.

Figure 10.3 shows the relationship of past experience and direct communications to the establishment of reference prices. It also identifies four approaches to adjusting reference price. The opportunity to influence the reference price is important to the sport, tourism, and leisure service manager, because the reference price is the price with which the objective price is compared in order to establish a subjective price. Purchase decisions are based on subjective price.

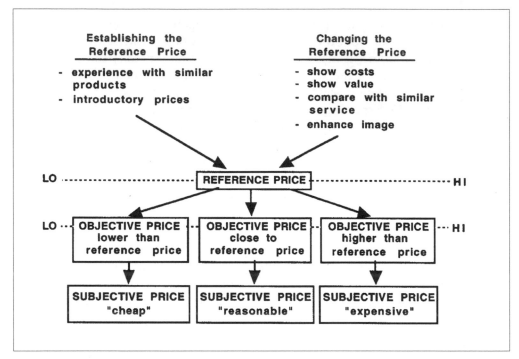

Figure 10.3. Relationship of Reference Price to Subjective Price

Summary

The price of a sport, tourism, or leisure service is the quantification of the level of exchange between the service provider and the customer. It is what the customer gives up in order to receive the service. In addition to financial resources, the price includes opportunity, effort, and psychological stress. Monetary pricing helps the organization to recover costs of production, manage consumer behavior, and establish value for the service.

Pricing of certain services is desirable and necessary, but others may not be suitable for direct pricing. There are several ways to establish a price, but the most common approach is to determine production costs and then price according to particular cost-recovery objectives. It is important for financial managers to understand and consider the sensitivity of sport, tourism, and leisure service consumers to price changes. Price changes will affect demand and consumption, which will ultimately affect revenue and profits.

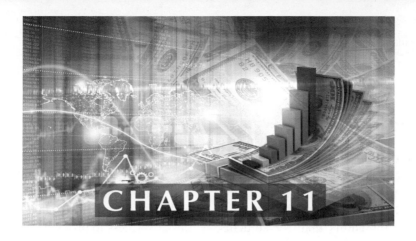

CHAPTER 11

Revenue Management

Introduction

In the 1989 movie *Field of Dreams* (based on W. P. Kinsella's novel, *Shoeless Joe*), the lead character is told by a mysterious voice, "If you build it, he will come." That optimistic forecasting statement has been used as a substitute for data-driven planning for decades, and the results have, at times, been disastrous. The landscape is strewn with sports facilities, tourist attractions and accommodations, commercial and public recreation venues, and leisure services that were created because investors believed that their mere existence was sufficient to guarantee financial success. Some have been successful, some have barely survived, some remain as a regretted financial burden, and others failed.

Wise capital development in sport, tourism and recreation requires objective evaluation of reliable and relevant information. It also requires a touch of passionate optimism that is checked by rational forecasting.

Likewise, effective operation of sport, tourism, and recreation enterprises requires reliable information about past, current and future use, as well as an understanding of potential efficiencies. Efficiency contributes to the bottom line in business, and to improve the bottom line, attention needs to be given to the potential maximization of revenues.

The traditional and simplistic approach to managing revenues is to set a price for a product (good or service) and then try to sell as much of that product as possible, thereby maximizing the revenue. This approach assumes a great deal, of homogeneity in the market as well as confidence in the ability of marketing and promotion to control or influence demand.

A slightly more sophisticated approach to managing revenues is to use pre-determined differential pricing to reflect and manage fluctuations in demand. Different prices may be charged for the same product depending on when it is delivered or who purchases it. For example, movie theater tickets may cost more on weekend evenings than during the day in the middle of the week. They may also cost more for adults than for students, children, or senior citizens. The reasoning behind such differential pricing schemes is that the movie will play as scheduled and any admission fees that can be collected are more than no admission fees at all. Therefore, using lower prices to entice customers who are willing to watch the movie at less popular times is better than losing those customers all together. Differential pricing schemes are typically applied with consistency, but not necessarily with efficiency.

Greater efficiency in revenue management is achieved through a process of revenue management that is dynamic and highly responsive to variations in demand.

Definition

Revenue management is a process designed to achieve an optimal level of net revenues and gross operating profit. This is done by offering the right product to the right customers, via the right distribution channel, at the right time, at the right price, and with the right communication. The process of revenue management recognizes that maximum revenue is not the same as optimal revenue. Sometimes the bigger cost of generating maximum revenue can negatively impact the bottom line or violate the social mandate of the enterprise. Therefore, this definition of revenue management links optimal net revenue and optimal gross operating profit.

Another aspect of the definition of revenue management is serving the "right" customer. The right customer is the one who an organization can properly and profitably serve. This, of course, implies that there are "wrong" customers and that revenue management practices will sometimes intentionally discourage or deny access to products.

Offered products should only be those that contribute to the profitability of the enterprise and are valued by the "right" customers. The value of a product to the customers is measured by their willingness to pay for it (directly or indirectly).

Delivering the right product to the right customer requires an effective distribution channel. Effective distribution channels are those that are affordable, sustainable, and provide access to the desired customers.

The "right" time to offer a product to the customer is when the customer is considering the purchase. The "wrong" time to offer a product is when the potential customer does not need, does not want, or cannot afford it. Offering a family vacation package at a classy resort in mid-September is an example of inappropriate timing. School obligations make it impossible for the children to get away, family budgets may still be recovering from summer expenditures, and the demands of employment often are not conducive to taking time off work at that time of year.

This chapter focuses on the "right price" aspect of revenue management. It will be shown that different prices can and should be charged to different markets and at different times in order to optimize revenue.

The purposes of generating revenue from sport, tourism, and leisure service enterprises are to cover the costs of providing service and, where appropriate, to generate profits. A wise financial manager will always look for ways to optimize revenues. Revenue optimization is accomplished by selling as much of the product as possible, at the highest price possible. This chapter examines a particular approach to revenue optimization that is used in the hotel industry but the underlying principles are applicable in other sport, tourism, and leisure service settings. The approach involves monitoring demand and adjusting prices to redistribute or increase demand while maximizing and optimizing revenues.

RevPAR (Revenue Per Available Room)

As discussed in Chapter 7, RevPAR is an important measure of financial performance in the hotel industry. It is a single metric that is a function of both room rates and occupancy. RevPAR is calculated by multiplying the average daily room rate times by the occupancy rate. A hotel's RevPAR can, therefore, be increased or decreased by changing either or both of the average daily price of the room or the hotel occupancy rate.

For example, if Lake Liahona Lodge has 200 rooms that sell for an average of $160 per night, and an average occupancy rate of 68%, then its RevPAR is calculated as follows:

$$RevPAR = \text{Average Daily Rate} \times \text{Occupancy Rate}$$

$$RevPAR = \$160 \times .68 = \$108.80$$

The daily revenue is calculated by multiplying the RevPAR by the number of rooms. At the above stated operating efficiency, daily revenue for Lake Liahona Lodge is $21,760 ($108.80 x 200 rooms).

One way to increase daily revenue is to undertake an effective marketing campaign that results in an increase in occupancy. If the occupancy rate can be raised to 72% without adjusting prices, then the RevPAR changes to $115.20 and the daily revenue increases to $23,040.

A marketing effort might also be designed to increase the perceived quality of the Lodge and thereby justify higher room rates. If the occupancy rate stays at 68% but the average daily room rate increases to $175, then the RevPAR improves to $119 and the daily revenue rises to $23,800. Of course, an increase in both occupancy rate and room rate will also increase RevPAR and total revenue (as shown in Table 11.1).

It is important to note that, while raising both price and occupancy seems like an obvious approach to increasing revenue, price and occupancy are often dependent on each other, and changing occupancy by changing price does not always work out as hoped. Lowering

Table 11.1
Sample RevPAR and Total Revenue Scenarios

Number of Rooms	Average Daily Room Rate	Occupancy	RevPAR	Total Revenue
200	$160	68%	$108.80	$21,760
200	$160	72%	$115.20	$23,040
200	$175	68%	$119.00	$23,800
200	$175	72%	$126.00	$25,200

the price usually generates increased occupancy, and a rise in price is likely to have an inverse effect on demand. Furthermore, the relative change in each may not be sufficient to generate increased revenue and the impact of either market response could be negative in terms of revenue generation. For example, when increasing the occupancy rate to 70% by lowering the average daily room rate to $140, the resulting revenue will be only $19,600. Likewise, if increasing the price to $190 results in a significantly lower (53%) occupancy, then the revenue will be only $20,140. The challenge of revenue management is to know when to raise or lower prices in order to influence demand and positively influence revenue.

Market Understanding

The question of when to raise or lower prices is really more a question of whom to target in offering a product at different price points. Some market segments are more price-sensitive than others and may disproportionately respond to changes in price. Some market segments are not sensitive to price but are constrained in their ability to consume at different levels. For example, a budget-conscious family might consider staying at a hotel for three nights when the daily room cost is $110, but would stay for only two nights if the room price is $135 per night. On the other hand, a businessman might be willing to pay $160 for the room, but only has time to stay for one night, no matter how much the hotel might offer to discount the room.

Revenue management requires a good understanding of who the customers are, what their sensitivity is to price, and what their opportunities for consumption are. Appropriate market information systems are essential to effective revenue management.

Market information that is useful in revenue management includes much of what might go into an individual guest/client history report. Details of when and for how long the guest stayed, cancellation or no-show ratio, room rates paid, type of room requested, dining-in behavior, hotel services utilized, and evaluation comments help the revenue manager to anticipate needs and respond to anticipated consumption patterns. In addition to understanding the needs of specific hotel guests, the revenue manager should develop more comprehensive profiles of the various market segments to be served.

Historical Performance Measures

Hotels and many other sport, tourism, and leisure service businesses have seasons or recurring periods of time during which demand can be predicted. Such prediction is based on history and can be very accurate. For example, a hotel in Washington D.C. can expect that every four years it will have one particular week where occupancy will be extremely high, guests will stay for several days, and the top room rate can be charged. During the Presidential Inauguration, there is little to be done to guarantee a high RevPAR for D.C. hotels. History has justified this expectation.

In a different situation, another hotel might have to be more deliberate in attracting guests to stay on another less eventful day. The hotel operator cannot afford to wait until that day to decide if he has met historical standards. If historical records indicate that, on the day in question, there are normally 260 rooms sold, then the operator should be able to decide 30 days or more ahead if he is on target to sell 260 rooms. He will need to know what the status of sales was at the same time last year, and in years before. Revenue management systems record such data and make them available for deliberative purposes.

The Yield Management Report

A simple tool for helping the revenue manager to determine if and what measures need to be taken in order to optimize revenue is the *yield management report*. An example is shown in Figure 11.1. For any given day in the future, a report can be generated that indicates, using historical comparisons, how well the hotel is doing in approaching its normal level of business.

The Inn at Cross Junction
Yield Management Report

Day of Arrival: April 1, 2019
Today's Date: March 1, 2019
Days until DOA: 31
Booking Pace: 124
Historical Average: 120
Total available rooms: 148

Figure 11.1. Sample Yield Management Report (Ahead of Pace)

As shown in the above example (Figure 11.1), the yield management report was prepared on March 1 and focuses on sales for April 1. There are 148 rooms available on April 1 and by this date in previous years an average of 120 have been sold. This year, 124 rooms

have been sold. The hotel is ahead of pace and little or nothing needs to be done to promote a greater rate of sales for that day.

If, however, the yield management report looked like the example in Figure 11.2, there would be reason to take corrective actions to promote sales.

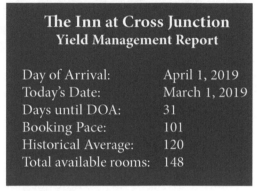

Figure 11.2 Sample Yield Management Report (Off Pace)

The yield management report in Figure 11.2 shows that sales by this date are off pace (i.e., are not as high as the historical average) and something needs to be done. Possible actions might include additional advertising and/or lowering room rates. By making adjustments 31 days ahead of the day of arrival, there will be sufficient time for the sales strategy (marketing effort and/or price reduction) to actually influence market behavior and meet occupancy and revenue goals. The yield management report helps the revenue manager to confidently sell rooms at a reduced rate today in response to a lack of demand tomorrow.

Sometimes, the yield management report will indicate that sales are well ahead of pace with many days to go. The example in Figure 11.3 illustrates such a scenario.

The Inn at Cross Junction
Yield Management Report

Day of Arrival:	May 10, 2019
Today's Date:	March 1, 2019
Days until DOA:	52
Booking Pace:	124
Historical Average:	85
Total available rooms:	148

Figure 11.3. Sample Yield Management Report (Significantly Ahead of Pace)

With 52 days until the date of arrival, the booking pace is much higher than the historical average. There is little question that the hotel will be fully booked by May 10. However, full occupancy does not necessarily equate to optimal revenue. Because the rooms are selling so robustly, the revenue manager could confidently raise the price of those that have not yet been sold and, thereby, increase the net revenue. With the booking pace so much higher than the historical average, the revenue manager can confidently give up selling a room at a low price today in order to sell it at a higher price tomorrow.

The yield management report should be generated and reviewed daily. It should also include data pertaining to many dates of arrival, thus affording a more complete picture of sales trends and opportunities for revenue optimization. Figure 11.4 is an example of a yield management report that covers a 14-day period. Most hotels use reports that extend well beyond 14 days into the future and may include dates of arrival that are months and years ahead.

Last-minute efforts to sell rooms are sometimes necessary, but careful attention to trends and future conditions will enhance the ability of the sales staff to develop and implement effective sales strategies that maximize net revenues.

Yieders Run Retreat					
Yield Management Report					
Date:	March 1, 2019				
DOA	Days till DOA	Avail. Rooms	Hist. Avg.	Booking Pace	Difference
2-Mar	1	95	81	80	-1
3-Mar	2	95	84	86	2
4-Mar	3	95	83	86	3
5-Mar	4	95	83	80	-3
6-Mar	5	95	78	79	1
7-Mar	6	92	77	77	0
8-Mar	7	92	76	75	-1
9-Mar	8	95	70	68	-2
10-Mar	9	95	70	66	-4
11-Mar	10	95	66	66	0
12-Mar	11	95	63	67	4
13-Mar	12	95	63	61	-2
14-Mar	13	95	57	59	2
15-Mar	14	95	57	60	3

Figure 11.4. Sample Yield Management Report Covering a 14-Day Period

Duration of Stay/Room rate

In discussing the need for revenue managers to understand markets, the example of a vacationing family and a business traveler was given. The price-sensitive vacationing family was willing to pay $110 per night for a hotel room but would not pay $135 per night for the same number of nights. The same room could be sold for $160 per night to a business traveler. On the surface, it would appear that pricing to sell to the business traveler is a better option. However, the duration of stay, as it is affected by room rate and other market characteristics, must also be considered. If the business traveler only needs to stay one night and then be somewhere else the next day, the revenue potential for that guest is only $160. If the family can stay for three nights at $110 per night, the revenue potential increases to $330. Even at $130 per night, the family might cut the vacation short and stay for only two nights, but still generate $260 of revenue. Three nights at $110 is better than two nights at $130, and better than one night at $160.

The preceding example assumes that the room sold to the one-night business traveler cannot be sold to a different guest at the $160 rate on the second or third night. Such an assumption is often justified, as there are certain days of the week when hotel demand arising from business travel is higher. When revenue optimization is the goal, it sometimes makes more sense to sell a room many times at a lower price than to sell it once at a higher price. Revenue managers are keenly aware of the fact that an unsold room generates no revenue at all. In the hotel industry, empty rooms equal money left on the table.

Discounting to Optimize Revenue

Because pricing and demand are so closely and predictably associated, the simplest sales strategy for optimizing revenue is to reduce or discount rates. The practice is effective but can have some negative impacts. For example, perceptions of quality are often influenced by price. It is natural to think that a less expensive hotel is not as good as a high-priced establishment. To avoid tarnishing the reputation or diminishing the quality perception of a property, discounting should be done in such a way that the discounted price does not become the reference price (see Chapter 10).

Additionally, deep discounts might not proportionally increase demand or occupancy and could have a negative impact on revenue. If the percentage decrease in the average room rate is greater than the percentage increase in occupancy, then a net decrease in revenue results.

On the positive side, a discounted sale is always better than no sale. An empty room generates no revenue. An occupied room adds minimal marginal cost that is more than balanced by the revenue it generates.

It should be remembered that the guest room may not be the only profit center in the hotel. Guests that occupy discounted rooms will often purchase meals in the hotel restaurant or pay for other on-site services.

Finally, a full hotel has a full parking lot. A full parking lot is free and credible advertising that the property is a popular place to stay. Being a visibly high-demand establishment contributes positively to occupancy, price, and revenue.

Summary

Revenue management is an active approach to manipulating demand and price in order to optimize revenue. This approach is used extensively in the hotel industry and has added much-needed sophistication to the management of marketing and sales. The underlying principles of revenue management are also applicable in other sport, tourism, and leisure service organizations. Revenue management involves understanding target markets, monitoring consumer behavior, and making price or supply adjustments to realize the greatest revenue potential. Yield management reports aid in sales strategy development. Along with historical data and market information, yield management reports guide the timing and focus of sales strategies, especially those that involve price increases or discounts. Effective revenue management results in the sale of unsold products, optimal pricing of high-demand products, and an increase in net revenues.

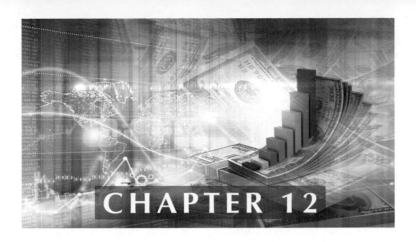

CHAPTER 12

Grantseeking

Introduction

Grantseeking is an area of financial management in which many sport, tourism, and leisure service professionals must develop proficiency. Grantseeking is a systematic, logical process of articulating and matching needs with the goals and expectations of a granting agency. Unfortunately, many sport, tourism, and leisure service managers are deterred from grantseeking by what they believe is complicated a process. While some granting organizations do require detailed proposals that are strongly supported by additional sources of information or money, there are many simpler grant proposals that can lead to equally successful results. There is no guaranteed formula for success, but there are procedures that, when followed, increase an applicant's potential for success. In today's competitive budget environment, it has become more common to use grantseeking as part of the sport, tourism, and leisure service organization's revenue plan. Successful grantseeking provides opportunities to extend programs and services in ways that might not otherwise be possible. This chapter describes the grantseeking process and suggests approaches that have proven to be successful in a variety of situations.

The terms *grantseeking* and *grantwriting* are frequently used interchangeably, but have different meanings. Grantseeking refers to the broader process of finding and securing a grant, while grantwriting is a particular reference to the process of writing a proposal.

Why Pursue Grants?

Indiana University's Bradford Woods Outdoor Center is a 2,600-acre outdoor campus located about 20 minutes south of Indianapolis. During its 65-year history, it has evolved from a youth camp facility to a multifaceted outdoor education resource and demonstration center that includes camping, professional development, environmental education, a retreat center, and a training center. For its first 35 years, Bradford Woods operated with little change. Its primary function was to provide summer camping opportunities and dedicated areas for outdoor youth-serving agencies.

By 1978, Bradford Woods was operating with a significant financial deficit. The university determined that changes needed to be made, and Bradford Woods was expected to become more financially self-sufficient. Divestiture of the property, which had been bequeathed to the university in 1941, was not an available option.

A new director was hired and given a charge to diversify operations and create new opportunities. One of the early strategies for increasing financial strength was the use of grants to support operations, programs, and capital improvements. This approach has made Bradford Woods increasingly more effective in securing short-term and multiyear grants. By 1998, almost 15% of revenue came from grants, and this change made it possible for Bradford Woods to undertake the kind of initiatives needed to move it towards self sufficiency. The 2014-15 revenue budget for Bradford Woods was more than $2.17 million, almost all of which came from program fees and only 2% from grants.

Bradford Woods is more successful in receiving grants in some years than it is in others. The management team's approach to grantseeking has yielded very positive results. Bradford Woods' need for and approach to grantseeking is typical of that experienced by many public and nonprofit organizations.

The Granting Environment

According to the Giving USA's *2017 Annual Report on Philanthropy*, the United States had nearly 78,000 granting foundations in 2016. That year, granting organizations awarded $59.3 billion in grants (Giving USA, 2017). Of that amount, nearly a third of the total value of all grants awarded went to education, human service, and arts, culture and humanities organizations. Granting organizations should be viewed as potentially important sources of income for sport, tourism, and leisure service organizations.

A foundation is generally organized as a nonprofit organization under appropriate state codes and registered as a 501(c)(3) charitable organization with the Internal Revenue Service. It typically has a board of directors and may hire an executive director. The board of directors makes decisions for grant awards. Foundation granting organizations are divided into three categories: independent foundations, corporate foundations, and community foundations.

Independent or *private* foundations are self-defining. They are not specifically connected with an organization, corporation, or community. Private foundations are usually created by an individual or family through a bequest of funds. These bequests frequently have restrictions placed on the granting. These independent foundations make grants to other tax-exempt organizations to accomplish their charitable purposes. They do not program directly, but provide money to organizations that do program.

A foundation invests its assets to generate revenue that is used primarily to provide money for grants. Independent foundations must make charitable expenditures of approximately 5% of the market value of their assets annually. If an independent foundation has assets totaling $100 million, it will need to award at least $5 million in grants. Of course, it may award more than that. Independent foundations award over 75% of foundation grants.

A *corporate foundation*, as the name suggests, is linked to a corporation and frequently focuses its giving in those communities where the corporation has operations such as offices, factories, or other interests. Funds for these foundations come primarily from the corporation, but granting decisions are, in most cases, separate from corporate decision-making processes and officers. Corporate foundations are the source of over 11% of foundation grants.

Community foundations represent a relatively new phenomenon. The focus of these locally instituted foundations is on their communities and on investing into the community. Some large corporate foundations, such as the Lily Foundation, have made major commitments to community foundations as a way of enhancing their efforts to achieve their purposes. The purposes of community foundations vary somewhat, and may appear as those articulated in the following example mission statement:

> The Community Foundation is committed to improving and strengthening the community of the metropolitan region. Our mission is to:
>
> - Develop the widest range of endowed funds and services to donors on behalf of the region and its counties and communities
> - Administer a growing granting program focused on helping where the needs are greatest and the benefits to the region are most extensive

> - Support the development of the services and institutions of the charitable sector of the region
> - Serve as a catalyst for community-based convening consensus building and problem solving in the region.

In today's rapidly changing and competitive society, securing grants is essential to fulfilling the missions of public and nonprofit sport, tourism, and leisure service organizations. The availability of traditional funding sources has forced organizations such as Bradford Woods to seek alternative funding opportunities. Simultaneously, the diminishing role played by government in social service areas has increased the demand upon granting organizations. It is, therefore, essential that grantseekers learn the art of matching their seemingly infinite needs with the finite offerings of grantmakers. The following step-by-step discussion of the grantseeking process is designed to help sport, tourism, and leisure service managers achieve proficiency as grantseekers.

The Grantseeking Process

Successful grantseeking preparation involves far more than just asking and writing. A well-planned grantseeking process involves six steps (Figure 12.1) that take the applicant from idea generation to grant administration. Each step requires the development and assessment of time-tested approaches to grantseeking. Grantseeking is an opportunity to increase resources and thereby allow the organization to accomplish its mission in ways not normally possible.

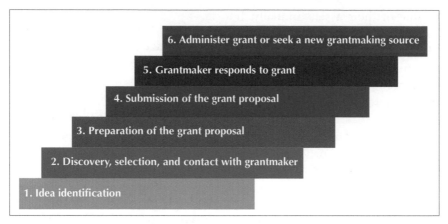

Figure 12.1. Steps of the Grantseeking Process (adapted from Smith and McLean, 1988)

Step 1: Identifying a Potential Idea

Beginning with the end in mind is a key element of grantseeking. Step 1 involves identifying an idea that lends itself to the grantseeking process. The identification of an idea is not as difficult as it may at first appear. There are many good ideas that are worthy of a grantseeking, but the key is to work the idea into a problem statement and then match it to a willing grantmaker.

The development of a good idea is a problem-solving process. It does not initially seek to match ideas with potential grantmakers, but instead seeks to identify ideas that cannot be met with existing resources. The following questions can assist an organization in determining whether the idea might have merit with a potential granting organization:

• Is the idea new or innovative, and does it meet an identified need among potential or existing constituents? Can it solve an existing problem or enhance the potential for the solution of a problem?

• Is there a general recognition of the need within the community or among organization members?

• Is funding available within the organization to support the idea? If no, then what external sources and amounts can be considered?

• Are local or organizational funds available as a matching support for a potential grant (e.g., other government or nonprofit organizations, individuals, in-kind contributions, etc.)?

• Are the community and the organization members willing to support a grantseeking process?

• Does the idea support the organization's mission and strategic plan?

Once an idea is generated, it needs to be refined. The most important part of this phase of the process is to clearly identify and describe the problem. This phase will require sound research to show that a problem exists. Just because someone may think this is a problem does not make it a problem in the eyes of the granting organization. It is becoming more common for grantmakers to require documentation of the needs and to justify the problem. If other, similar types of projects already exist in other organizations, the grantseeker may be asked to show how his proposal is different. At this stage of the process, the development of the idea should be the primary focus. Collection of data to justify the need should be started, but only sufficient to begin phase 2 of the process.

Step 2: Discovery, Selection, and Contact with a Granting Agency

Of the thousands of grantmakers serving U.S. communities, grantseekers must identify those that are most closely linked in their purposes for applying for the grant. Grantmakers can be classified as (1) government organizations, (2) corporations, (3) national or international philanthropic organizations, (4) regional or local or community philanthropic organizations, and (5) individual foundations. Identification of the philanthropic organization that best fits your problem can be daunting, but fortunately, assistance is available.

There are several organizations that assist grantseekers in their search for the perfect match. For example, the Foundation Center has branch libraries with staff in Atlanta, Cleveland, New York, San Francisco, and Washington, D.C. In addition, there are cooperating collections in over 200 public and university libraries, where support materials and publications are available. The Foundation Center publishes several directories, including *The Foundation Directory*. The Foundation Center suggests that, through its resources, searches can be accomplished by using one of three criteria: geographic location, subject, or type of support.

The *Chronicle of Philanthropy* is another source of information about grants. The *Chronicle* is especially useful if the intent is to make grantseeking a part of the organization's funding and growth strategy. The *Chronicle* is a monthly magazine that tracks what is going on in the philanthropy arena and provides detailed information about grantmakers, types of grants that are being awarded, trends in grants, and so forth.

The same resources are available on the Internet. Users can access the Foundation Center (foundationcenter.org), The *Chronicle of Philanthropy* (philanthropy.com), and The Grantsmanship Center (tgci.com). Each site provides information for the grantseeker to assist in this search for granting organizations. Most grantmakers also maintain a web presence. These are accessed by conducting an Internet search for a specific foundation, for a specific type of grant, or for a type of foundation. Searches can be conducted through a foundation support site, such as the Foundation Center, or using a common Internet search engine.

Searching for grantmakers. There is no single best way to search for a foundation that supports an identified problem. Finding the right grantmaker can be a time-consuming and sometimes frustrating process. This discovery phase is a necessary second step. The search can be conducted by looking through the various resources available from one of the previously mentioned sources, by making direct contact with foundations, or by securing support and ideas from other individuals. No single source will be sufficient. It requires a combination of sources to identify and select the one or more grantmakers that match a particular problem statement.

The search will likely turn up several potential grantmakers from whom some basic information should be secured. First, the name, contact person, and address of the foundation should be noted. Second, financial information related to the organization should be collected. This information should include the total assets of the grantmaker, the total grants awarded in the most recent reporting year (many foundations issue annual reports), the dollar value range of grants awarded (high to low), and the average period of time for which the grantmaker is willing to fund a project. Total assets consist of the economic resources available to the grantmaker. They make up the principle that the grantmaker has available for investment purposes and from which

they draw interest income. Third, the grantmaker's areas of focus (in order of importance). Fourth, the grantseeker needs to know if funding is restricted on the basis of geographic locations. Private grants are frequently restricted to the area where the benefactor either lived or had some special ties. Fifth, there may be restrictions or specific types of support that are identified by the grantmaker. The population that is served, such as children, the disabled, or the elderly, is another important piece of information. Finally, identify the types of recipients that the grantmaker has made awards to in recent years. Figure 12.2 depicts the results of this information search as applied to The National Parks Foundation.

Year: 2017
Total Assets: $195.7 million
Grants Payable: $2.3 million
Funding focus:
    Historic preservation
    Protecting national treasures
    Engaging future generations
Grant ranges: $40,000 - $1.5 million
Funding period: Up to 5 years

www.nationalparks.org

Figure 12.2. Example of a Search Result

Selecting a grantmaker. Selection of the appropriate grantmaker is based on the research completed in the early part of this step. If the research has been thorough, then the grantseeker can make an informed judgment. Most likely, several grantmakers will emerge as potential sources of funding. If this occurs, the grantseeker must determine how to select the grantmakers with the highest potential to fund the project. Using the collected information, the grantseeker compares the various grantmakers with the specific criteria for the grant and the grant's goals and outcomes.

Table 12.1 provides an example of how to evaluate the gathered information. The decision to select a single grantmaker is based on finding the one most closely matching the funding problem. If there are no foundations matching the funding problem, then maybe it is appropriate to rethink the problem or to rethink the type of grantmaker being sought. While some grantmakers may seem better suited to a particular problem or idea, there may be other grantmakers who have not yet been considered.

Figure 12.3 is a prospect worksheet that grantseekers can use to assist in the decision-making process. Grantseekers could carefully deselect potential grantmakers at this stage in the process. Keeping options open and being creative in the approach to seeking a grantmaker allows an organization a higher degree of potential success. Many grantseekers are not successful in their first try, so an attitude of perseverance becomes an essential quality for all good grantseekers.

Contacting the grantmaker. Depending on the type of grantmaker that is contacted, the nature of the relationship between the would-be grantseeker and the potential grantmaker will vary. Large

Table 12.1
Grantseeking Selection Criteria

Grantseeker	Grantmaker	Criteria
Problem statement	Focus	The problem statement and grantmaker primary focus should match
Appropriateness	Examples of recipients	Examples provide additional information to the grantseeker depicting how previous resources were awarded. This is a guide to the grantseeker who recognizes that funding priorities do change.
Location of need	Geographic limits	Many grantmakers geographically restrict their awards. Use this as a quick eliminator of potential grantmakers.
Required support	Types of support	Provides detailed discussion of types of support the grantmaker might provide. Grantseekers need to match needs with willingness.
Population in need	Population served	Address the target of the grantmaker. Does the grantseeker population in need match the population that the grantmaker is willing to serve?

Date:	Funder:	Your Organization
1. Name Address, Contact Person		

2. Financial Data:
    Total Assets
    Total Grants Paid
    Grants Ranges/Amount Needed
    Period of Project Funding		

3. Subject Foucs		
4. Geographic Limits		
5. Type(s) of Support		
6. Population(s) Served		
7. Type(s) of Recipients		
8. People (Officers, Trustees, Staff)		

Application Information
    Does the funder have printed guidelines/applications forms?
    What type of initial approach is required?
    What are the deadlines?
    Board meeting dates?		

What are the sources of information?		
Notes:		
Followup:		

Figure 12.3. Funding Prospect Worksheet

grantmakers may send a packet with a form letter telling about themselves and their expectations. Smaller, specialized, or regional grantmakers may take a more personal interest. In one community, the grantseeker made personal contacts with the grantmaker over a period of several years and had established a credible relationship. Many have done the same thing with local foundations in their areas.

When contact is made, some questions need to be addressed by the grantseeker. The questions include the following: (1) How do they want the proposal written? (2) Do they provide technical assistance, including a review of proposal drafts? (3) How are proposals reviewed and decisions made? and (4) Are there budgetary requirements and preferences (examples include matching funds, in-kind services, payment preferences, and so forth)? The contact is an important source of information and future reference for the grantseeker.

Securing grant guidelines. It is important to secure a copy of the grantmaker's published grant guidelines from the potential grantmakers. Many grantmakers have their guidelines printed and available for distribution. Figure 12.4 provides an example of the grant guidelines from a philanthropic organization that supports nonprofit agencies.

Guidelines for Prospective Applicants

We strongly recommend that prospective applicants submit the following in the form of a letter of inquiry before a full proposal is sent:

- Information about the organization's purposes and specific activities.
- A brief description of the program for which funds are being sought, including the time period to be covered.
- The principal outcome(s) expected. Budgets for the program for which funds are sought, as well as for the organization.
- The amount being requested of the Foundation.
- Funding received to date for the program, as well as sources from which funding is being sought.
- The names and qualifications of the key personnel who will be responsible for the program.
- The most recent audited financial statements of the organization and its operating subsidiaries, if any.
- IRS certification of 501©(3) status of the organization.
- E-mail address for contact person at the organization.

Figure 12.4. Grant Guidelines from a Typical Foundation

Step 3: Preparation of the Grant Proposal

A grant proposal has several elements. Collectively, they provide a comprehensive justification and plan for what the grantseeking organization sees as a problem and for which it hopes to secure funding. Unfortunately, there is no standardized format for preparing grant proposals. One grantmaker may require an extensive funding proposal, while another may require a single-page summary of the proposal. Paying careful attention to the grantmaker's guidelines increases the chances that the proposal will be given serious consideration. Figure 12.5 illustrates elements of a grant proposal as suggested by four different grantmakers and grantwriting support organizations.

The elements of a grant proposal will vary according to the grantmaker's requirements, but there are some commonly agreed upon elements of a proposal. The eight common elements are a cover letter, an executive summary, a statement of need, a project description, organizational information (including key personnel and/or credentials), a budget, an evaluation process, and the grantseeker's commitment and ability to complete the project.

Cover letter. The cover letter is the formal introduction of the grantseeker to the grantmaker. It should be a clear and concise statement about the organization's purpose and why a grant is being sought. The grantseeker's needs are written in a manner that matches the grantmaker's purposes. This match clarifies the grantseeker's intentions and provides a

The Foundation Center	Corporation for Public Broadcasting	LRR.net	The Grantsmanship Center
		Cover letter	Cover letter
Executive summary		Summary of cover sheet	Abstract/Summary
			Introduction
Statement of need	Statement of need	Problem statement	Need
Project description	Approach	Methodology	Plan of operations
	Methods of evaluation	Evaluation	Evaluation
	Project timelines	Program goals and objectives	Budget and cost effectiveness
Budget	Budget	Budget	
Organizational information	Credentials	Qualifications	Key personnel
Conclusion			Commitment and capability
	Supporting materials	Appendices	

Figure 12.5. Comparison of Elements of a Grant Proposal

gateway to the grantmaker's goals and objectives. The cover letter should be addressed to a specific person, rather than to the grantmaking organization, and it should include a brief description of the content of the proposal. The letter should not be overly long. One page normally suffices.

Executive summary. The executive summary is a one- or two-page descriptive summary of the project. It contains all of the essential information present in the full proposal. This snapshot of the proposal allows the grantseeker to set the stage for the proposal in a clear and concise way. It provides a narrative explaining the problem, its importance, the proposed solution (the projects and anticipated results), budget needs (including what has already been committed), and information about the organization and its competence. The executive summary should be written last and requires considerable thought and framing. It is often easier to write the proposal than an executive summary. It takes practice and

several rounds of editing to write a good executive summary.

Statement of need. The statement of need is the most critical part of the grant proposal. It provides a description and justification of the need and/or description of the problem the project will resolve. The statement should enhance the reader's understanding of the issues. It presents facts in support of the project's need and validates the grantseeker as the best organization to meet the need. It provides information about five areas: (1) involvement of beneficiaries of the grant, (2) statement of need in terms of the participants or beneficiaries, (3) explanation of how needs were identified, (4) supporting statements and statistical data and authoritative documentation or statements, and (5) linking the needs and proposed solutions to the goals and strategic plan of the organization. The Foundation Center's Proposal Writing Short Course suggests six points to follow in preparing the arguments:

1. Determine which facts or statistics are going to best support the project. Emphasis in this section is on accuracy and detail to ensure that a valid case is built for the issue or problem. Eliminate information that is not germane to the proposal.

2. Determine whether it is reasonable to portray the problem as acute. If this is an acute problem, then explain why the organization should receive the grant.

3. If the problem is an issue that may seem unsolvable, then give the reader hope about the organization's involvement and potential to solve the problem.

4. Could the project be presented as a model solution? Determine if that is the best approach for this grant. If the grantseeker has a model solution and it fits the grant proposal, then include it. If not, then don't make it part of the proposal. Using a model solution can increase the base of potential grantmakers.

5. Demonstrate that the project addresses the need differently or better than other projects that may have preceded it. Be sure not to be critical of other projects that are competitive or have preceded this proposal. Show collaboration where possible. This characteristic is frequently viewed as a strength by grantmakers.

6. Avoid circular reasoning, where the absence of a problem is presented as a problem. For example, "The problem is we have no community center in our community. Building a community center will resolve that problem." It is better to focus on what a community center would mean to the community. "The problem is the lack of available facilities for community members to use, and especially youth-at-risk and gang-related issues."

Project description. The project description should contain three subsections: (1) goals and objectives, (2) methodology, and (3) staffing and administration. The proposal has already dealt with need. This section describes how the proposal, when funded, will operate and solve the problem. It provides sufficient detail, facilitating a clear understanding of the process and how the project will meet the described need. Goals and objectives establish a basis for measuring outcomes of the project. Each provides a clear level of distinction. Goals separate the problem or need into achievable work units. For example, a problem statement that reads, "How can we reduce the rise in juvenile crime and its impact upon at-risk youth in our neighborhood?" might generate several goals that could read:

1. To determine the at-risk youth population and who among the population has the greatest potential to engage in criminal behavior.

2. To establish an outreach program to reach targeted youth.

3. To establish a collaborative program of after-school activities and neighborhood resources meeting the needs of targeted youth.

Goals provide a general direction. They take the broader problem or need statement and divide it into workable units. For the grantmaker, it shows that the organization has established a direction and a plan leading to a solution.

Objectives are a natural subdivision of goals and more clearly delineate how the goal will be established. Objectives are more specific, are based on a goal, and are measurable. There are four common types of objectives. *Behavioral objectives* suggest some type of human behavioral impact. An example would be, "Over a period of nine months, targeted youth will exhibit a more positive feeling about themselves." Objectives should address a single outcome. An objective stating, "Over a period of nine months, targeted youth will have a more positive feeling about themselves and about their families" should be written as two separate objectives. *Performance objectives* deal with proficiency or skill development. For example, "At-risk youth participating in the program over a six-month period will develop and exhibit study skills resulting in improved school performance." The objective may appear to have two outcomes, but the actual outcome is improved school performance. This is a measurable outcome. The development and exhibiting of study skills are processes that facilitate the measurable outcome. *Product objectives* suggest a deliverable item or hands-on product that other people can use or that is used by the grantseeker. An example is the statement, "To develop a manual for outreach workers that provides proven approaches to reaching at-risk youth." Both the product and the users of the product are clearly defined. A *process objective* looks at how a methodology was implemented and modified. It suggests, in many cases, an assessment process (e.g., "Methods used in the outreach program will be documented and assessed to determine which are most effective").

Methodology describes how the problem will be solved once the grant is awarded. This should be clearly stated in terms that are generally understood.

Administration of the grant (if awarded) should be discussed. Smith and

McLean (1988) suggested several items should be included in the discussion:

1. The overall design of the project should include an overview of how the project will be administered from start to finish. This is a narrative beginning with a restatement of the problem followed by a summary of the entire design process.
2. Specific activities that are planned, and the sequencing of the activities within the project.
3. The relationship between planned activities and the stated goals and objectives. Linking the activities with the goals and objectives is essential to the grantmaker's understanding of how outcomes are achieved. Goals and objectives do not stand alone. They must always be tied to process.
4. Identify the specific procedures used to implement the program. A discussion of how the procedures will operate, as well as when they will be implemented. This may include a discussion of the sequencing of actions occurring before planned activities are implemented.
5. Explain how program participants are selected.
6. Identify project completion timelines for each phase of the grant.
7. Discuss plans for collaborations with other organizations.
8. Describe the project "deliverables," such as newsletters, process manuals, training materials, publications, seminars, and workshops.

Staffing and administration are important parts of any grant proposal. This section explains the competence of the organization's members who will be administering the grant. One of its purposes is to convey to the grantmaker confidence in the organization's capability to successfully carry the project to completion. Included are key people involved in the project, their experience, education, and training as related to the project. Résumés for existing staff should be included in the appendix with a narrative summary in the text.

When new staff members are proposed as part of the grant project, it is appropriate to justify the positions and demonstrate how the staff will have adequate responsibilities related to the project. Projects that propose new positions but fail to provide for continuation of the positions after the conclusion of the grant may find it a detriment to successful grantseeking. Finally, a project relying primarily on new staff will be less attractive than one that uses a mix of permanent and new staff.

Organizational information. The introduction to this section is a description of the grantseeker's qualifications or evidence of credibility for the proposed project. The introduction tells the grantmaker about the organization, its mission, its purpose, a brief history, and its general goals and objectives. There is a discussion about the organization's current programs, activities, service statistics, strengths, and accomplishments. This section needs to focus on the strategic plan and progress toward achieving it. Also included is a discussion about the function and size of the governing board and its involvement in the organization. The grantmaker should be able to get a feel for the composition, commitment, and involvement of that governing board. Any special constituent groups serving as volunteers are identified and it is stated how they support the project's goals. How the staff will be involved in the proposed

project and in the variety of activities focusing on the organization's mission will also be articulated. Finally, a description of the organizational activities and the identification of the services provided to the various constituencies should help to emphasize the appropriateness of the expertise of the organization as it fits with the proposal.

Budget. The budget can be a key factor in successful grantseeking. Convincing the grantmaker that the budget effectively and efficiently responds to the needs related to the grant is important. A well-constructed budget with a strong supporting narrative is a positive reinforcement to the grant proposal. Budgets normally identify two primary sources of funds: those requested from the grantmaker, and those provided by the grantseeker. The grantmaker normally provides money, but may also provide other types of resources. The grantseeker can provide a variety of different types of resources. These include money from the operating budget, in-kind services (such as staff or secretarial assistance), or external resources (such as sponsors or volunteers). In-kind donations are services rendered by individuals who are members of the organization, the cost of their services, and contributions of services such as office space, utilities, telephone service and so forth. The total in-kind contribution is determined and added to the budget as part of the grantseeker's contribution. For example, a secretary who makes $30,000 a year and has 10 percent of her time assigned to the project would represent $3,000 in in-kind services. Office space might be priced at $500 month with utilities adding another $30 monthly for an annual in-kind contribution of $6,360. The budget should clearly reflect the types of in-kind services provided. The budget process follows the budget procedures explained in Chapter 4. As a guide, the budget should do the following:

- Address (in financial terms) exactly what the narrative of the grant has proposed
- Provide complete compensation information about each staff position, including rate of pay, percent of time allocated to the project, fringe benefits, mileage rate, per diem rates, honorariums, and so forth
- Include actual costs for supplies and services related to the project
- Include items paid for by other sources

Figure 12.6 shows how a sample budget for a project might be formatted. A supporting budget narrative would only be necessary to explain unusual or unclear costs. A budget narrative is framed in one of two ways: a footnote style providing a description of different budget items, or the budget narrative could be written as part of the document. In some cases, grantmakers provide a budget form for grantseekers to complete.

Evaluation process. The evaluation section of the proposal explains how project outcomes are assessed. It provides the grantmaker with measures of effectiveness for grant dollars awarded. Grantmakers increasingly demand accountability. Evaluation is integrated throughout the project. The evaluation process should include an assessment of the process and continuous progress toward intermediate and final outcomes. A well-prepared evaluation process is an important criterion in their decision making. A checklist for the evaluation narrative, at a minimum, includes the following:

Item	Number	Item Cost	Total Cost
Printing of envelopes & stationery	300	$80.00	$24,000.00
Questionnaire printing	150	$3.00	$450.00
Postage for questionnaire	150	$2.75	$412.50
Data input (student hours)	40	$8.50	$340.00
Data analysis (student hours)	40	$8.50	$340.00
Telephone interview	60	$10.25	$615.00
Qualitative date analysis	120	$15.00	$1,800.00
Travel			$0.00
Dissemination of data - conference	partial	$1,500.00	$1,500.00
Dissemniation of data - conference	partial	$1,500.00	$1,500.00
Sub-total			$30,957.50
Overhead	40%	$12,383.00	$12,383.00
Total Requested			$43,340.50
In-kind Contributions			
Co-primary research time	12%	$72,000.00	$8,640.00
Co-primary research time	8%	$65,000.00	$5,200.00
Benefits	28.70%	$13,840.00	$3,972.08
Clerical	23.10%	$732.00	$169.09
Total In-Kind Contributions			$18,713.17

Figure 12.6. Sample Grant Budget

- Explain how the evaluator and the process will be selected.
- Include an evaluation procedure for each goal and objective.
- Identify interim outcomes and match them to timelines for the project and reporting periods.
- Describe data-gathering methodology and connect it to goals, objectives, and timelines.
- Describe any instruments or tools used and how they support the project.
- Explain how evaluation data are used and disseminated to stakeholders.
- Describe the evaluation reports.
- Explain how evaluation is used to enhance the project's progress and outcomes.

Commitment and capability. The grantmaker appropriately asks, "What is the potential for success of the project?" The answer to this question comes only after a careful review of the grant proposal reveals soundness in conceptualization, effectiveness in design, and confidence in delivery. Confidence in delivery comes, in part, from demonstration of the grantseeker's commitment to and capability of achieving success. The grantseeker explains how similarly funded projects have been successful, how the presence of staff, facilities, and other resources all contribute to the potential success of the proposed project. A concise discussion of strengths, resources, and successes allows the grantmaker to gain a clearer picture of the grantseeker's capability. This section of the proposal is not long, but provides critical support to the preceding sections.

Step 4: Submitting the Grant Proposal

The culmination of the grantwriting process is the submission of the grant proposal to a grantmaker. All of the components described in Step 3 are included in the proposal. The submitted proposal must have a professional look. It should be bound if it is large, should conform to rules of good grammar, and be easy to read. Before sealing the package for delivery to the grantmaker, the grantseeker should complete one final review, ensuring that all materials are included and in the requested/intended order.

Step 5: Grantmaker's Decision

The grantmaker can make one of several decisions regarding a proposal. The grantmaker may (1) award the grant in full, (2) make a partial grant award, (3) defer consideration of the proposal to a later date, or (4) deny the grant request. If the final option is taken, the grantmaker is under no obligation to explain why the proposal was rejected. In the same regard, the grantseeker should not read a lack of worthiness or value into a rejection. A grant rejection may be due to a lack of available funds, an overabundance of similar proposals, or it may have fallen outside the guidelines of the grantmaker. In some cases, the grantmaker will ask for changes in the proposal with a resubmission. Regardless of whether the grant proposal is rejected, funded in part, or needs modification, the grantseeker should call the grantmaker and ask how the proposal might be strengthened. This feedback may be important in strengthening the grant proposal for future submissions.

In cases where only portions of the grant were funded or where there was a decision to defer to a later time, the grantseeker must decide whether to accept the decision of the grantmaker or to withdraw the proposal and seek another grantmaker. This can be a difficult decision, as the grantseeker has invested considerable energy in the process. If the grantseeker determines that it may have a better opportunity elsewhere, then it may be appropriate to seek another grantmaker.

Even when full funding is awarded, the grantseeker still must choose to accept the grant. A grantmaker may attach conditions to the funds, and the grantseeker will have to determine if they are appropriate. An important deciding factor in the acceptance of a grant is whether the project can be accomplished and whether it remains consistent with the values and mission of the organization.

Step 6: Grant Administration

Grant administration involves managing the project for which the grant was awarded, along with maintaining appropriate communications with the grantmaker. Some grantmakers choose to have little contact with the organization after an award is made, but most require some type of ongoing contact. The grant administrators should consider the following:

- Where feasible, have a single point of contact from the grantseeking organization to the grantmaking organization. This simplification enhances communication and reduces the potential for confusion.
- Don't leave questions about the grant unanswered. Make contact with the grantmaker to resolve issues before they become problems.

- Always make contact with an individual, and not with an organization.
- Include the project name and grant identification number on all correspondence.
- All correspondence should be clear and specific. Do not assume people know the issue that is being discussed.
- Always seek permission before making changes in the budget.
- Make regular progress reports to the grantmaker. Any deliverables such as newsletters, reports, brochures, and annual reports should be provided.
- Stick to the timeline. If schedule changes are required, seek approval from the grantmaker before making them.
- At the conclusion of the report, submit all required information in a timely and complete manner.

Knowledge of all the requirements of the grantmaking organization, as well as the criteria of the grant, will ensure a more effective administration process.

Summary

Grantseeking is neither a complicated nor a mystical process, but it can be a time-consuming process. Successful organizations have implemented the steps outlined in this chapter. Identifying potential grantmakers, paying careful attention to detail, and taking time to learn the grantseeking process frequently results in successful receipt of grants. Thankfully, most worthy ideas can be matched to the interests of generous, willing grantmakers. The decision to award a grant is based on the sustained efforts of the grantseeker to find a grantmaker that is a good match for a proposed project.

References

Giving USA. (2017). *2017 Annual report on philanthropy.* Chicago, IL.

Smith, S. H., & McLean, D. D. (1988). *ABCs of Grantsmanship.* Reston, VA: American Alliance for Health, Physical Education, Recreation and Dance.

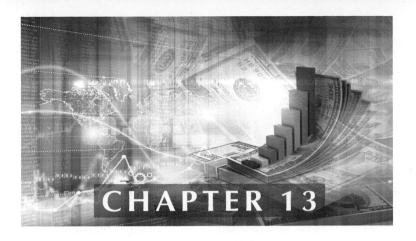

CHAPTER 13

Philanthropy and Fund-Raising

Introduction

In contemporary government enterprises, supporting sport, tourism, and leisure services wholly from the general fund is a thing of the past. Although the expectations for meeting social needs that are placed on many allied public and nonprofit organizations are increasing, budgetary resources are becoming more competitive as demands upon local government finances increase. Partnering with philanthropic and nonprofit organizations is increasingly becoming an attractive and necessary approach to securing additional resources. Many and varied training programs addressing how to conduct fund-raising for sport, tourism, and leisure service professionals are offered by professional fund-raising organizations, private corporations, and universities. This chapter addresses philanthropy and the process of fund-raising.

Philanthropy

A charitable act is a social exchange that occurs each time a gift is made. The decision to make a gift usually comes after someone trusted by the donor asks. A gift implies a considerable level of confidence and trust in both the asker's and the charitable organization's ability (and ethos) to do what is "right" with the donation.

Philanthropy is synonymous with charitable giving. While charitable giving is perceived as giving for the social good, the social good is increasingly being interpreted in a broader context of issues. In the narrowest sense, charitable giving is giving resources to those in need or to organizations that assist those with needs. This perspective of giving has been broadened to include all types of philanthropy, which can be defined as an act of trust on the part of a donor toward the organization that will receive and use the donation.

The philanthropic process that is discussed here is uniquely American. No other region in the world has the same level of giving, nor the social and governmental structure to allow such massive levels of giving. In 2016, over $390 billion were donated to charitable causes. Of that amount, $281.86 billion were donated by individuals. Foundations gave $59.28 billion, bequests (a unique form of personal giving) accounted for $30.36 billion of the giving total, and corporations contributed a further $18.55 billion for charitable causes (Giving USA, 2017).

Philanthropy is an activity of and resource to individuals and nonprofit organizations. It involves more than just giving and receiving money. It involves a short- or long-term commitment to the nonprofit organization. It is nonprofit organizations working in conjunction with individuals and public and private organizations that secure donations from individuals, other nonprofit organizations, foundations, and corporations. Sometimes referred to as the third sector, philanthropic organizations primarily focus on meeting social needs that are neglected by other sectors. In public park and recreation organizations, for example, there has been a steady decline in financial resources made available from public funds to fulfill the public park and recreation mission. To counteract this, public agencies have turned to the philanthropic sector. The National Park Service is probably the leader in this movement, although other federal land-managing agencies, state park agencies, public recreation departments, and many nonprofit sport organizations are close behind. The Florida Park Service produces a *Citizen*

Support Organization Handbook for the express purpose of extending its resources through philanthropic partnerships and providing a better experience for visitors. Hundreds of American cities have developed foundations to support their social service programs. Many state and local-level sport-based nonprofits are highly dependent on charitable giving for their ongoing operations. During the last decade, philanthropy has become increasingly intertwined with daily services and programs provided by sport, tourism, and leisure service organizations.

Both independence and volunteerism characterize philanthropy. Independence is a characteristic in the sense that individuals and organizations making donations give independently of conditions that could have been associated with the gift. In philanthropy, the gift is given voluntarily; that is, the donor does so of his or her free will with the intent of promoting a particular purpose or meeting a particular need.

Why Fund-Raising is Important

There are many good reasons for using fund-raising activities to develop and sustain public and nonprofit sport, tourism, and leisure service organizations. Ross (1997) suggested several reasons why organizations should include fund-raising in their revenue structure plan. Those reasons have been refined, revised, updated, and modified to fit the 21st Century realities and are covered in the following:

1. Public agencies, at all levels of government, are increasingly dependent upon external philanthropic support. Traditional government funding levels for many services offered by

public agencies are either dwindling or being replaced by for-profit enterprises. Nonprofit support has become an essential revenue source to maintain services.

2. Philanthropy is one of America's most distinctive virtues. Giving to public/society benefit purposes and giving to leisure, sport, and environment and wildlife continues to increase annually.

3. The "Greening of America": Contributions to environmental causes, including our parks, forests, open spaces, and wildlife, is big business—over $11 billion annually. The numerous nonprofit environmental and park support organizations hope to benefit as current generations pass unprecedented wealth from the baby boomer generation—an estimated $30 trillion to subsequent generations.

4. Sport, tourism, and leisure service organizations are well positioned to make the case for philanthropic support. They are in the quality-of-life and resources business.

5. Socially and environmentally oriented public service professionals have those desired qualities to make fund-raising a success: a dedication to fulfilling a public trust; a desire to work with both the general public and those with affluence or influence (hopefully, both); a willingness to ask the hard questions; and an ability to communicate a sense of urgency.

6. Partnership building is critical in obtaining the diverse philanthropic support available. If individual giving decreases, as projected, these partnerships will become increasingly important.

7. Individual citizen donors and volunteers have come to expect accountability, ownership in what they give to, and a direct voice in how the philanthropic dollars are spent.

8. From fund-raising to the stewardship of gifts received, sport, tourism, and leisure service organization professionals demonstrate their public trust.

9. A caution: Tax-law changes could potentially have a significant negative impact on the amounts and kinds of gifts Americans have traditionally made.

The Benefits of Philanthropic Fund Development

The benefits of philanthropic fund development are many. Regardless of how the organization is structured, of greatest importance is how the philanthropy dollar is used and how effective the donor or potential donor perceives its use to be. Some of the benefits include the following:

Building community. Sport, tourism, and leisure service organizations have long been involved in building communities. They are seen as contributing to the quality of life of communities. The Highland Ranch, Colorado Parks and Recreation Foundation has raised over $600,000 in 18 years to provide support for recreation programs, park amenities, youth scholarships, and other programs and services. Community foundations typically focus on improving the community in general, but can also target a specific site or issue, such as a river front, sports complex, cultural arts, and the like.

Investing in human capital. This is a frequently cited benefit of giving. Sport, tourism, and leisure service organizations have their foundations in human services and continue to strengthen their involvement in this area.

Facilitating the accomplishment of objectives. Many sport, tourism, and leisure service organizations are unable to achieve their goals with traditional funding models. They need fundraising to make accomplishment of their objectives possible. For example, St. Louis, Missouri's Forest Park is a major community park. With an area of 1,300 and serving over 130,000 visitors annually, it is considered an essential community resource. The city, working with the Forest Park Forever Conservancy, a private foundation supporting the park, undertook a $130 million fundraising initiative. Traditionally, donors have provided up to 50% of the cost of operating the park. However, there were still insufficient budget funds to maintain and improve Forest Park. In 2018, the successful campaign closed, having exceeded its goal (Forest Park Forever, 2018). This is an excellent example of the power of a foundation to work with local government.

Providing a means for donors to fulfill their aspirations. Friends of the outdoors, friends of parks, friends of wildlife, sport corporations, state tourism bureaus, and similar types of friends groups provide donors with the opportunity to realize their altruistic aspirations and give of both their time and money for a cause about which they feel passionate. "Friends of ..." foundations are among the most popular mechanisms for giving in the United States.

Boys & Girls Clubs of America: There Because of Giving.

The Boys & Girls Clubs of America are an example of a nonprofit organization that is focused on the community good and is dependent upon philanthropy. The Boys & Girls Clubs of America are ranked by *Forbes* magazine as the 12th largest charity in the United States in 2016 and the second largest youth serving charity behind the YMCA of America. The mission of Boys & Girls Clubs is to *enable young people, especially those who need us most, to reach their full potential as productive, caring, responsible citizens.* This is a mission that finds resonance in the nonprofit fundraising sector. In addition, the Boys & Girls Clubs report that 5 million young people are served through 4,300 clubs housed in rural areas, public housing, Native American lands, schools, and U.S. Military installations worldwide. Among nonprofits, the Boys & Girls Clubs have done an excellent job of telling their story. Their vision is to *provide a world-class Club Experience that assures success is within reach of every young person who enters our doors, with all members on track to graduate from high school with a plan for the future, demonstrating good character and citizenship, and living a healthy lifestyle.* The organization's success has helped it to excel in serving the community as well as gaining the generous support of donors.

Why People Give

Understanding why people give is as important as knowing how to ask for money. Not all people have the same motivation for giving. There are several reasons for giving. For some, it fulfills social, religious, or philosophical obligations. Religious organizations receive the largest amounts of charitable contributions annually. Social conscience and philosophical reasons move many in society to give of their means for the benefit of others. Small charities and large foundations such as the Bill and Melinda Gates foundation provide billions of dollars in funding based on their belief that every life has equal value.

The government has traditionally made charitable giving an obvious tax advantage, both at the federal and state levels. Some donors contribute funds because doing so puts them in a preferred tax status and thus saves them money. Every philanthropic organization makes sure its potential and actual donors understand the tax advantages of giving.

Sometimes individuals hope to directly or indirectly gain appreciation and public recognition for their efforts or the contributions of others. Some philanthropists want to create a memorial to themselves or others who are dear to them. Many buildings, parks, monuments, and tourist attractions are created as memorials to an individual or a family (e.g., Rockefeller Center, Carnegie Hall). An observant walker on any college campus or public park will note the names on benches, fountains, and buildings that were made possible by the generosity of a successful alumnus, family, or friends.

Others give because it makes them feel good. Some have a strong attachment to their community or the work of a social group, or of some other type of organization and give in support of their efforts. A few people give because of guilt or competitiveness when challenged by others to give at the same level or by inducement of a matching grant. Finally, some donors want to keep their life's work in the family and make sure it is perpetuated for future generations through the creation of philanthropic foundations.

Charitable Organizations

Most American charitable organizations are organized under the United States Internal Revenue Service (IRS) tax code with a 501(c)(3) classification. In order to qualify for 501(c)(3) status, an organization must meet specific requirements. Foundations must have articles of incorporation that have been filed with the appropriate state authorities. Requirements for incorporation vary by state. The IRS also requires that the organization provide a detailed narrative of all of the activities of the organization—past, present, and future. The National Park Foundation has provided the following brief narrative as an example:

> The National Park Foundation raises private funds that directly aid, support, and enrich America's 417 national park units and related programs, so that they may be experienced by current and future generations. Chartered by Congress as the nonprofit partner of the National Park Service.

A charitable organization is required to identify sources of income, describe actual and planned fund-raising programs in detail, and provide the names, addresses, and titles of the officers of the board of directors. If public officials are involved in the organization, they must be identified by title. Many of these charitable organizations receive all or part of their administrative support from the nonprofit or public organizations that they serve. If so, this must be noted in the IRS Form 990. Additional information requested by the IRS includes activities and operational functions focusing on the assets of the organization, as well as financial data for the current year and the three previous years.

The greatest advantage to achieving IRS 501(c)(3) status as a charitable organization is the increased attractiveness of donating to the organization. Individuals and corporations that donate to recognized charities are able to claim the amount of their donations as a tax deduction when filing with the federal and state governments. By so doing, they can significantly reduce their tax liability while concurrently being good corporate citizens in their communities.

Fund Development

Fund development is the core of the philanthropic process. Philanthropy suggests individuals engage in voluntary action for a common good and involves contributions of time and/or money. Fund development is an essential part of philanthropy and is, in fact, what makes sustained philanthropic support possible. Philanthropy connects individuals over a cause or causes of mutual interest and concern. Individuals who show an interest in a particular project or cause become prospects and can eventually become donors who are willing to invest financially in the cause. Ideally, donors become committed to the cause or organization and continue to make investments. Figure 13.1 depicts the donor pyramid, illustrating, in a simplistic manner, the progression of donors from knowing the organization to giving to the organization.

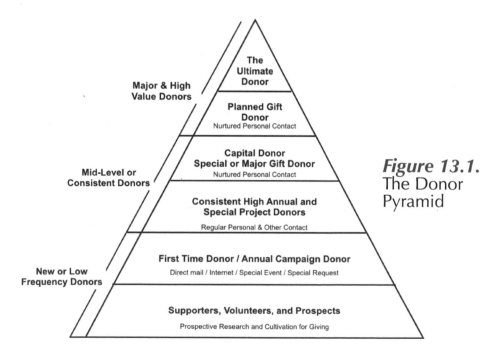

Figure 13.1. The Donor Pyramid

Fund development is a process of relationship-building. Development involves a process of initiating, creating, and strengthening relationships with individuals who are potential donors. More specifically, it is a process of building their interest in the mission and services of an organization, allowing them to develop a passion for the organization's mission and future, then getting them to make a gift. It continues to require maintaining a relationship leading to further gifts and giving. It involves a time-consuming process of introducing potential donors to a cause and/or nonprofit or government organization, helping them to build an interest and commitment to the organization and causes, to make an investment in the organization, and ultimately to make multiple investments over a period of time.

Development suggests a broader vision than the term fund-raising. Development is a process of engaging individuals, nurturing their interest, building understanding, matching their personal interest to the organization, and building a long-term relationship with the potential donor. Often, donors are drawn to a specific program or an activity, as opposed to the organization itself. Fundraising has a narrower interpretation, that of only addressing the giving component of development. Giving is an important and essential part of development, but giving is tactical whereas development is strategic. This, development involves the long-term engagement and nurturing of the potential donor, whether it is an individual, commercial organization, or grant-making group.

In addition to a phase where contact is made, the development process involves three stages (indicated by the behavior of donors) as shown in Figure 13.1. The *initial contact stage* focuses on

new or low frequency donors. The *growth stage* focuses on mid-level or consistent donors. The *commitment stage* is the time when the nurturing of major and high value donors is the primary activity. Fund development is a process of finding and nurturing potential contacts until they become donors committed to the cause of the organization. Such a process can take years to complete.

Fund development can be compared to a permission marketing process designed to bring together potential donors with the nonprofit or government organization in such a way that both benefit from an exchange. Permission marketing is a form of marketing where people opt in or opt out. It is the privilege of delivering anticipated personal and relevant messages to people who actually want them. It involves treating people with respect and gaining their attention.

A donor may be giving for altruistic reasons or for financial benefit. The development process is different from the consumer or internal marketing that a commercial organization practices. While there are some similarities, there are significant differences. The product that a commercial organization sells is a tangible benefit or commodity to the customer. In some sense, charitable organizations provide the same advantages, in terms of tax benefits, but they also provide some philosophical, social, and cultural benefits that commercial organizations are not well suited to provide. Individuals give because the opportunity is related to their personal goals. It directs attention and interest on the part of the potential donor, and arouses the need for action. In a sense, when the project or opportunity for giving arouses the potential donor it is because it stirred a sense of meaning in the individual. Thus "meaning making," targeted to specific individuals, is at the core of securing donations. Meaning is not easily identified or quantified for an individual. Data can provide lists of potential donors, but without creating meaning for the potential donor. At the core of fund development is the creation of meaning making for individuals.

The fund development process of a charity-seeking organization focuses on securing committed donors. A committed donor is one who is willing to make a long-term commitment to the organization's vision, goals, and objectives.

Within the three stages of fund development depicted in Figure 13.1, there are six classes of potential donors.

Supporters, volunteers, and prospects. The universe of prospects, or consumer base, is seen as all individuals who might be contacted. This is a global population of potential donors from which the organization could potentially draw. In reality, only a small part of the population is going to become committed

donors. The most promising candidates are already involved with the organization as supporters or volunteers. With limited funds available for the search for new donors, the charitable organization must begin to narrow its list of potential donors. Most nonprofit organizations maintain profiles of donors to assist in efforts to target other prospects. The profile might include age (or generation), and known giving behavior (as illustrated in Table 13.1) can be considered in prioritization of fund development activities.

Table 13.1 illustrates the levels of giving by generational cohorts in 2017. Comparatively, Boomers contributed the most money in that year. That was expected since they were at retirement age, represented the largest percentage of wealth in the United States, and had shown a propensity toward community engagement. Clearly, nonprofits and government organizations desire to target those individuals with wealth, but need to nurture other younger generations, as their wealth will eventually exceed the wealth of the current older generations.

Table 13.1
Giving Propensity of Selected Generational Cohorts

Generation	Percent Give	Years
Matures	26%	1945 and earlier
Baby Boomers	43%	1946–1964
Gen X	20%	1965–1976
Millennials	11%	1977–1995
Gen Z	0%	1996–present
Total 100%		

Source: https://www.classy.org/blog/infographic-generational-giving

First-time donors. These are the lifeblood of an expanding donor pool. Not only does this group represent a new source of funds, but also new contacts. The size of the first donation may not be large, but the number of first-time donors is important. The narrowing of the population of potential donors to those who actually give is critical. Whether the winnowing is done through a mass mailing, telephone calls, or individual contact, the sport, tourism, or leisure service organization needs to maximize the efficiency and effectiveness of the contact. Researching and knowing potential donor sources is critical and is discussed in more detail in the upcoming section on annual campaigns. The key challenge is the ability to identify the donors that will move forward into the mid-level or consistent donor phase. Sometimes this does not occur for years.

Consistent high annual and special project donors. In the mid-level or consistent donor phase, the donor begins to receive more frequent or sustained contact from the charitable organization through the Internet, by mail, through newsletters, and by personal contact from the foundation director or designated representative. The intent is to encourage the donor to change from a once-a-year minimal contributor to one who makes multiple annual donations. The goal is to create a commitment to the charitable organization's goals and mission that will continue to grow, along with donation size. Only a small number of donors will move up beyond the annual campaign donor. The annual campaign donor is the foundation of the organization's fund-raising, but without individuals or external foundations and support groups making larger donations as mid-level, consistent, or major and high-value

donors, the organization cannot achieve many of its major goals. In other words, in the absence of the high-value donors, the organization is restricted in its ability to serve its intended audience and achieve its goals.

Donors might remain at the mid-level or consistent giving phase for many years. In this phase, matching of donors' desires with organizational needs is the greatest challenge/opportunity. Growth in this phase comes when the donors see their gift as something that meets their desires. They have become committed to the charitable organization or some aspect of its operations and are willing to commit some of their financial resources to it. At this level, regular personal contact becomes more and more important to the success of the effort.

Capital donor/special or major gift donor. A few donors will move along to higher involvement as mid-level or consistent donors and, as might be expected, the size of their gifts will increase. The frequency of gifts may decrease, although this is not always the case, but the size of their gift and its impact on the charitable organization will be significant. These are the donors who will give $1 million or more to a major project, or $500,000 to build a community structure, or $200,000 to endow a scholarship fund.

Planned gift donor. As illustrated in Figure 13.1, the once-large pool of donors continues to get smaller as the organization nurtures donors who make regular, ongoing and automatic gifts of significance in support of its important work.

The ultimate donor. The willingness of a donor to give is a function of both economics and commitment to the charitable cause. An individual with a desire to give much, but whose economic resources are limited, may always be a special or major gift donor. The ultimate donor has the economic resources to make a gift that has a major impact on the charitable organization's ability to achieve its mission. As each organization strives to develop the ultimate donor, it would be unwise for it to focus all of its energies on this limited field of donors. It must rely on diverse, multi-tiered fund-raising and donor development efforts.

Fund-Raising Sources

A successful fund-raising program draws upon at least seven different potential sources of funds. These include individuals, boards and board members, corporations and industry councils, foundations, special events, government, and planned giving.

Individuals constitute the most significant source of all philanthropic dollars available to charitable organizations. Major donors are cultivated over a period of time and provide the core of success to many charitable organizations. These individuals are important because they generate an enduring personal loyalty to the charitable organization. Typically, these individuals have the interest and wealth necessary to act on their enthusiasm for the benefit of the charitable organization. Major donors have become benefactors for risky projects, providing necessary capital to successfully undertake a project that the charitable organization might not otherwise fund. Finally, these individuals have extensive contacts and can bring others (and their money) to the charitable organization. Although they will be few, the major individual donors should be recruited and nurtured with great care.

Individuals are drawn to charitable organizations because they believe that they have the ability to make a difference.

Boards and board members are an important source of income and prospective donors. Board members of charitable organizations have usually made large donations or are expected to contribute during their tenure on the board. Equally important, board members identify and work with potential major gift givers.

Corporate and industry councils have been consistent givers to philanthropic causes. Since 1950, they have given about five percent of total contributions (about $18.5 billion in 2016) (Giving USA, 2017). Many corporations restrict their giving to local communities where they have operations. They do so for many reasons, including strengthening the community, enhancing board connections, stimulating economic development, and providing educational outreach. It is becoming increasingly common for corporations to have a separate corporate foundation into which they make contributions, to be dispersed by the foundation. Gaining access to corporate foundation grants is facilitated by continuous nurturing of a relationship between the foundation and the sport, tourism, and leisure service organization. The Kellogg Foundation has a long history of supporting parks and recreation. In 2006 it gave the Kalamazoo County Parks Development Foundation a 7-year, $2 million grant that created and fostered the care of a nonmotorized trail for transportation and recreation (Parks Foundation Kalamazoo County, 2018).

Charitable organizations and support foundations occasionally reach out to other foundations as sources of funds. Many foundations only give to intermediary foundations or charitable organizations. A notable example is the Lilly Foundation.

Built with funds from the Indianapolis-based Lilly Pharmaceutical Company, the foundation has made serving Indiana a major focus. In the early 1990s, it recognized great need across Indiana, especially in rural communities. Lilly saw many local groups asking for support and realized it was not in the best position to judge who should and should not receive a grant. Initially, Lilly established a system where each county that wanted to receive funds must create a community foundation. The community foundations were separate from any governmental body. Any nonprofit in the county seeking funds from Lilly was referred to the community foundation. Lilly then funded county-based community foundations. Its belief was that funding decisions are best made at the local level. When the process began in 1992, there were fewer than 12 community foundations in the state with assets of less than $30 million (not including Indianapolis). By 2016, each of the 92 counties had a community foundation and had collectively received over $2.4 billion from the Lilly Foundation (Lilly Endowment Inc., 2018). The search for and use of foundations as a major income source requires considerable effort, but can result in sizable contributions.

Special events can be a major source of income for some charitable organizations. The extent to which special-event fund-raising is used depends upon the purpose and focus of the charitable organization. Sport organizations, cultural groups, and symphonies are a few examples of groups that use special events extensively. Whether it is a run for youth or a jazz festival in the park or a riverwalk festival, the purpose is the same: to raise community awareness about the charitable organization and its function

and purpose, and to raise money. Special events bring in diverse donor groups that might not otherwise be interested in the charitable organization. A positive spin-off of special events is the publicity it generates and the potential it offers for board development. On the negative side, the cost-benefit ratio of a special event is sometimes quite low. Special-event fund-raising is not always an effective long-term single-focus strategy, but it does serve as an important ingredient in the mix of effective fund-raising.

Governments often have special grant programs designed to support economic and social development. Desiring to maximize the effect of the government contribution, there is frequently a matching condition to a grant. That is, each dollar of government funding must be matched by donations from individuals or other sources identified above. The opportunity to double the impact of a donation also enhances the attractiveness of giving.

Planned giving is discussed later in this chapter. It is an approach to philanthropic fund-raising that establishes donations as an ongoing commitment to a cause or project. Individuals and corporations often prefer to deal with their endless giving opportunities by establishing and following an annual or multi-year giving plan.

Goal Setting, Relationships, and the Gift Pyramid

Any successful fund-raising effort is grounded in goal setting. Figure 13.2 illustrates the relationship of organization goals to gift-giving potential, as well as to the organization's mission statement, to the board, and to the staff.

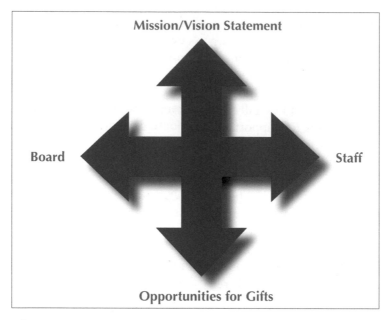

Figure 13.2. Goal Relationships in Fund-Raising

A sport, tourism, and leisure service organization's *mission statement* answers the following: (1) who is served, (2) what services are provided, and (3) how the services are delivered. The mission statement is a starting point for the charitable organization's fund-raising efforts. Some charitable organizations call their mission statement a "statement of purpose." The Parks and Wildlife Foundation of Texas, Inc., identifies its purpose as being "to provide private support for the efforts of Texas Parks and Wildlife Department." It further states that its intent is "to ensure that all Texans, today and in the future, can enjoy the wild things and wild places of Texas" (Texas Parks and Wildlife Foundation, 2017).

This nonprofit's *staff* play an important and ongoing support role in fund-raising. The annual giving program is a major focus of the work of the organization's employees and volunteers. They are the behind-the-scenes workforce ensuring the success of the campaign without becoming directly involved in the publicly visible parts of the process. Public appeals are reserved for the CEO, members of the board of directors, or honorary spokespersons. The activities of the staff will vary according to the size and nature of the organization, their level of expertise in fund-raising, and the expectations of the board when it comes to staff involvement.

Opportunities for gifts represents the range of potential program areas and services to which donors might give. They are defined by the charitable organization and represent the development and accomplishment of their mission. The leaders of the organization develop and implement strategies that build on their individual and collective strengths. Such strategies might include signing letters, attending top-level meetings with potential donors, making strategic calls, attending media opportunities with donors, attending receptions, and generally creating a high level of public visibility. The board defines the opportunities for gifts with the help of significant input from the chief executive officer and the support staff. The strategy to actually receive the proposed gifts is part of organizational goal development.

Each charitable organization has a unique perspective on its expectations of the *board's* role in fund-raising. Boards of directors typically have multiple responsibilities. The Georgia Center for Nonprofits, for example, suggests that the board's role in fund-raising is to provide leadership, financial support, and connection to donors and potential donors. The board must be structured to meet the primary needs of the organization. And it needs to be prepared to effectively pursue the fund-raising goals that it establishes in support of the organization.

Boards have a general responsibility to govern the organization in such a way as to ensure the success of its mission—which also assumes a fiduciary, programmatic, and capital responsibility. Secondly, the board is responsible for the recruitment and selection of board members who are committed to the mission of the organization, are willing to give financially, and will actively work with potential donors. Most boards have some type of annual retreat, where they discuss the charitable organization's mission and functions, build board relationships, and strengthen staff and board relationships. Board members are expected to make major efforts in securing funds for the charitable organization. These efforts may include an expectation for them to personally make donations.

Goal Setting

The annual fund-raising campaign involves the establishment of fund-raising goals. The goals should be realistic and designed to meet the sport, tourism, and leisure service organization's identified needs. Goal setting begins by examining the organization's financial needs for the coming year. This examination involves constructing an operating budget that shows all committed and desired services and programs. If the organization is committed to providing funds to another organization, this is taken into account as part of the committed funds. Another goal-setting activity is the identification of programs and functions that will require external funding and which can be supported either by internal funding sources or through direct cost recovery from sales, fees, etc.

The act of setting an achievable goal for contributed income is based on several factors, such as the history of giving to the organization, the level of current giving, current economic conditions, the frequency of past appeals and their effectiveness, and the attractiveness of the programs to be funded.

Table 13.2 presents a budget that establishes a gift goal. In general, projected contributed income should be set at 90% of the previous year's donation level. This practice allows that some donors may not continue contributing to this organization. The remaining 10% of the gift goal must be met through the contributions of new donors, or else the need projection should be reduced.

Gifting: How Many Donors Are Required?

Traditionally, many fund-raisers have used a rule of thirds to guide them in securing contributions. The rule of thirds suggests that a third of the funding goal will come from 10 to 15 gifts; the next third will come from the next 25 donors; and the final third will come from all other gifts. For a small campaign, this

Table 13.2
Example Goal Setting Using a Budget

Budget	Amount	Totals	Goal
Expenditures			
Committed Funds	$750,000		
Desired Additional Funds	$450,000	$1,200,000	
Income			
Earned Income	$350,000		
Deferred & Investment Income	$600,000		
Special Events & Fundraising	$50,000	$1,000,000	
Proposed Contribution Income Goal			$200,000

makes sense, but for a larger campaign the rule of thirds places too much stress on the lower third of the giving pyramid. The number of individuals required for funding in the lower third can become a burden, if a solid base of potential givers is not present. Fund-raisers typically spend the bulk of their time focusing on the top and middle tiers of giving. These individuals or corporations take more time and nurturing in the giving process, but when a contribution is made, it is worth the investment.

Table 13.3 depicts the *rule of thirds* when used for a small campaign. In this example, 68% of the giving comes from 40 donors. The final 40% comes from many donors at the lower tier. These are individuals who are contacted by telephone, mail, email, special events, or

Table 13.3
Rule of Thirds: Example of Gifts/Prospects Needed for a $2.5 Million Capital or Endowment Campaign

	Gift Level	Gifts Required	Prospects Required	Total Contributions	Percent of Goal
Top Third	$21,000	2	4	$42,000	
	$10,500	4	8	$42,000	
			Subtotal	**$84,000**	**33%**
Middle Third	$9,000	5	8	$45,000	
	$4,500	9	20	$40,500	
			Subtotal	**$85,500**	**34%**
Lower Third	$1,500	20	75	$30,000	
	$1,000	40	100	$40,000	
	Under $1,000	Many	Many	$14,000	
			Subtotal	**$84,000**	**33%**
			Grand Total	**$253,500**	**100%**

by electronic device. They can also come from contacts and recommendations made by other donors.

Table 13.4 illustrates a different goal-setting percentage, focusing on a larger campaign. In this campaign, 92% of the proposed funding sources come from the top 2 levels. At the top tier, the contribution represents 64% of the goal. The emphasis on a few key donors is typical for any successful campaign, but especially large campaigns. There are no hard and fast rules for determining where funding should come from, but most campaigns are reliant on one or more significant donors (top tier) and key second tier donors. Regardless, at the end of the fund raising campaign all donors should feel good about their contribution and that they were part of a significant opportunity to help an organization to meet its goals and serve others.

Fund-Raising Strategies

A successful fund-raising process requires a variety of strategies designed to take advantage of different donor levels. A fund-raising campaign recognizes different types and levels of donors and makes appropriate overtures. While online contacts, email, direct mail, or telephone solicitation will secure a first-time donor and may retain a donor, it is not likely to entice individuals at the top of the gift pyramid. Diversifying fund-raising strategies is essential. This section looks at annual campaigns, planned giving, special events, and support organizations as differing strategies. The strategies do not represent all those available, but constitute effective strategies that many sport, tourism, and leisure service organizations utilize.

Table 13.4
Rule of Thirds: A Top Tier-Focused Example of Gifts/Prospects Needed for a $2.5 Million Capital or Endowment Campaign

	Gift Level	Gifts Required	Prospects Required	Total Contributions	Goal
Top Tier	$500,000	2	3	$1,000,000	
	$200,000	3	6	$600,000	
			Subtotal	$1,600,000	64%
Second Tier	$85,000	5	10	$425,000	
	$50,000	7	15	$350,000	
	$25,000	11	18	$275,000	
			Subtotal	$700,000	28%
Third Tier	$10,000	8	16	$80,000	
	$5,000	10	20	$50,000	
	$2,500	15	30	$37,500	
	Under $1,000	Many	Many	$32,500	
			Subtotal	$200,000	8%
			Grand Total	$2,500,000	

There are four types of fund-raising campaigns. The *annual* campaign focuses on raising funds that are typically needed for annual operating expenses. *Planned* giving focuses on a longer-term perspective and on different types of gifting that may provide direct funding for several or many years. *Special events* are a less effective way of securing income, require significant time and energy, but do raise the level of community awareness and can open doors to more donors at all levels. *Capital campaigns* (discussed in Chapter 16) reflect the need for organizations to invest in construction, land acquisition, or other major purchases.

Annual Campaigns

Annual fund-raising campaigns are the primary source of income for annual operating funds for many nonprofit organizations. An annual campaign is an organized process that raises a specific amount of money over a specified period of time. Examples of organizations that depend heavily on annual campaigns include the United Way, public radio and television stations, the Red Cross, Boys & Girls Clubs, and the Girl Scouts. The development of a well-planned annual campaign requires considerable effort on the part of the nonprofit organization's staff, its board, and volunteers. The annual giving campaign has two primary functions: (1) to acquire new donors and (2) to retain donors and upgrade their level of giving.

The annual giving campaign generally results in low value of donations ($1 to $1,000), but this is offset by the higher number of donations made. Annual giving campaigns are seen as a predictable source of income because need tends to fluctuate minimally. The donations received are intended to provide a short-term benefit to the organization focusing

on ongoing operations. These donations are usually unrestricted, allowing the organization's managers to determine how to best use the money. There is still a fiduciary responsibility to use the contributions to serve the specific programs and clients identified in the campaign literature.

The two most common methods of conducting an annual campaign were mail and telephone solicitations. These methods are still effective. However, the use of email and Internet-based solicitation has grown dramatically in the last few years and provides fund-raisers with additional effective strategies. Most organizations now use a mix of all four strategies. Direct mail is the least expensive annual campaign fund-raising methodology. Most annual campaigns use some type of direct mail strategy. The development of a successful mailing and/or email list requires considerable effort. Returns from cold, or untested, lists can be as low as one percent, while on a more predictable, or tested, list, as high as 66 percent. The more refined the list, the higher the expected return. Greater accuracy and currency in the mailing leads to a higher rate of return. Another factor affecting the rate of return is how well those who receive the mailing know the charitable organization. This factor is termed "name recognition." Organizations with greater name recognition can expect a higher rate of return from direct mailings.

When retention is the goal of the mailed message, additional strategies are developed. The strategies should include multiple (two or more) mailings (or contacts requesting donations) per year, thank-you notes, newsletters, and other methods of communication. Effective direct mail and email campaigns should do the following:

- Raise funds efficiently but not usually in large amounts.
- Increase the number of donors to an organization.
- Increase the visibility of the organization among those targeted by the campaign.
- Help identify prospects for other giving strategies.
- Identify potential volunteers and new workers for the organization. This is dependent upon the strategy used and the intent of the campaign.
- Reach a greater number of the target prospects in an appropriate way.
- Focus on development.
- Provide instant gratification for the donor.
- Give the nonprofit organization the opportunity to tell the full story. The story focuses on how important the donor is and less on how much the organization needs the money. This is a form of flattery, and when done well can encourage the donor to give. Donors should be cast as "the heroes," because without them the organization cannot achieve its goals.
- Be individualized/personalized and segmented to a specific audience. The audience is composed of those who donated before and those who have not. Those who have donated before may give without even reading the letter.

Telephone solicitations have a higher rate of return, but are more difficult to conduct. They are usually reserved for those individuals from whom a donation is realistically anticipated. As more and more solicitations are conducted by telephone by competing organizations, people are not responding as effectively as they did a decade ago. Often a letter to the potential donor precedes the telephone campaign. Telephone campaigns are more costly and time-consuming than direct mail campaigns and are therefore expected to result in larger donations and provide a greater percentage of revenue. Staff, volunteers, and board members should all be involved in telephone campaigns.

Planned Giving

Planned giving is an inclusive term addressing a scope of philanthropic giving. It may involve the annual campaign, but more frequently, planned giving is associated with other major fund drives. Planned giving is an effort by the organization to ensure its future through a program where potential donors are identified, contacted, nurtured, and made part of a giving program that benefits the organization and the individual. In many instances, the results of the planned giving are deferred, with the actual donation occurring years in the future.

Table 13.5 identifies and compares six approaches to planned giving.

Outright gifts are gifts of money or other tangible property given with an immediate benefit to the nonprofit sport, tourism, or leisure service organization. Such gifts may be given without regard to how they will be used, or the donor may choose to put specific conditions on the gift. The larger the gift, the more likely some application parameters will be established.

Bequests, by contrast, are made available to the charitable organization only after the donor dies and the will has gone through probate. Bequests are the single most important source of income for charitable organizations. Bequests allow the donor to retain control of the donation throughout his lifetime while simultaneously reducing the estate tax for the donor's heirs. Bequests come in many

Table 13.5
Overview of Some Planned Giving Instruments

Type of Gift	Form of Gift	Benefit to Donor	Benefit to Nonprofit
1. Outright Gift	Cash Securities Real securities Insurance Personal property	Deductible for income tax purposes	Funds available for immediate use by the organization Frequently without restrictions or terms of trust
2. Bequest: Anything one owns at the time of the death may be passed on to an organization or person through one's last will and testament. Moreover, all forms of life income gifts may be in testamentary form to benefit family or friends and will then become available for use by named organizations.			
3. Life Income Gifts			
A. Pooled income	Appreciated securities Cash	Variable income that may provide hedge against inflation No capital gains tax on appreciated gift	Ensures future funding
B. Charitable remainder unitrust	Real estate Securities Cash	Same as pooled income funds, *plus* can be tailored to donor's situation Permits deferred income Includes real estate	Ensures substantial future funding
C. Charitable remainder annuity trust	Cash Securities	Fixed income Tax deduction in year the gift is made No capital gains on appreciated gift; alternative mimimum tax may apply	Ensures substantial future funding
D. Charitable	Cash Securities	Fixed income for a lifetime Tax deduction early years of gift	Portion of funds are available to organization Ensures future financing Upon death of insured, remaining payable to the organization
4. Charitable Lead Trust	Real estate Securities Cash	Allows property to be passed to other with little or no shrinkage due to taxes	Provides organization with current income for the length of the trust for a period of 10 years
5. Revocable Charitable Trust	Real estate Securities Cash	All or part of amount placed in trusts is available if needed by donor Removed burden of managing assets	Very high percentage of revocable trusts are not revoked and thus provide future funding
6. Insurance Policies			
A. Organization is made owner and beneficiary of policy current in force	Life insurance	Donor gets income tax deduction for value of policy when transferred Future premium payments may be deducted as gift Donor can make large future gift at small present cost	Organization may borrow on policy Organization may cash in policy Organization may receive full face value of policy at insured's death
B. Paid-up policy is given to an organization	Life insurance	Tax deduction based on current value of policy	Organization may keep policy and receive face value upon death of insured
C. Organization is named beneficiary of policy, but not owner	Life insurance	Enables donor to make large future gift at small present cost Donor may change beneficiary later Donor may borrow on policy	Upon death of insured, organization will receive face value of policy

Source: KPMG Peat Marwick, *Management Issues*
Note: This table was revised by the AAFRC Trust for Philanthropy. The trust gratefully acknowledges the advice of the National Committee on Planned Giving. The contents of the table are the responsibility of that trust. This table is for information purposes only and is not a substitute for legal or professional advice.

forms. They may include a fixed amount of money, a percentage of the total estate or a part thereof, or a specific item in estate (e.g., land, stock).

A *life income gift* is given to the charitable organization as an irrevocable gift. The asset is invested by the organization, with all or part of the income earnings paid either to a single beneficiary or to multiple beneficiaries for a specified period of time. The charitable organization can use the part of the investment income from the gift that is not given to the beneficiary. Once the beneficiary dies or the predetermined period of income to the beneficiary expires, the full benefit of the gift is made available to the organization.

A *pooled income fund* can be compared to a mutual fund in the sense that the contributions of multiple donors are pooled together and managed as a single investment. The obvious advantage is the size of the fund, allowing for a greater return and broader investment opportunities. The investment generated from the principal provides support to the charitable organization after the donor's death.

The *charitable remainder annuity trust* provides income to both the charitable organization and the donor. The donor makes a fixed contribution to the nonprofit organization with the opportunity to contribute additional funds. The organization manages the contribution, and the donor receives a guaranteed annual return on the investment. The donor can determine when the return begins (e.g., after retirement) or can set it for a fixed length of time (e.g., 20 years). This is known as deferring income. If the return on the investment is greater than the amount promised to the donor, then the organization retains it as earnings.

The organization eventually receives the returns. *Charitable remainder unitrusts* are very similar to a charitable remainder annuity trust, except that, instead of a fixed amount, the return to the donor will vary, depending on the market.

The final type of life income gift is a *charitable gift annuity*. This is a combination gift and investment, and it is among the oldest and most popular of the methods of making a life income gift. While similar to the others previously presented, the charitable gift annuity immediately becomes the property of the organization, which then guarantees the donor a lifetime income.

A *charitable lead trust* provides assets to the charitable organization for a specified period of time, but not indefinitely. It allows the donor to preserve assets for himself while providing income for an organization. The income received by the organization is either a percentage of the trust assets (as annually revalued) or a fixed dollar amount. A charitable lead trust can be in the form of property, securities, or cash.

A *revocable charitable trust* puts the resources (real estate, cash, or securities) in control of the organization, but allows the donor to access the trust. The donation is placed in a trust so it might be available to the donor, if desired. Not only does this type of trust remove the burden of the donor managing assets, but the trust may ultimately be given to the organization.

When *insurance policies* are given, they are placed wholly or partially in the control of the organization. There are three methods of providing life insurance proceeds to such a sport, tourism, or leisure service organization. The first is to make the organization the owner and beneficiary of a policy currently in force. The donor secures an income tax deduction for the value of the policy when transferred, and all future insurance premiums are treated as charitable donations by the IRS. The organization has the option of cashing in the policy for its current value, borrowing on the policy, or waiting until the death of the original beneficiary to receive its value. The second method is for a original beneficiary to give a paid-up policy to a organization. To the donor, the advantage is a tax deduction based on the market value of the policy. The organization benefits immediately by knowing, upon the death of the donor, that it has a certain level of guaranteed income. The third method is for the organization to be the owner and the beneficiary of the policy. In this instance, the donor can make a large future gift at a small present cost. The sport, tourism, or leisure service organization receives the face value of the policy upon the death of the donor. One problem with this, however, is the possibility that the donor will borrow against the policy or change the beneficiary at any time.

Special Events

Special events provide a unique opportunity for an organization to put its mission forward to the public, to secure new potential donors, and to generate a profit. Special events come in many forms and might include fun runs, festivals, dinners, social outings, golf tournaments, dances, and other types of creative approaches to raising money. Special events are seen as an attractive and relatively easy method of raising money, and they are appearing with increasing frequency. However, they are time consuming, requiring considerable effort to achieve success, can be financially risky, and may not generate a profit. The

easiest way to ensure the financial success of a special event is to have someone underwrite it. When this occurs, all the proceeds become profit. An underwritten special event can also put a higher level of pressure on the organization to be successful. It also increases awareness when a local television or radio station co-sponsors the event.

Support Organizations

Support organizations are increasingly popular among sport, tourism, and leisure service organizations. At the federal, state, and local levels, "Friends of the Park" or "Friends of the Zoo" or "Friends of the Botanical Garden" or "Friends of the Sports Club" have grown dramatically. The National Park Service has over 70 co-operating associations (Natural History Wanderings, 2013). In California, the state park system has over 40,000 volunteers who annually contribute over one million hours of service (California Department of Parks and Recreation, 2018). In Oregon, a state parks trust program has been established and has grown from 4 to 14 affiliated organizations since the mid-1970s. The Oregon trusts receive financial donations, land, and gifts for the state park system. In Indiana, the state park division of the government co-operated with a private foundation to develop a new state park. The state purchased the land, and the foundation undertook a major development (White River State Park, 2018).

The Florida Park Service views support groups, or citizen support organizations, as valuable sources of volunteers to support ongoing operations. There are currently 86 parks with "Friends..." groups. These support organizations may provide guides, as well as brochures, exhibits, interpretive areas, and conduct tours or special programs. All support groups are member based and may or may not have a membership fee. Members of the support groups can provide special educational needs, serve as a communication liaison to the community, develop special exhibits, and help in other ways. In addition, most support groups are organized in such a way that they are able to receive funds, seek grants, and accept gifts and bequests of money or tangible property.

Support groups are usually organized as tax-exempt organizations under the umbrella of the parent public or private nonprofit organization. Each support group must operate according to rules and procedures approved by the parent organization. Funds, volunteers, members, and potential partners are directed to the parent organization in order for it to fulfill its mission. Generally, the parent organization has developed a set of priorities and has identified needs to be met (such as volunteers for special events, funding for capital and interpretive projects, operation of concessions areas, etc.). Priorities are generally agreed upon in advance by the support group and the parent organization. A well-organized support group has a board of directors and a variety of committees that focus on meeting the needs of the parent organization. The committees work interdependently and independently on different projects. The committees become highly engaged in the process and meet the needs of individual members, as well those of the support group and the parent organization.

Support groups require the same care and nurturing that annual campaigns and planned giving programs require. Members of support groups are donors and often give considerably more than just their time. The sport, tourism, and leisure service organization should find effective ways of nurturing support group members. These can include member-only lectures, special recognition, newsletters, group travel tours, estate planning seminars, and others—all designed to keep members active.

Although such groups are formed to support the parent organization, they require a certain level of independence and autonomy. The delicate balance between independence and interdependence is an ideal that parent and support organizations need to achieve. Some parent organizations have complained that they have lost control of their support groups, and some support groups protest that they are just rubber stamp organizations. Not only should there be sufficient independence to allow the support group to make decisions and be flexible enough to respond to changing demands and economic conditions, but there should also be accountability and shared vision.

Retention of Donors

Retention of donors is a key component of a successful planned giving program. Significant time, money, and effort are committed to acquire donors. Initial donors are difficult to acquire and a challenge to retain. The results of one study on donor retention showed that only 43% of donors in one year continued as such in subsequent years (CauseVox, 2016). That percentage varies dramatically from organization to organization. The study found that only 19% of new donors were retained, while 63% of repeat donors were retained (Ibid). It is important to work with donors and keep them aware of the organization's goals and activities, how donations are used, and how important those donations are. It is easy for an organization to focus on their major donors, and they must do this to be successful, but there must be a strategy present to retain new and repeat donors. Donors are retained at a higher rate (76%) when they make larger ($250 or more) contributions (Ibid).

If an organization chooses only to touch base with donors during the campaign, the likelihood of retaining donors will be low. If there is a consistent plan to report, provide information, and share successes, then the donor's awareness and commitment is increased. The emphasis is dual: first focusing on the value of the donor and how important they are, and second on the successes of the organization, brought about by donor giving.

Selecting Fund-Raising Strategies

At some point an organization must select a fund-raising strategy. The challenge is to determine the most appropriate strategy for the needs. For example, should the annual campaign be used for the purchase of new land or for the board to secure operating dollars for day-to-day support? While there are no formal rules, there are suggestions for the use of various kinds of fund-raising

Table 13.6
Suggested Applications of Fund-Raising Strategies (adapted from the River Network's River Fund-Raising Alert)

Best Strategies	Start-up	General Operating Support	Projects	Building/ Equipment Purchase	Crises	Reserve Fund /Endowment
Bank loan/line				X		
Bequests						X
Board requests	X	X		X	X	X
Annual campaign		X	X		X	X
Capital campaigns				X		X
Corporate proposals			X	X		
Earned income		X				
Foundation proposals	X		X	X	X	
Government proposals			X			
In-kind requests	X	X	X	X		
Local business memberships	X	X				
Major donor requests	X	X	X	X	X	X
(Employee) matching gifts		X				
New members and renewals		X				
Organizational memberships		X				
Special appeals		X	X	X		X
Special events	X	X			X	
Workplace campaigns		X				

strategies presented in this chapter. Table 13.6 identifies 18 approaches to fund-raising and six scenarios to use the strategies.

River Network (a nonprofit organization supporting the development of clean rivers) also poses some questions that can be very helpful in selecting an appropriate fund-raising strategy:

1. Does this strategy fit with the vision and mission of the organization?
2. Is this strategy cost effective (as a general rule, will it bring in at least twice what it will cost)?
3. Will our target constituencies (those we are asking for donations from) respond well to this strategy?
4. Do we have the organizational skill and expertise that we need to carry out this strategy?
5. Do we have the resources (money, people) to carry it out?
6. Does this strategy build or strengthen our organization and its staff/board/volunteers?
7. Does this strategy represent a stable (repeatable) source of income? Does the strategy strive to build repeat donations, even for one-time activities?
8. Can this strategy be integrated into program activities already planned? If there is an ongoing fund-raising program, how does this strategy fit into the existing program?
9. Has this strategy worked well for us or for groups like ours in the past?
10. Does this strategy take advantage of our special fund-raising assets (a celebrity on the board, a member who owns a restaurant, a large group of volunteers, etc.)?
11. Timing: does this strategy fit well with other activities that we have planned?
12. Are there other benefits accruing from this strategy beside money (media exposure, good will, etc.)?

How Technology Is Impacting Philanthropy

Across the nation and in almost every home, hardly a day goes by without one or more telephone calls asking for support. Telephones and mail are traditional approaches to gaining new donors, but in today's fast-paced society, the old ways are no longer as effective as some new smartphone-targeted approaches. One of the more successful approaches has been used by the Mobile Giving Foundation. It links potential donors with opportunities for giving. As a foundation, it retains no portion of donations generated, instead passing 100% of the funds to the needy recipients (Mobile Giving Foundation, 2018). The Mobile Giving Foundation led the effort for mobile giving for major disasters in Haiti and Japan in 2014. Nonprofit organizations are becoming tech savvy and are allowing donations to be made via text and other mobile opportunities.

Nonprofits are increasingly aware of the potential for positive and negative publicity shared on social networks. Individuals are quick to share their negative experiences online and influence others' giving behavior. In response, nonprofits are creating greater transparency and accountability. Additionally, online guides are available, such as Charity Navigator (charitynavigator.org), the BBB Wise Giving Alliance (give.org), and GiveWell (givewell.org). They help would-be donors to determine the appropriateness of giving to certain organizations.

Nonprofits and foundations are increasingly influenced by mobile communications, the presence and availability of information on the Internet, the expectations of donors for detailed information, and the challenge of operating in our connected society. Balancing the need to raise funds, expend funds on programs, and provide an up-to-date and relevant technological presence, will challenge fund-raisers into the future.

Summary

Philanthropy and fund-raising are an essential part of the budget and fiscal operations of sport, tourism, and leisure service organizations that are private nonprofit or government entities. Managers of these organizations must be well versed in the different strategies and methodologies of fund-raising and know how philanthropy can assist their organizations. Sport, tourism, and leisure service organizations have been among the recent beneficiaries of support groups and philanthropic efforts. Sport, tourism, and leisure service organization managers who ignore the impact of philanthropy will find their organizations left out of a key source of income.

References

California Department of Parks and Recreation. (2018). Volunteers in parks. Retrieved from https://www.parks.ca.gov/?page_id=886

CauseVox. (2016). Four surprising donor retention statistics. Retrieved from https://www.causevox.com/blog/donor-retention-statistics/

Florida Park Service Citizen Support Organization Handbook. (2018). Retrieved from https://www.floridastateparks.org/content/cso-handbook

Forest Park Forever. (2018). Forest Park Forever meets and exceeds $130 million fundraising goal to improve Forest Park and expand endowment for long-term care. Retrieved from https://www.forestparkforever.org/news/2018/campaign-exceeds-130-million-fundraising-goal

Giving USA. (2018). Highlands Rance Park and Recreation Foundation.Retrieved from http://www.highlandsranchparkandrecreationfoundation.org/about-us/projects-andaccomplishments

Golan, J. (1998.) Comments on fund-raising: Winning strategies and practices with a special eye to Carnegie Hall. From notes of November 10, 1998, lecture notes given to a graduate philanthropy course at Indiana University.

Greenfield, J. M. (1994.) *Fund-raising fundamentals.* New York, NY: John Wiley & Sons.

Lily Endowment Inc. (2018). Homepage. Retrieved from https://lillyendowment.org/our-work/community-development/strengthening-indianapolis/

Mobile Giving Foundation. (2018). Homepage. Retrieved from https://mobilegiving.org/

Natural History Wanderings. (2013). List of National Park Associations. Retrieved from https://naturalhistorywanderings.com/2013/07/21/list-of-national-park-associations/

Parks Foundation Kalamazoo County. (2018). Homepage. Retrieved from https://www.parksfoundationkalamazoo.com/

River Network. (2004.) Choosing your fund-raising strategies. River Fund-raising Alert 11(1 & 2). Retrieved from http:www2.rivernetwork.org/library/fra2004_v11n2.htm.

Ross, J. R. (Ed.). (1997.) Philanthropy and Americans outdoors: Fund-raising and partnering workshop. Bloomington, IN: Indiana University.

Texas Parks and Wildlife Foundation. (2017). Who we are about. Retrieved from https://www.tpwf.org/who-we-are/about-us/

White River State Park. (2018). About the park. Retrieved from https://www.whiteriverstatepark.org/about-the-park/

Additional Resources

https://www.forestparkforever.org/news/2018/campaign-exceeds-130-millionfundraising-

https://www.gatesfoundation.org/Who-We-Are/General-Information/Foundation-Factsheet

https://www.floridastateparks.org/content/cso-handbook#1.2.

https://www.qgiv.com/blog/donor-stewardship-guide/#pyramid).

https://bloomerang.co/blog/14-basic-principles-of-fund-development/ - funddevelopment.

https://lillyendowment.org/our-work/community-development/strengtheningindianapolis/

https://www.tpwf.org/who-we-are/about-us/

https://www.gcn.org/articles/what-role-do-boards-and-individual-board-members-havein-nonprofit-fundraising

https://bloomerang.co/blog/15-odd-things-that-make-direct-mail-fundraising-appealssuccessful/

The 2016 Planned Giving Study. Indiana University Lilly Family School of Philanthropy.

https://www.issuelab.org/resources/25928/25928.pdf.

https://www.floridastateparks.org/get-involved/friends-groups.

https://www.causevox.com/blog/donor-retention-statistics/

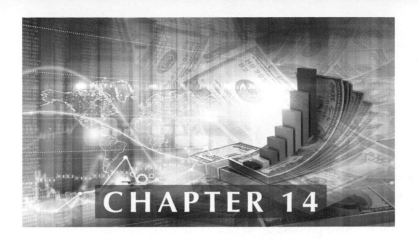

CHAPTER 14

Sponsorship

Introduction

Event or team sponsorship, as a communication vehicle for companies to reach targeted consumers, has been growing rapidly for the last 35 years. In sports alone, global spending for sponsorship contracts has increased from $2 billion in 1984 to approximately $65.8 billion in 2018 (Statista, 2018). More than a third (36.8%) of sport sponsorship spending was in North America (Statista, 2018). Sponsorship spending in Europe accounted for over a quarter (26%) of the global total, and a further 25.2% of the spending was in the Asia-Pacific region. Sport-related sponsorship agreements in the U.S. alone to hit a record amount of $17.1 billion in 2018 (a 5% increase over the previous year) (Statista, 2018).

Sponsorship can be described as a "mute" or "nonverbal" medium that targets active sport participants, spectators, and media followers in order to enhance the sponsors' brand awareness and image, and consequently, increase the sponsor's product or services sales (Cornwell & Maignan, 1998). It is formally defined as "a cash and/or in-kind fee paid to a property (typically sports, arts, entertainment, or causes) in return for access to the exploitable commercial potential associated with that property" (Uckman, 1995). It is, in other words, the acquisition of rights to affiliate or directly associate with a product or event for the purpose of deriving benefits related to that affiliation or association. These benefits may take the form of brand image enhancement, retailing opportunities through point-of-sales and various promotional activities, naming rights for a sport facility and/or sporting event, acquisition of media time for direct advertising, signage, and hospitality. Specifically, sponsorship agreements provide the legal foundation for the following:

- The right to use the sport property's brand associations (name, logos, trademarks, mottos) in order to accentuate the sponsor's direct association with the property (exclusive association within a product or service category, official sponsor/supplier/product, etc.) through advertising spots, promotional activities, publicity opportunities, or any desired means of communication.
- Naming rights for the sporting event, or the facility.
- The right for the sponsor to execute promotional happenings (e.g. contests), direct advertising, and sales-focused activities in conjunction with the sporting event, the facility and/or the web presence of the property.
- Hospitality benefits for the sponsor's customers and/or employees.

Sport sponsorship has its roots in ancient Greece, where cultural and religious events (often games to honor the deities) were financed from Chorigia (sponsorship) by wealthy citizens of the City-Republic. This practice was also observed in ancient Rome, where Roman aristocrats (patriarchs) sponsored gladiator games and spectacles to attract public support and recognition. In modern times, and until the early 1980s, corporate sponsorship had the form of donations to various cultural and sporting events with no specific expectations, on behalf of the sponsoring company, of taking anything in return for their support. However, after the financial success of the 1984 Olympics in Los Angeles, and the wide acceptance of tobacco corporate sponsorship in motorsports events worldwide (due mainly to U.S. government regulations against cigarette advertising on radio and television), the nature of sponsorship dramatically changed. A market-driven approach replaced the previous philanthropic nature of sponsorship activities, and involvement in sponsorship agreements and relations is now considered as business-related behavior (Uckman 1995). Corporations can utilize sponsorship as a strategic marketing tool to reach their targeted markets of consumers, helping the organization in its quest for a sustainable competitive advantage (Amis, Slack, & Berrett, 1999). As more management executives become aware of the numerous advantages of sponsorship over the traditional forms of direct advertising, approaches to sponsorship from sponsors, sport properties and consultants are becoming more professional, research, and results-oriented.

In an era of escalating advertising fees around mega sport events, where a 30-second ad during the 2018 Super Bowl half-time period had a price tag of $5.2 million (Michaels, 2018), sponsorship advantages are very difficult to ignore. Sponsorship offers higher levels of visibility for the sponsor, extensive media coverage, and increased publicity opportunities (all of them leading to brand awareness). However, the greatest of all advantages is the potential for brand image enhancement, and as a result of this, fan loyalty to the sponsor's products and/or services.

Product loyalty is a sought-after marketing objective for corporations because it is easily transformed into repeated sales and increased revenues. Sports are often associated with fan engagement and loyalty. As sport spectators are exposed to corporate messages under the favorable conditions of excitement and enjoyment that sporting events generate, they are more receptive to those messages (Dolphin, 2003). In addition, fans tend to appreciate and reward with their loyalty corporations that financially support their favorite club, team, or athlete, thereby securing their success in and out of the sport arena. The NASCAR case, where racing fans not only are highly associated with the league, but also fanatically support a specific driver (and the products he endorses), is the desired outcome all corporations wish to achieve through their sponsorship agreements.

Causes of Sport Sponsorship Growth

There are several factors contributing to the growth of sport sponsorship for the last 25-30 years. A list of the most significant factors is discussed below.

The U.S. Government Ban on Tobacco and Alcohol Advertising

The ban of tobacco advertising on TV in the early 1970s forced tobacco firms to redirect marketing budgets and brand-building efforts in promotional methods other than direct advertising. The tobacco industry now spends well over $300 million in sport sponsorship, most of it in motorsport-related events.

Excessive "Noise" in the Print and Electronic Media

With the increase of channel availability through cable television, the expansion of the Internet and world wide web, and the growing number of special-purpose magazines and newspapers, direct advertising in recent years has ex-perienced a substantial growth. As a result of the plethora of print and electronic media, the average consumer is bombarded with thousands of messages for commercial products and services every day. That situation creates "noise" in the consumer's mind, which does not allow advertising messages to achieve their full potential. In such noisy environments, advertising dollars are almost wasted. Today, companies try to identify methods that overcome these noise obstacles and allow their messages to reach the targeted consumers with as little noise as possible. Sponsorship is a great alternative because, under certain circumstances, it can minimize the noise effects observed in direct advertising (i.e., exclusivity clause in sponsorship agreements, purchase of naming rights, designation of the company as the official sponsor/provider of a product/service, etc.).

Rising Advertising Costs for Television Exposure

Advertising costs for companies that want to secure exposure in media with national appeal continue to rise. The cost of a 30-second advertisement in the 2018 NFL Super Bowl was $5.2 million, a significant increase since the first Super Bowl game when the same airtime cost just $40,000. This situation led corporations to the realization that advertising may not be the cost-effective proposition that it was in years before. Involvement in sponsorship partnerships with sport properties has been proven to achieve a higher level of exposure for corporate partners and, in most cases, at lower costs compared to exposure gained through traditional advertising campaigns.

The Increasing Commercialization of Sport

Sponsorship became an acceptable form of support for amateur sports as their National Governing Bodies found in corporations the ideal partner to help them realize their organizational goals and growth plans. The financial success of the 1984 Summer Olympics held in Los Angeles was the very first successful example of the tremendous potential this partnership might have for sport properties all over the world. Until then, mega sporting events such as the Olympics were mainly financed by public subsidies and by the International Olympic Committee (which, at that time, was at the verge of bankruptcy). The 1976 Olympics in Montreal is a vivid example of financial failure; it took the city of Montreal more than 30 years to pay off the debts generated to stage those games (Guardian, 2016). Peter Ueberroth, president of the Los Angeles Olympics Organizing Committee (LAOOC), faced the resulting reluctance of public authorities to financially support the Games and developed a different vision for the event. His vision called for corporations to become partners by developing a mutually beneficial relationship. One of his actions was to limit the number of Olympic sponsors to 30 in order to reduce the clutter (noise effect) of advertising. He also established category exclusivity, where a corporation could buy the right to become the only sponsor within that product/service category. The adoption of these actions allowed Ueberroth to significantly increase the sponsorship fees that corporate sponsors had to pay, thereby securing the viability and financial success of the Games. At the same time, sponsors realized the increased benefits that Olympic sponsorship had to offer, as sponsors and property worked together to achieve common goals (e.g., securing Games exposure, increase in sponsors' brand awareness and positive image, prevention of ambush marketing, success of hospitality events, achievement of outstanding event management etc.) (IOC, 2018). The realization of corporations that sponsorship is the desired platform of corporate exposure was given another boost after the IOC president's decision to allow professional athletes to participate at the 1992 Olympics in Barcelona, Spain. The participation of high-caliber professional players for the first time in history was received with much enthusiasm and positive feelings from the public, and subsequently from major corporations, which saw in this action, a unique opportunity for exposure to greater consumer masses all over the world.

The Increasing Media Interest in Sport Programming

The public interest in sports has been growing steadily for the last 40 years as a result of changing lifestyles, availability of leisure time, and increasing participation in fitness and sporting activities. This interest is also translated into interest for additional sport programming. The advent of cable television as well as the growth of new media sources (the Internet, subscription services via satellite, pay-per-view channels, etc.) were instrumental in satisfying the public's desire for more sports programming, and, at the same time, the needs of sponsors for additional means of exposure through them. These reasons, along with the fact that networks find sporting event broadcasting less costly to produce compared to sitcoms, shows, or documentaries, create a formula of success that media outlets find difficult to ignore. The example of the X Games, created by ESPN, demonstrates how a nontraditional sporting event, influenced by the alternative lifestyles characterizing Generation X, found viewership success in mainstream media surrounded by devoted fans and major corporations and brands sponsoring its activities, with a loyalty that is admirable in the sponsorship business.

Changes in Governmental Policies Related to Sport Activity Around the World

Although in the United States funding for the national governing bodies (NGBs) of various sports is coming from private sources (through fund-raising events, institutional grants, and other various activities), in other parts of the world, government funding for the development of grassroots programs is the primary source of support. In difficult financial times, where public sources are scarce, NGBs felt the need to look for other sources of funding in order to cover their budgetary deficits. Corporations and private institutions were then targeted to contribute financially in exchange for media exposure. Companies were, through sponsorship, also able to improve their public image by demonstrating good corporate citizenship.

The Globalization of Sports, and Corporate Desires to Successfully Penetrate Foreign Markets

Doing business in a foreign country is a challenging experience for many corporations, since they have to overcome cultural and language barriers, and adapt their production, employment, and marketing practices to the local customs

and traditions. The global appeal of sports has presented a unique opportunity to those corporations operating in foreign markets. Sport sponsor partnerships enable corporations to use sport properties as promotional vehicles in their attempts to successfully penetrate foreign markets. The 2008 Olympic Games in China, for example, were viewed by many international companies as the golden opportunity to promote, through sponsorship partnerships, their products in an emerging marketplace. The same purpose was served by the $400 million sponsorship of the national soccer team of Brazil by NIKE. The company accomplished a number of goals by signing a 10-year sponsorship agreement: (a) it established NIKE as a reputable manufacturer of soccer equipment, a reputation the company's rivals, ADIDAS and PUMA, have enjoyed for years; (b) it allowed the company to penetrate (through joint promotions, grass roots tournaments, charity events) not only the Latin American market, but also the global market due to the international appeal of the sport property-partner; and (c) it enhanced the company's brand image through the association with one of the most beloved and successful teams in this very popular international sport (Magnay, 2014).

Setting Sponsorship Objectives

When clear objectives for involvement in sponsorship have been articulated, potential sponsors are better able to assess the value of their direct financial participation in a sponsored event. The selection of a sponsored activity requires that sponsoring companies first decide which objectives they desire to achieve through the partnership. Sponsors then choose the activity that is most likely to enable them to achieve their predetermined objectives. Setting clear objectives beforehand enables sponsoring companies and sport properties to evaluate all related activities and actions more easily and more effectively.

It is obvious that one of the key objectives for any sponsoring company is to increase its ability to reach, influence, and involve existing and/or potential customers in something that excites them and attracts them to the company's brands (or services) and thereby establish a competitive advantage. Another key objective is to provide the sponsor with a desired return on their investment. This return on investment (ROI) may be expressed in monetary terms (e.g., increase of quarterly sales and revenues) or in a variety of other ways (e.g., quantity and quality of broadcast coverage). Sponsoring companies need to attach great importance to objective quantification in order to be able (during the post-event evaluation) to assess ROI. Sponsors may need the sport property's assistance in undertaking that task. Each objective should be as clear and as specific as possible. Generalizations and/or ambiguities will almost guarantee that the primary results of a sponsorship will be unquantifiable. Even if the event or property performed well in terms of attendance, etc., it may be impossible to prove that the sport property has delivered on the objectives of most interest to the sponsor.

As an example, consider an international company, such as Samsung, that manufactures electronics. If one of its sponsorship objectives is to increase sales for the brand, then that objective needs quantification. The company needs to determine the expected or desired impact of sponsorship using the following measures:

- Type of sales/markets affected (new customer, repeat, extended)
- Distribution channels enhanced (retail, web, catalogue)
- Time frame (duration of the sponsorship)
- Benchmarks (successes of comparable activities)
- Other critical success factors

Determining the corporate objectives to be accomplished through sponsorship is a challenging, time-consuming, and strenuous situation. Every corporation, based on its size, resources, and appeal to regional, state, national, or global markets, has different marketing issues to address through sponsorship. Researchers agree that there is an integrated and complex set of objectives that potential sponsors consider when deciding if and how much sponsorship to extend.

Ukman (2003) divided sponsorship objectives into three major categories: (a) image objectives, (b) sales objectives, and (c) media/promotional objectives.

By meeting *image objectives*, sponsors expect to do the following:

- increase awareness of their brand
- showcase their social responsibility
- change or enhance their corporate image
- build relations with external communities and public policy makers
- build relations with employees, their unions and other stakeholders
- increase the relevance of their brand to specific markets
- increase brand loyalty

Through meeting *sales objectives*, sponsors expect to do the following:

- stimulate retail and distribution channels
- expand their customer database and generate new leads

- find new/incremental business opportunities from major clients
- display products or services
- build business with co-sponsors
- stimulate their sales force
- increase sales to end customers

Finally, companies set *media/promotional objectives* in order to garner promotions in new distribution channels, and to reduce marketing costs.

Tripodi (2001) further suggested that sponsorship objectives can be grouped into two major categories: (a) corporation-related, and (b) product/brand-related. *Corporation-related* objectives refer to increasing public awareness of the corporation and its products/services, enhancing company image, altering public's perceptions, fostering community involvement, building business/trade relations and goodwill, and enhancing staff/employees' relations and motivation. *Product/Brand-related* objectives serve the purposes of increasing target market awareness, building brand image within the target market (positioning), increasing sales and market share, and blocking/preventing competition from being successful within that target market. These objectives might be used for positioning or re-positioning products and/or services for a targeted market.

Sponsorship research identifies the following list of corporate objectives that most influence management's decisions to enter into a sponsorship relationship with a sport property (Clark, Cornwell, & Pruitt, 2002):

- To increase public awareness of the product (brand), the company, or both
- To change or enhance product (brand) and/or company image and reputation by fostering favorable associations with the sporting event

- To improve the company's community relations (demonstrating good corporate citizenship)
- To identify the company with the targeted consumer segments
- To create promotional opportunities for the company's products and/or services
  To stimulate sales of products and/or services
- To enhance employee motivation, involvement, and loyalty, and to facilitate staff recruitment
- To generate media exposure through publicity
- To create opportunities for hospitality and entertainment for the company's business partners, clients, and workforce, thereby influencing key contacts
- To develop business-to-business relationships (networking, cross-promotions) with other sponsoring companies that support the same sport property
- To create and sustain a competitive advantage through exclusive association with a sport property
- To demonstrate unique product features, advantages, and innovations
- To develop a database of prospective customers and leads for the company's sales executives
- To build a new customer base

Sponsorship: The Corporate Perspective

When corporations consider sponsorship activities, they look for sport properties that can make a significant, valuable, and measurable contribution to current and future brand communications. They believe the following:

- The property (team, athlete, facility, or event) should demonstrate a good fit with the brand (or company) image and, ideally, be unique to that brand so that there is no confusion in the minds of the consumers (Meenaghan, 2002; Sports Sponsorship, 2007)
- The geographic reach of the sponsored activity should cover an appropriately matched target market
- The timing and duration of the sponsorship (multiyear contract, seasonal event, etc.) should fit in with the company's overall promotional campaign (Simpson, 1999).

Taking the above noted factors into consideration, sponsoring companies normally apply the following process in selecting the right property, event, or organization for their anticipated "win-win partnership" (Martin, 1996):

Phase 1

(a) Assess customers' perceptions and attitudes (through survey instruments, informal interviewing, or focus groups).
(b) Management team agrees on the desired image of the brand and/or company that is to be promoted through the sponsorship partnership.

Phase 2

(a) Identify all potential sponsorship partners.
(b) "Short list" the sport property/events that have an image that most nearly fits the desired image of the company/brand.

Phase 3

Meet with the most promising partnership candidate(s) and closely examine the following:

(a) Communication objectives
- What does the company want to accomplish through that sponsorship agreement?
- What communication outcomes (brand awareness, brand image enhancement, hospitality opportunities, etc.) does the company seek?
- Does the existing image of the sport property best fit the desired image of the brand/company? (Jobber, 2001).

(b) The targeted consumers
- What target group of consumers is the company trying to reach?
- Where are these customers located?
- Does the audience/fan base for the sponsored event match the company's customer base?

(c) The inherent risks associated with the sponsorship partnership
- What are the associated risks for either the sport property or the sponsoring company?
- Are there any image-related risks associated with the termination of the sponsorship agreement?

(d) Promotional opportunities
- What are the promotional opportunities for the company's products and/or services?
- What are the promotional opportunities for the sport property/event?

(e) The sport property's past record in sponsorship success
- What does the property's record with past sponsors look like? If sponsoring companies had withdrawn in the past, what were the reasons behind that development?

- What were the results of previous sponsorship partnerships with that property? Did the sponsors meet their desired objectives?

(f) The overall cost of this partnership
- Does the cost of entering into and participating in the sponsorship agreement justify the expected return on investment (ROI)?

Phase 4

Undertake a formal sponsorship agreement. Be sure to include a statement of purpose, objectives, terms and conditions, and a description of the process by which the partnership will be evaluated.

Sponsorship Acquisition: The Sport Organization's Perspective

Before looking for a sponsorship deal, the sport property needs to evaluate what it has to offer to prospective sponsorship partners. It must be realistic in determining what it can deliver and what market it can reach.

The sport organization will need to know how many events will be held, how many people will be involved as participants and spectators, and how extensively participation is shared through broadcast media. Not only is it important to know how many people can be reached by the corporate sponsor through the sport organization, but relevant details about those people must also be understood. Age, gender, family stage, income, and education are just a few of the demographic characteristics that might be of interest to a potential sponsor.

In addition to knowing what markets can be offered to the sponsor, an inventory of all marketable assets, such as signage, media opportunities, naming rights, hospitality events, promotions, etc., should be compiled.

The sport organization must then find potential sponsors. It begins by looking at existing sponsorship activity in order to get a sense of what types of corporations are involved in sponsorship. Note the type of organization, not just the specific company. Sometimes a company will extend its sponsorship activity, and sometimes a currently involved sponsor's competitor will be eager to get involved in sport sponsorship. Never offer sponsorship opportunities for the same event to competing corporations!

All of the information that the sport organization collects in determining its sponsorship offering and potential sponsors is used in developing the sponsorship package. The sponsorship package is a top-quality presentation that outlines the sport organization's offer of benefits to sponsors, and a set of proposed partnership actions. Sponsorship packages "may be tiered to reflect levels of expenditure that would just 'make it happen,' to more sophisticated versions that reach more people with extensive publicity" (Sports Sponsorship, 2007).

Selling the Sponsorship Opportunity

When it is time for the provider of a sponsorship opportunity and the potential sponsor to get together and make a deal, the matter of "selling" the sponsorship should be relatively simple. After all, the advance work and preparation should have served to bring together partners with reciprocal interests and mutually beneficial resources, and the sponsorship agreement is just the expression of details of how those interests will be satisfied.

Not all potential sponsors, however, readily see the benefits being offered to them through sponsorship opportunities. The sponsorship sales strategy that a sport organization develops must account for this, and the individual who presents the proposal to enter into a sponsorship agreement will have to be very well prepared. Proper preparation includes thinking of ways in which the sponsorship partnership would be integrated in the marketing campaigns of the targeted companies, as well as reading annual reports, company newsletters, trade organizations, media reports, etc. in order to more fully understand the target corporation's objectives, activities, priorities, and circumstances. Preparation also includes deciding what products may be sponsored (collectively or exclusively), finding out who to contact, and estimating the level of sales to be realized.

After the sport property has decided the sales strategy it will follow in order to successfully attract sponsors, it is time to initiate the sales process. Typically, the sport property will begin by approaching major companies first in order to sell its best (and most expensive) inventory (naming rights, exclusivity packages, event TV rights, etc.). In addition to securing large sponsorship contracts early in the sales process, selling to major sponsors first has the advantage of momentum and example. That is, the property can take advantage of name recognition of major corporate sponsors and more easily convince smaller companies of the good business practice of being part of its sponsorship program.

The sales process usually involves the following:

- Soliciting interest in a face-to-face meeting with prospective sponsors using a proposal brief (a one-page document that contains basic information about the sponsorship opportunities with the sport property).
- After the prospective sponsor expresses an interest, scheduling a meeting with management executives who have decision power over sponsorship partnerships. At this first meeting, it is imperative for the seller of sponsorship opportunities to spend most of the time listening to what the prospective sponsor has to say.
- Preparing for the meeting by learning about the prospective sponsor. Answers to the following questions should be known:
  (a) Where does the sponsoring company spend its marketing budget at that point in time?
  (b) Does the company have sponsorship partnerships with other sport properties?
  (c) What does the sponsoring company think about these relationships? Have they been satisfied with the outcomes/met their sponsorship objectives?
- After the initial meeting is over, assessing the situation and examining if the property can realistically deliver what the sponsor wants. If the assessment is positive, a follow-up meeting is scheduled (usually within the next 7-10 days following the first meeting).
- Returning to the second meeting with a detailed sponsorship proposal; this is a multipage document that includes the offer letter with all supporting information. Sponsoring companies use this document to facilitate their internal decision-making process.

- Allowing the prospective sponsors to intervene and modify the "draft" proposal in order to meet their organizational needs.
- Negotiating the final terms of the agreement and closing the deal.

The Sponsorship Proposal Document

A sponsorship proposal may address various issues depending on the needs of the sponsorship company and the complexity of the agreement (multiyear contract, parties involved, etc.). The following elements are usually included in a sponsorship proposal document:

- Property facts (i.e., history of the organization, organizational chart, contact info, etc.)
- Event(s) schedule
- Photographic displays
- Audience demographics, purchase behavior, and loyalty studies
- List of existing sponsors
- Sponsor case histories and clients' testimonials
- Naming rights and/or exclusivity categories
- Sponsorship packages
- Post sponsorship evaluation processes
- Summary of rights and benefits for the sponsor
- Sponsorship fee information

The proposal should be written in such a way that it captures the attention of the audience. Use of irrelevant data in order to impress the audience will have a negative effect. Judicious use of attractive graphics is encouraged, and care should be taken to incorporate only the information that is necessary for the sponsor to assess the value of the sponsorship deal. Descriptions of activities and benefits should be precise and related to the interests and uniqueness of the prospective sponsor. The proposal also needs to be so thorough that the prospective sponsor is left with very few or no unanswered questions.

Marketing Benefits of Sponsorship

The main motivation for corporations to sponsor a sport, tourism, or recreation event or facility is to gain access to the vast number of individuals that are exposed to the events being sponsored and, by association, to the corporation or its products. The most common ways of promoting corporations through sponsorships include the following:

- Stadium signage (score boards, advertisement boards, etc.)
- Branding opportunities (logo placement, promotional giveaways, uniforms, etc.)
- Corporate hospitality opportunities (luxury suites, premium-level season tickets, ticket discounts, etc.)
- Naming rights
- Advertising (and virtual advertising)
- Publicity opportunities (radio, television, print media)
- Promotional events and contests
- Cross promotions
- Direct marketing, personal selling, and retail promotions

All these methods are used by most properties to maximize the marketing benefits of sponsorship. Three of the above noted methods are deserving of further discussion.

Cross Promotions

Promotion is the critical mechanism for positioning a product or service in the minds and the hearts of the consumers. Cross promotions is where two or more sponsoring companies develop a business relationship with the sole purpose of creating a joint-promotion themed around the sponsored property. This mutually beneficial solution allows sponsors to exchange their resources, so that they both efficiently advance their business objectives.

Virtual Advertising

In virtual advertising, virtual images can be projected and broadcast on top of existing inventory (ads, posters, and signs) or digitally inserted into previously untouchable areas, such as the playing field. This type of advertising allows a sport property to carve up its international TV footprints and sell multiple narrowcast advertising packages worldwide. It also allows a sport property to remove all in-stadium advertising and provide its TV partners with "advertisement-free" stadiums and arenas. In this instance, virtual advertisements can be superimposed onto blank advertising boards, allowing for animated messages and, more importantly, the same space to be sold many times over. Virtual advertising technology allows a sport property and its TV broadcast partners to define advertising on the same board according to the needs of advertising companies across different regions in the country. Virtual advertisement digital boards are actually less costly than rotating boards, and are much more versatile.

Hospitality

Hospitality benefits provide sponsors with unique opportunities to get to know clients in a relatively informal atmosphere and develop a relationship that may otherwise have taken a significant amount of time and resources to nurture. The opportunity to impress clients while they are attending a sporting event (especially when the event has a wide appeal, like the Super Bowl or the Olympic Games) can be substantially increased. Hospitality deals also allow a large number of people (clients and sponsors' employees) to be invited to an event for which tickets may be scarce and interest high. The appeal of hospitality benefits is significant for both the property (low cost of offering) and the sponsor (high return on investment through nurturing business relationships or improving management-employee relations).

Evaluation

The effectiveness and value of a sponsorship partnership should be regularly evaluated. Evaluations should generate formal reports that are studied by the sponsoring company and the sport property. Evaluation reports can be highly effective not only in securing the sponsor for the following year, but also can be used as a marketing tool in recruiting new sponsors. In times when sponsoring companies are forced to look closer at the cost effectiveness of their investments, it is imperative that sport properties are fully engaged in post event evaluation activities.

A meaningful sponsorship evaluation begins with the decision about what is to be measured and against what criteria those measurements will be assessed. Jiffer and Ross (1999) suggest the following as essential elements in an event sponsorship evaluation:

1. **Exposure**—How well was the sponsors' brand positioned in the mind of the consumer?
2. **Attention**—What level of customer attention was given to the company's products and/or services?
3. Knowledge/Awareness—What is the level of customers' basic or extensive knowledge regarding the company's products and/or services?
4. **Attitudes**—How well did the sponsorship enhance the sponsor's ability to influence customers' perceptions regarding its products?
6. **Behavior**—Did the sponsored event stimulate positive changes in the consumers' consumption patterns?

Several methods can be employed in measuring the success of a sponsorship agreement. These are discussed below.

Print press monitoring. Monitoring the press media and collecting any press clippings that refer to the sponsored event and the sponsoring company.

Photographic record. Recording all activity related to sponsors exposure using digital photography and/or even video clips with participant and spectator comments regarding the event and the affiliated sponsoring company.

Television exposure. Measuring and reporting the amount of broadcast time given to the event, the number and reach of the channels that carry the event, and the estimated number of viewers watching the event.

Telephone interviews. Assessing the awareness level for a sponsor in a very quick and inexpensive way.

Mailed survey instruments. Using surveys to measure consumers' knowledge and attitudes regarding the sponsor's products.

In-depth interviews and focus groups. Qualitative research involving samples of target markets and highly focused discussion about the desired outcomes of the sponsorship arrangement. The discussion is focused on generating new ideas to be used in future sponsorship partnerships through open-ended questions, and circulation of opinions and suggestions from participants.

SPINDEX Method. A method that is used in measuring the exposure time obtained by each of the sponsors in all TV broadcasts and on all broadcasting channels. SPINDEX values are calculated by employing four measures: advertising time obtained throughout the television broadcast; the number of times that an advertisement was shown; the duration of the broadcast; and the number of viewers watching the broadcast. The resulting SPINDEX scores provide the sponsoring company with an accurate idea of the cost per advertising second, the cost per television viewer, and the cost per SPINDEX point (i.e., the cost per 30-second TV spot).

Evaluation reports are a tool to gauge what the sponsorship has actually done for a sponsor. However, some sport properties have been reluctant to get involved in the post-sponsorship evaluation measurements in fear of losing the sponsor if the research shows that the partnership has not generated the hoped-for benefits. In addition, some sponsoring companies are reluctant to undertake evaluation research because of the monetary cost and time factors involved in this process. Other concerns are the danger of getting conflicting data through the surveys and the challenge of deciding what information is relevant.

The drawbacks to sponsorship evaluation are outweighed by its positive aspects. The formal report of the evaluation is "hard copy" evidence that the sponsorship agreement between the two parties either did or did not meet the original objectives. It serves as evidence of the property's commitment to the sponsorship partnership, and it shows the sponsoring company that the property cares how the relationship is affecting the company's bottom line.

Summary

Sponsorship in sport, tourism, and leisure service organizations is an effective way to generate revenues and create synergistic relationships within the community. Sport sponsorship, in particular, has made millions of dollars available for sport properties and provided corporations with additional marketing opportunities. The objectives of both the sponsor and the sport property should be clearly articulated before entering into a formal sponsorship agreement. Those objectives should also be understood early in the process of identifying and securing potential sponsors and sponsorship situations. That process involves many steps.

Sponsorship can manifest itself in many ways, but it always includes providing the sponsor with unique opportunities to promote its corporate image or product line. How well the company or its products are promoted is the main question to be answered in the formal sponsorship evaluation process.

References

Amis, J., Slack, T., & Berrett, T. (1999). Sport sponsorship as distinctive competence. *European Journal of Marketing, 33* (3/4), 250–272.

Clark, J., Cornwell, T. B., & Pruitt, S. (2002). Corporate stadium sponsorships, signaling theory, agency conflicts, and shareholder wealth. *Journal of Advertising Research,* 16–32.

Cornwell B., & Maignan, I. (1998). An international review of sponsorship research. *Journal of Advertising, 27*(1), 1–21.

Dolphin, R. (2003). Sponsorship: Perspectives on its strategic role. *Corporate Communications: An International Journal, 8* (3), 173–186.

Guardian. (2016). The 40-year hangover: How the 1976 Olympics nearly broke Montreal. *The Guardian.* Retrieved from https://www.theguardian.com/cities/2016/jul/06/40-year-hangover-1976-olympic-games-broke-montreal-canada

IOC (2018). The Olympic Partners Programme. The International Olympic Committee. Retrieved from https://www.olympic.org/sponsors

Jiffer, M., & Roos, M. (1999). Sponsorship: A way of communicating. Stockholm, Sweden: Ekerlids Förlag, S-Comm.

Jobber, D. (2001). *Principles and practice of marketing* (3rd ed.). Berkshire: McGraw-Hill Publishing Company.

Magnay, J. (2014). The real value of a World Cup sports sponsorship. INTHEBLACK. Retrieved from https://www.intheblack.com/articles/2014/07/01/the-real-value-of-a-world-cup-sports-sponsorship

Martin, J. H. (1996). Is the athlete's sport important when picking an athlete to endorse a nonsport product? *Journal of Consumer Marketing, 13*(6) 28–43.

Meenaghan, T. (2002). From sponsorship to marketing partnership: The Guinness sponsorship of the GAA all-Ireland hurling championship. *Irish Marketing Review, 15*(1), 3–23.

Michaels, M. (2018). The price of a 30-second Super Bowl ad has exploded, but it may be worth it for companies. *Business Insider.* Retrieved from https://www. businessinsider.com/super-bowl-commercials-cost-more-than-eagles-quarterback-earns-2018-1

Simpson, C. (1999). A sporting try. *NZ Marketing Magazine, 18*(8), 34–37.

Sports Sponsorship. Retrieved from http://www.sports-sponsorship. co.uk/sponsorship.htm

Statista. (2018). Global sponsorship spending by region. Retrieved from https://www.statista.com/statistics/196898/global-sponsorship-spending-by-region-since-2009/

Tripodi, J. A. (2001). Sponsorship: A confirmed weapon in the promotional armory. *International Journal of Sports Marketing & Sponsorship*, 1–20.

Ukman, L. (1995). *IEG's complete guide to sponsorship.* Chicago, IL: International Events Group.

Ukman, L. (2003). *Measuring the result of sponsorship.* Chicago, IL: IEG Valuation Services.

SECTION E

Investment

The four chapters in this final section explore the nature of entrepreneurship and examine some of the key aspects of capital budgeting and business planning. Because a basic understanding of economic principles is so important to managing financial resources in sport, tourism, and leisure service organizations, a chapter on economics is also included.

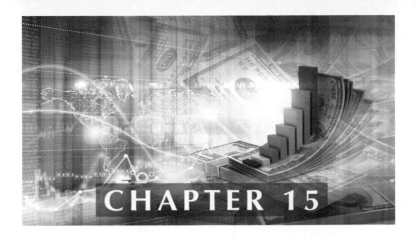

CHAPTER 15

Entrepreneurship

Introduction

Sport, tourism, and leisure service organizations exist because someone saw an opportunity to satisfy personal or social needs in a financially viable way. Much is owed to those who blazed the paths within the public, private nonprofit, and commercial sectors and created the agencies, businesses, departments, and programs that serve the leisure needs of society. Much is also expected of those who will yet blaze new paths in this dynamic field of human services. The creators, initiators, risk-takers, and pioneers of sport, tourism, and leisure industries are all entrepreneurs. In this chapter, the nature of entrepreneurship is discussed and the personal characteristics and essential skills of entrepreneurs are identified. Entrepreneurship, as it may apply differently to sport, tourism, and leisure service organizations is also explored.

Definition of Entrepreneurship

While the most obvious example of entrepreneurship is the starting of a new business, the entrepreneurial approach to service delivery can be just as obvious in existing enterprises. Entrepreneurship is the capacity and willingness to develop, organize, and manage a business venture and assume any of its risks in order to make a profit (or meet a greater non-financial need). The entrepreneurial spirit is characterized by innovation and risk-taking, and is an essential part of a sport, tourism, and leisure service organization's ability to succeed in an ever changing and increasingly competitive marketplace.

Most simply defined, an entrepreneur is a person who identifies a need and starts a business or program to fill that void. However, there is more to an entrepreneur than the act of starting a business. Entrepreneurs have particular skills and qualities that help them to make those new businesses or programs financially successful.

The Importance of Entrepreneurship

In capitalistic societies, the entrepreneur is seen as a national asset and, at the regional level, is considered to be a critical factor in economic development. The entrepreneurial spirit is also highly valued because of its contributions to social development and community growth. Entrepreneurs can improve the way we live and work by raising our standard of living. In addition to creating wealth from their entrepreneurial ventures, they also create jobs and the conditions necessary for a flourishing society.

Four reasons why entrepreneurship is important to the economy and to society in more general ways are discussed next.

Entrepreneurs Create New Businesses and New Employment

When entrepreneurs create new goods and services, the result is often new employment, which can produce a cascading effect or virtuous cycle in the economy. The stimulation of related businesses or sectors that support the new venture add to further economic development.

For example, a new tourist attraction in a community requires employees to operate it. New jobs are created directly by the new tourism business. However, tourists who come to the attraction need places to eat, hotels rooms to sleep in, and retail stores in which to shop. They need gas stations to fill up their cars and parks or theaters for their relaxation or entertainment. Indirect employment in all of these related businesses is positively enhanced. Both direct and indirect employment because of the new tourist attraction also affects employment in other areas as additional homes, police services, schools, churches, health services, etc. are needed for the new employees.

Entrepreneurs Add to Local Income

Existing businesses are confined to existing products and markets. Entrepreneurs add new products and new markets and, therefore, generate new income opportunities. Some of the new income may be from existing income sources, but it is rare that new businesses will create a net loss of income due to competition. The new income will also generate additional taxes that the government can invest in other struggling sectors and in human capital.

For example, a sporting goods store can only sell watercraft that exist, and only to the limited number of people who want such vessels. When an entrepreneur develops a new way to enjoy boating, such as by standing on a board and paddling instead of sitting in a canoe, kayak, sailboat or motorboat, the sporting goods store now has a range of new products to sell to an expanded market. New sales (i.e. new income) are thereby generated.

Entrepreneurs Can Create Social Change

Sport, tourism, and leisure service organizations exist because society changed in ways that give people time and other resources necessary to play, travel, be creative and relax. This change is due, in large part, to the work of entrepreneurs who devised technology to provide abundant clean water, reliable power, healthy foods, safe transportation, education, security, and all of the other features of modern living that are generally taken for granted. Society is freed from most of the challenges of survival and has the luxury of focusing on improving the quality of life.

For example, the pioneers of low-impact camping equipment were instrumental in facilitating the trend toward "21st century camping." In the past, camping involved activities that were harmful or, at least, disruptive to the natural environment (e.g., campfires, pit toilets, soil compaction, devegetation, etc.). Modern lightweight stoves, food products, packaging, footwear, and lightweight equipment developed by entrepreneurs have greatly reduced the environmental impact of this popular outdoor adventure activity. The use of these improved products allows individuals and outdoor recreation organizations to redirect their "overcoming nature" efforts to "enjoying Nature while protecting it."

Entrepreneurs Get Involved in Community Development

Entrepreneurs often play a nurturing role in entrepreneurial ventures by other like-minded individuals. They are committed to improvement and advancement and also invest in community projects. Entrepreneurs often provide generous financial support to local charities. They are interested in further development beyond their own ventures.

For example, technology entrepreneur and Microsoft founder Bill Gates has used his money to promote further technology advances and to finance good causes, from education to public health. The qualities that make one an entrepreneur are the same qualities that motivate entrepreneurs to move the community forward.

Myths about Entrepreneurs

Entrepreneurs are often inappropriately and inaccurately portrayed using stereotypical descriptors. These illustrative myths, include the following:

1. **He's the undisciplined kid who dropped out of high school and made millions of dollars.** False. There may be a few examples in history of individuals who abandoned formal education and used their cunning, charm, or undeserved good luck to get rich, but they are rare and not representative or idealistic of the successful entrepreneur. Education, discipline, and managed opportunity are still the most valuable tools at the disposal of the entrepreneur.

2. **She's a sociable huckster who has no guilt and exploits friends and swindles strangers.** False. Entrepreneurs rely on others to be successful and, therefore, will not and cannot take unfair advantage of others for their own potential gain.

3. **He is someone who gambled the family fortune on a business long shot and got lucky.** False. Luck plays a part in everyone's success story, but so does failure. Entrepreneurs are very careful with personal or family resources and are unlikely to make high-risk business decisions. They are risk-takers, but entrepreneurs operate best in the moderate-risk realm.

4. **She has a "Midas touch" instinct for business and, therefore, does**

not need to be analytical. False. An entrepreneur's success is the result of careful analysis, sound decision-making, hard work, and an appropriate amount of luck. The risks associated with impulse business decision or operating based on "gut feelings" is too high for most entrepreneurs.

5. **He will do anything to make a dollar. False.** Entrepreneurs act with conscience and have a high degree of personal ethics. While they may be rewarded with money for their success, entrepreneurs are more invigorated by the sense of accomplishment and the satisfaction of having overcome a business challenge. An entrepreneur would view financial success through unethical practice as a hollow victory or, more likely, a personal failure.

The Characteristics of an Entrepreneur

Having debunked the myths of what an entrepreneur is, attention will now be turned to what research has identified as the characteristics that are common to successful entrepreneurs. Not all entrepreneurs will fit the profile exactly, but the following attributes have proven to be both consistently present in and clearly related to the success enjoyed by entrepreneurs. Following the discussion of each attribute are related quotes from several innovative corporate executives who were asked to describe the main qualities of entrepreneurs (Fernandes, 2018).

Confidence

The successful entrepreneur has confidence in his/her abilities, resources, and accountability. Entrepreneurs are self-confident but not to the point of being unrealistic about their abilities. They know their strengths and weaknesses, and know how they might influence the success of their business ventures. Entrepreneurs also accept that they are responsible for making the business successful and rely on their own abilities to generate the required resources. They do not look to someone else to "make it happen." Likewise, entrepreneurs are prepared to take personal responsibility for the success or failure of the business.

"It's about blazing new trails, about believing in yourself, your mission and inspiring others to join you in the journey."—Derek Hutson, CEO of Datical

"It's about having the creativity to question, the strength to believe and the courage to move."—Jordan Fliegel, co-CEO of DRAFT

Involves Others in the Business Concept

Entrepreneurs are not usually loners. The original business idea may be theirs alone, but they are open to sharing the idea and receiving feedback and advice. During business operation, the entrepreneur builds the work team by sharing the goals and, to some degree, the risks of the enterprise. Entrepreneurs also share the risks by seeking partners and investors as they build the business.

"It is important to balance strong vision with a willingness to embrace

change. *The ability to listen, whether it be to the opinions of customers or employees, is also integral to success."* —Tirath Kamdar, founder and CEO of TrueFacet

"To be a successful entrepreneur you must have a passion for learning— from customers, employees and even competitors."—James Bedal, CEO of Bare Metal Standard

"An entrepreneur has to be able to build a team that cares about their work, and to do that you have to care about how you create your team."— Jonathan Barnett, founder and CEO of Oxi Fresh Carpet Cleaning

Realistic

The entrepreneur has a grasp on reality, even the parts that are uncertain. Entrepreneurs have a strong reality orientation. They are dreamers in many ways, but they are grounded in the practical realities of the business environment. They do not believe in "crazy ideas," but, rather "good ideas that nobody else has considered." Entrepreneurs also recognize that reality includes uncertainty and ambiguity. They have a high tolerance of both and do not let doubt or lack of complete knowledge hinder decision-making.

"Fundamentally, entrepreneurship is about ... the ability to recognize [and] methodically analyze [an] opportunity, and ultimately, to capture [its] value."— Bruce Backenheimer, Executive Director of the Entrepreneurship Lab at Pace University

"Being an entrepreneur is like heading out into uncharted territory." —Amanda Austin, founder and president of Little Shop of Miniatures

Risk-Takers

The successful entrepreneur is a moderate risk-taker. Risk is inherent in business. If there is no risk, there will be little or no return on an investment. However, there are different levels of risk and the highest levels are not in a comfort zone for most entrepreneurs. They are moderate risk-takers, demonstrating their desire to be as well informed and analytical as possible while still showing tolerance for reasonable uncertainty. They also feel that no greater level of risk should be imposed on others with whom they have vested interests. Entrepreneurs are moderate risk-takers and moderate risk-sharers.

"Successful entrepreneurs ... have the guts to take a calculated risk and the tenacity and persistence to keep going even when there are bumps in the road."—Eileen Huntington, co-founder and CEO of Huntington Learning Center

"To be a successful entrepreneur, you have to be someone who is able to risk failure at the deepest personal levels." — Steven Benson, founder and CEO of Badger Maps

Low Need for Status and Power

Some people are motivated by titles, influence, or financial compensation. While entrepreneurs do want to make a great deal of money from their business activities, they do not feel the need to be seen as a powerful person or someone who is honored publicly at every turn.

They are motivated by their passion, by their desire to succeed, and by their quest to improve something.

> *"Entrepreneurship is the persistent progression towards an innovative solution to a key problem. It's the constant hunger for making things better and the idea that you are never satisfied with how things are."*—Debbie Roxarzade, founder and CEO of Rachel's kitchen

> *"Successful entrepreneurs look past [the] 'quick buck' and instead look at the bigger picture to ensure that each action made is going toward the overall goal of the business or concept, whether or not that means getting something in return at that moment."*—Allen Dikker, founder and CEO of Potatopia

Reliable and Acts with Integrity

Entrepreneurs understand that, without integrity, they are nothing. They know that integrity is essential to good human relations and to business success. They take commitments seriously, especially when they are the one who has promised to do something. They respect other people trust in them.

> *"It's hard work and persistence to leave the world a better place once your time here is done."*—Konrad Billetz, co-founder and co-CEO of Offset Solar

> *"These things take determination and a strong focus on the end goal."*—Stacey Kehoe, founder of Brandlective Communications

Maintains a Success Orientation

Every entrepreneur enters into a business venture with an expectation of success. However, sometimes they fail —it's only natural, given the uncertainty of the business environment and key markets. Entrepreneurs respond to failures by treating them as lessons for success and learning from them in order to succeed the next time. Entrepreneurs are problem solvers and they have a high need to achieve what others have not been able to do. Success invigorates them and failure informs them.

> *"What sets [entrepreneurs] apart is the will, courage, and sometimes recklessness to actually do it."*—Derek Hutson, CEO of Datical

> *"To me, entrepreneurship means being able to take action and having the courage to commit and persevere through all of the challenges and failures."*—MJ Pedone, founder and CEO of Indra Public Relations

> *"You need to be able to bounce back from losses if you want to be successful. There will be much more disappointment than progress when you first start off, and you need to have a short memory in order to put the past behind you quickly."*—Vip Sandhir, founder and CEO of HighGround

Opportunity and Goal Oriented

Entrepreneurs are constantly looking for opportunities to improve a product, solve a problem, or satisfy an unmet need. Their goals are always action oriented and they measure success by those goals and actions.

> *"At its core, [entrepreneurship] is a mind-set—a way of thinking and acting. It is about imagining new ways to solve problems and create value."* —Bruce

Backenheimer, Executive Director of the Entrepreneurship Lab at Pace University

"Entrepreneurship is the ability to recognize the bigger picture, find where there's an opportunity to make someone's life better, design hypotheses around these opportunities, and continually test your assumptions."— Konrad Billetz, co-founder and co-CEO of Offset Solar

"Entrepreneurship is the mind-set that allows you to see opportunity everywhere. It could be a business idea, but it could also be seeing the possibilities in the people that can help you grow that business." —Preeti Sriratana, co-founder and COO of Sweeten

"Entrepreneurship is seeing an opportunity and gathering the resources to turn a possibility into a reality. It represents the freedom to envision something new and to make it happen. It includes risk, but it also includes the reward of creating a legacy."—Maia Haag, co-founder and president of I See Me! Personalized Books and Gifts

Entrepreneurship—Self-Assessment

One does not just decide to become an entrepreneur. An entrepreneur does entrepreneurial things because of personal characteristics that have developed from family experiences, personal activities, and lifestyle circumstances. Investopedia (2018) suggests that would-be entrepreneurs ask themselves the following questions to assess their personal suitability to the world of entrepreneurial business:

- Do I have the personality, temperament, and mind-set of taking on the world on my own terms?
- Do I have the required personal circumstances and resources to devote all my time to my venture?
- Do I have an exit plan ready with a clearly defined timeline in case my venture does not work?
- Do I have a concrete plan for next "x" months or will I face challenges midway due to family, financial, or other commitments? Do I have a mitigation plan for those challenges?
- Do I have the required network to seek help and advice as needed?
- Have I identified and built bridges with experienced mentors to learn from their expertise?
- Have I prepared the rough draft of a complete risk assessment, including dependencies on external factors?
- Have I realistically assessed the potential of my offering and how it will figure in the existing market?
- If my offering is going to replace an existing product in the market, do I know how my competitors will react?
- To keep my offering secure, will it make sense to get a patent? Do I have the capacity to wait that long?
- Have I identified my target customer base for the initial phase? Do I have scalability plans ready for larger markets?
- Have I identified sales and distribution channels?

Entrepreneurship in Sport, Tourism, and Leisure Services

In sport, tourism, and leisure service organizations, entrepreneurship is not just about coming up with the next great idea that is going to capture the interest of massive markets. In fact, most entrepreneurs in these fields will never do that. What they will do is continually improve and innovate in ways that benefit their customers, clients, and guests while improving the financial position of their organizations.

For example, consider the inspiring yet simple story of Judi Sheppard Missett who, after retiring from professional dancing, taught dance classes in order to earn some extra cash. Her market was comprised mostly of adult women, most of whom were not learning to dance for performance purposes. Judi realized that the women were less interested in form and precision than they were in socializing, losing weight, and toning up. She developed dance-based routines that served those interests, trained instructors to teach the routines, and incorporated her new business under the name of Jazzercise. Franchise deals followed, and there are now over 8,000 Jazzercise locations in the United States and abroad (O'Connor, 2017).

Judi Sheppard Missett did what could be considered the defining act of an entrepreneur. She made a well-thought-out shift of resources from an area of low productivity to an area of high productivity.

There are many opportunities for entrepreneurs in sport, tourism, and leisure services. There are opportunities in the public, private nonprofit, and commercial sectors. There are opportunities in small, medium, and large organizations. Whatever the setting, the entrepreneur is always watching for change, responding to it, and exploiting it as an opportunity. The sport, tourism, and leisure service entrepreneur constantly studies the environment, trends, and conditions, and finds and manages new resources in response thereto.

Summary

Entrepreneurship plays an in important role in sport, tourism, and leisure service organizations. Entrepreneurs are valued in these organizations because of their ability to identify needs and opportunities, and because of their willingness to take risks in implementing well-thought-out plans to find new or re-allocated resources that can be directed to satisfaction of needs or capitalization of opportunities. Entrepreneurs possess unique attributes and skills and can thrive in a corporate environment that supports entrepreneurism. They have much to contribute to the success of a sport, tourism, or leisure service organization.

References

Fernandes, P. (2018). *Business News Daily* Contributing Writer February 19, 2018.

Investopedia. (2018). Retrieved from https://www.investopedia.com/terms/e/entrepreneur.asp

O'Connor, T. (2017). Jazzercise. Franchising Today. Retrieved fromhttp://www.franchising-today.com/sections/profiles/198-jazzercise

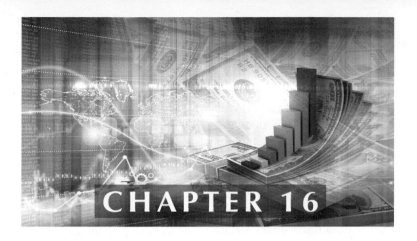

Capital Budgeting

Introduction

Capital budgeting addresses a sport, tourism, and leisure service organization's major expenditures for equipment, buildings, and land. For the most part, sport, tourism, and leisure service organizations manage two budgets—one for operations and another for capital expenditures. Capital budgeting is not directly concerned with the costs of daily activities and functions. It concerns the management of debt and investments in capital resources. Capital budgets are generally approved annually at the same time as the operating budget, but annual capital budgets are just a part of a larger Capital Improvement Program (CIP) that may represent a five- to 10-year period of time. The CIP pulls together all of the identified major asset desires and needs of the organization over a predetermined period of time. Although the CIP extends over a period of years, it is reviewed and updated annually. Capital budgeting is conducted in similar ways in the public, private nonprofit, and commercial sectors. In the public and commercial sectors, sport, tourism, and leisure service organizations may issue bonds for short- or long-term debt, while nonprofit sport, tourism, and leisure service organizations would more likely use a capital campaign, which is an extension of the fund-raising processes discussed in Chapter 13.

Benefits of Capital Budgeting

The use of capital improvement programs and budgets provides some important advantages to organizations. Several of the most important reasons for adopting a capital budget are described below.

High-cost items could have a negative effect on operating budgets if they are included in an operating budget. Organizations desire a level of stability in their operating budgets that shows minimal fluctuation from year to year and responsiveness to public demand. Removing capital items eliminates major fluctuations in the operating budget and presents a more accurate projection of actual operating costs. For example, a public parks and recreation department has an annual operating budget of $2 million, and it constructs a new band shell in a city park at a cost of $450,000. The construction of the band shell is financed through a five-year loan. If this capital expenditure was included in the operating budget, it would increase that annual budget significantly and give a false picture of the organization's financial health. Placing the same $450,000 in a separate capital budget allows the observer and budget manager to readily see how money is being used for operations and for capital development. Capital projects are normally funded from separate capital improvement funds rather than from the operating budget. Some funds and sources may be similar, but other funds, such as general obligation bonds, revenue bonds, and special assessments, are specifically designed for capital projects.

Capital budgeting allows for planned growth and spending. It strives to anticipate specific needs of the organization and to budget for those in advance. If land is to be purchased in the future, current planning can anticipate that and set the stage for securing funds and planning for short- and long-term debt.

Capital budgeting provides focus. It allows the organization to put its energy into a few well-conceived capital projects and purchases rather than be distracted through an inefficient "shotgun" approach.

The Capital Budgeting Process

Capital budgeting allows for planning of expenditures that may have a significant impact on the sport, tourism, and leisure service organization's budget. Capital budgeting is a four-step planning process that involves inventory of capital assets, needs analysis, cost analysis, and financing.

Inventory of Capital Assets

An inventory of capital assets is an essential first step in any capital improvement program. An inventory should include, at least, the following: (1) a description of the type of facility, land, or equipment; (2) the purchase price; (3) any improvements that were made; (4) its current condition; (5) the projected replacement cost for equipment; (6) the depreciated value; and (7) the projected end of the useful life.

The inventory allows the sport, tourism, and leisure service organization to know, at any given point, the status of its capital assets. For example, if vehicles are purchased on a five-year cycle, the inventory can show what year each vehicle was purchased, how many will have to be purchased in the next five years, and any unanticipated need to purchase in advance of the five-year cycle. For a building, the inventory can show the date it was built, the dates and types of renovations made, its current condition, and its current use.

Needs Analysis

A needs analysis looks at the future needs of the organization and attempts to identify how those needs will be met and what capital investments will be required. For example, if a fitness club owner determined she needed to expand her facilities in the next five years, the needs analysis would be a part of the process of determining the type and size of the expansion. A needs analysis also looks at replacement needs. Most organizations assume a certain life span for the equipment that they purchase and use that consideration as they plan for the eventual replacement of that equipment.

Strategic Plan

The strategic plan should be a key element in the needs-assessment process. The strategic plan looks three to five years into the future, providing vision, purpose, goals, and objectives. It provides direction to the capital budgeting process. There are a number of factors that influence the outcome of the needs-analysis process. They include demographics; cultural changes; the local, regional, and national economy; legislation that has an impact (such as the Americans with Disabilities Act); community growth or lack thereof; technological obsolescence; disaster planning; and replacement schedules. Each must be taken into account in the needs assessment.

Cost Analysis

Cost analysis is a decision-making process that helps to pinpoint where to spend available funds for capital improvements. It is not very different from most decision-making processes. The crux of the cost analysis is the determination of where to allocate limited resources in response to seemingly unlimited demands. The inventory and

needs analysis set the stage for cost analysis.

Cost analysis provides key information for the prioritization of projects. There is no single method for establishing priorities. Organizations must take into account a number of variables and weigh each of them accordingly. Some of the variables to consider in the prioritization process include the following:

- Relationship of the project to future needs
- Legal mandates
- Capital costs versus operating costs
- Costs relative to the benefits of competing costs
- Political costs and benefits
- External funding potential
- Impact on improved effectiveness and/or efficiency
- Spin-off benefits
- Costs relative to competing costs
- Financial impact on defined stakeholders
- Relationship of the proposed asset to defined beneficiaries

A four-part approach to cost analysis is suggested. *Part 1* involves determining the turnkey cost of the project. For a new facility, such as a family aquatic center, the turnkey costs would include costs for services, construction, and fees as identified in Figure 16.1.

While those represented activities may not account for all of the costs, they represent a major share of the anticipated costs. Table 16.1 depicts the projected costs, as presented in a capital budget, for a proposed water playground. The budget includes all of the expected costs of the project.

The proposed Family Aquatic Center will have a capacity of 4,200 people (4% of the population) and be open from Memorial Day through Labor Day (99 days). The facility will include a wave action pool, zero-depth leisure pool, activity/water play pool, lazy river with zero-depth entry, flume slide, water-play apparatus, and a flo rider. In addition, the 16-acre facility will have parking for 1,000 cars, internal and external landscaping, support facilities, concession operations, a bath house, wet sand play, sand volleyball, and other amenities. The projected cost of the facility, less administrative costs, utility hookups, and access is $14,700,000.

Land acquisition	**Platting fees**	**Furniture and equipment**
Architectural fees	**Bringing utilities**	**Attorney's fees to the site**
Engineering fees	**Cleaning**	**Interim construction interest**
Debt financing	**Construction costs**	**Landscaping**
Contingency fees	**Project management fees**	**Insurance**

Figure 16.1. Cost Items Associated with a Capital Development Project

Part 2 involves estimating the annual operating costs of the project. Operational costs occur after the purchase or after the project is completed and are typically funded from the operating budget. They include the cost of utilities, staffing, insurance, maintenance, equipment repairs, etc. While construction is a major cost to the organization, operating the facility requires a long-term commitment. The operating budget can begin as a "rough estimate" and then be formalized into a more detailed analysis later. Table 16.2 presents sample data collected from four comparable facilities/sites that can be used in estimating operational costs and revenues for a new family aquatic center.

Always remember that, after building a facility, there will be an ongoing additional cost of operating it. Failure to take the added operational requirements into account could result in serious budget problems. One Midwestern community constructed a 50-meter indoor aquatic complex. When it was completed, the leisure service organization discovered that it had not adequately prepared itself to meet the new operating costs. In order to cover those operating costs, two full-time positions were eliminated.

Part 3 of the cost analysis is a review of the qualitative and quantitative benefits to be derived from the project. In some cases, projects offer a monetary return that may be estimated and compared with their cost. In commercial enterprises, the cost of capital projects is frequently evaluated in terms of the estimated payback period (i.e., the

Table 16.1

Projected Capital Budget Costs for a Water Playground

Item	Size	Estimated Amount	Total
Pre-construction work			**3,500**
1. Topographic survey	Allowance	2,000	
2. Soils Investigation	Allowance	1,500	
Demolition			**40,000**
1. Demolition of existing bath house and pool	L.S.	40,000	
Earthwork			**4,500**
1. Cut and fill on site	350 cu. yd.	4,500	
Water playground			**40,000**
Water play equipment	40,000		
Tee cup (1)			
Tumble buckets (1)			
Rain drop (1)			
Pool Construction			**50,000**
1. Concrete zero-edge pool		50,000	
Water depth 0-18"			
Gals., 28,500			
Bathers, 250-300			
Support Elements			**231,635**
1. Perimeter decks	2,804 sq. ft.	16,824	
2. Admission/Mech./rest rooms	1,296 sq. ft.	142,560	
3. Landscape and restoration	8,360 sq. ft.	25,080	
4. Perimeter fence 6' high, vinyl	356 lin. ft.	7,170	
5. Pool mechanical	L.S.	40,000	
Utilities and Infrastructure			**75,000**
Construction Sub-total			**444,635**
Contingency and Fees			**102,265**
Estimated Project Budget			**$546,900**

Table 16.2

Comparative Data to Help in Estimating Costs of and Revenue from a Family Aquatic Center

Comp. Site	Capacity	Avg. Daily Attendance	Total Season Attendance	Cost Per User	Total Operational Costs	Revenue Per User	Total Revenue
A	4,200	2,115 (50%)	209,385	9.80	2,051,973	10.50	2,198,542
B	3,800	2,020 (52.9%)	198,990	2.30	457,677	4.00	795,960
C	4,400	1,985 (45.1%)	196,515	7.40	1,454,211	8.50	1,670,378
D	4,000	2,300 (57.5%)	227,700	8.00	1,821,600	10.00	2,277,000
Mean	4,100	2,103 (51.3%)	208,148	6,88	1,430,997	8.25	1,717,221

number of years it takes for net revenue from the project to equal or exceed the initial capital investment). In public projects, the payback period may be only one of several considerations. As part of this step, a cash-flow analysis should be conducted (see sample depicted in Table 16.3). Because the proposed project has not incurred costs or received income, the cash-flow analysis uses projections that are based on communities or facilities of comparable size and with similar services (such as in Table 16.2).

Public organizations also consider the social benefits derived from projects. This is less a concern for commercial sports, tourism, and leisure service enterprises. That is why, for example, there are no commercial fire stations in most communities. They simply are not profitable, but their social benefit warrants their public cost. Assessment of the qualitative benefits of a capital project should include consideration of the following:

- Congruence with the vision and mission of the organization.
- Long-range impact on the organization's strategic plan.
- Effect on the organization's image.
- Influence on stakeholders, including primary customers.
- Compliance with mandatory requirements or policy.

Part 4 of the cost analysis requires an evaluation of the project and should be conducted when both the project's costs and the detailed operational and revenue budgets are available. There are two analyses that can be conducted that will help in evaluating the project. The first analysis addresses the need to earn back, in a reasonable amount of time, the original money invested in the capital project. This method of evaluation tells the organization how long it will take for the project's newly generated cash flow to pay for the cost of the capital development that generates the increased cash flows. If a new indoor tennis complex adds a fitness center at a cost of $1.6 million, and it generates revenue of $200,000 per year (after paying operating expenses), then the payback period is eight years.

Payback period = Capital cost/ estimated annual net revenue

Note that the payback period assumes a constant value of the dollar throughout the payback period. There are other ways to calculate the payback period that also account for the impact of time on the value of the dollar. Is a payback period of eight years good or bad? That is for the investor to decide. Whether it is good or bad depends on how long the organization wants to wait to recover its capital development investment.

Table 16.3

Basic Cash Flow Analysis

Month	Jan	Feb	Mar	Apr	...	Dec
Projected Revenue	280,000	300,000	370,000	350,000	...	200,000
Projected Expenses	360,000	320,000	250,000	240,000	...	235,000
Cash Flow	(80,000)	(20,000)	120,000	110,000	...	(35,000)
Net Cash Flow	(80,000)	(100,000)	20,000	130,000	...	266,000

Evaluation of the project can also be facilitated by calculation of the *internal rate of return* (IRR). This provides another way of assessing the investment opportunity cost of the project. The IRR is calculated by equating the initial investment with the present value of the returns and solving for interest rate that validates the equation.

Initial Investment = Annual returns
$$\times\ ((1-(1+i)^{-n})/i)$$

Where: i = the interest rate (IRR), and n = the number of years of receiving the return.

Interest Table C (in the appendices) provides values for $((1-(1+i)^{-n})/i)$. Therefore, the formula can more simply be rewritten as:

Initial Investment = Annual returns
$$\times\ T_C$$

In the above example, a $1.6 million fitness center addition with a projected life of 10 years that generates net revenue of $200,000 per year would have an IRR of approximately 4%. This is calculated as shown below:

Initial Investment = Annual returns
$$\times\ T_C$$
$$\$1,600,000 = \$200,000\ T_C$$
$$T_C = 8.00$$

From Table C, when $n=10$ years and the tabulated value is 8.00, i=approximately .04 (or 4%).

Once the calculations of the two methods are made, projects can be ranked. The payback method is the more common approach in this early judgment phase. If the IRR is calculated, then that figure should be compared to the organization's cost of borrowing. If the IRR is lower than the cost of borrowing, then the project may not be advisable. If, for example, the cost of borrowing the $1.6 million was 7%, then the fitness center addition at the tennis complex would not be built (they are paying 7% to borrow money that pays back 4%). However, a 3.0% interest rate for borrowing capital funds would greatly improve the chances of the fitness center project being approved (they are paying 3% to borrow money that earns 4%).

There are two major approaches to financing any capital project in the public sector. They are referred to as *pay-as-you-go* and *pay-as-you-use*. The pay-as-you-go approach is the most conservative. It requires all the money needed for the project to be available before it is started. The advantage of this method is the avoidance of debt (and the costs of debt servicing). With the entire cost of the project being paid for in advance, there is no concern for the payback period. A disadvantage to pay-as-you-go is, however, that many of those in a mobile and aging population who contributed to building up the cash fund for the project may not ever benefit from its use. Additionally, the time that it takes to save up the needed cash may, because of inflation, erode its purchasing power (see Chapter 18).

The pay-as-you-use approach requires getting into debt for the capital project. Pay-as-you-use allows for the cost of the project to be paid while it is being used. Payments are made from revenues generated by the project or from funds generated through taxes, special levies, fees and charges for services, fund raisers, investors, etc. The argument in support of the pay-as-you-use approach is that those who benefit from the capital asset will be the ones who pay for it. The contrary argument focuses on the increased cost of the project due to debt servicing.

Capital Improvement Revenue Sources

Capital improvements usually require different sources of income than what is used for general operations. Table 16.4 illustrates some of the sources of income used for public capital improvement funding. While some public agencies may use the general fund to provide the necessary revenue for capital improvements, the nature and size of many capital improvements frequently make it inadvisable to rely on this fund.

Table 16.4

Revenue Sources Used by Public Agencies for Capital Improvements

Financing Source	Provides Funds	Re-payment	Advantages	Disadvantages
General Obligation Bond (GOB)	Immediately	All taxpayers over a 5- to 30- year term	• Funds available immediately •Payments tied to benefits received •Potentially lowers interest costs	• Increased property taxes • Competes with local services for limited resources • Separates payment from benefit
Revenue Bonds	Immediately	By users over 5-30 years	• Funds available immediately • Payment linked to benefits • Payment may be linked to users	• Increases rates or fees • Interest costs potentially higher than GOB
Tax Increment Financing Bonds	Immediately	By all taxpayers within defined boundaries	• Ties benefit to specific geographic area • Reduces impact on overall capital budget • Reduces competition for limited resources	• Revenues dependent upon willingness and ability of individuals in area to make payments • Revenues dependent upon growth in assessed values
Bond Banks	Varies	By all taxpayers over 5- to 30- year period	• Particularly helpful for small communities • Lowers cost of insurance	• Bond issuance may be delayed until enough communities apply
Certificates of Participation	Immediate use of land area	By all taxpayers over a defined period of time	• Allows land purchase over a period of time • Payments made annually • Not recommended as formal debt • Does not impact community's debt limit	• Hides debt of community from bond appraisers • Less public control, no vote required
Lease Purchase and Certificates	Immediate use of facility or equipment	By all taxpayers over a 5- to 10-year period	• Provides a way to purchase without issuing debt	• High interest rates • Payments may not be related to benefits

Table 16.4 (cont.)

Real Estate Transfer Tax	Immediately	By individuals transferring or purchasing real property	• Provides income every time property is sold • Places burden for development and renovation on real estate purchases	• Unfairly taxes purchasing and selling homeowners for benefits received by entire community
Impact or Dedication Fees	Immediately	By those purchasing property sold for first time, or by developer	• Allows for new residents in fast-growing areas to pay for improvements, rather than the whole community • Easy to administer and collect • Promotes growth management	• One-time tax only – does not provide for ongoing maintenance • Unfairly taxes developer and new owner for benefits received by entire community
Mitigation Financing	Immediately	By those developing property	• Places burden on developer to provide open space in new development • Takes burden off taxpayer for infrastructure development • Provides local government with flexibility in land acquisition	• Places unfair burden on developer • Allows developer to provide land within development or another location
Revolving Loans	Immediately	By ratepayers over 12-20 years	• Makes funds available immediately • Ties payment to benefit received • Could lower interest costs	• Increased rates or fees and charges • Reporting and administration may be cumbersome • May not be consistent with agency priorities

Most capital improvements involve taking on short-term debt and, in some cases, long-term debt. One of the reasons for taking on debt is that taxpayers and others who will contribute to the cost will not have to suffer a significant financial burden over a short period of time. A $10 million recreation center paid for over 15 years places considerably less annual burden on taxpayers than does the same recreation center paid for in three years. It places the debt into a longer payback period, allowing the agency to structure the debt so it has minimal impact on those who will assist in retiring it. While Table 16.4 demonstrates most of the commonly accepted ways of financing debt, it is not all-inclusive.

Bonds

The traditional source of capital improvement revenue for governments is bonding. Bonding allows public organizations to borrow large sums of money without a significant impact upon the community's tax ability. Bonding provides immediate funding to a state, county, or community at a level it could not achieve in any other way. A bond comes in many forms, but there are two ways of classifying bonds. The first is according to the sources of revenue for repayment by the government, and the second is according to the method of retirement of the bond. They are named, respectively, *serial bonds* and *term bonds*.

Serial Bonds

Serial bonds allow public sport, tourism, and leisure service organizations to make regular payments, usually annually, on both principal and interest for the life of the bond. A serial bond is similar to installment buying; however, governments typically pay a much smaller interest rate because their bonds are guaranteed by the taxing power of the legislative body. *Straight serial bonds* make annual equal payments of principal until the bond maturity is paid. Since the principal payments are made equal, the interest paid is much higher at the beginning of the period and much lower toward the end. This approach to bond payment suggests that the highest payments are made when the facility is new and has the greatest opportunity for revenue generation. The overall value of the payments by the government gradually diminishes over the life of the bond, even though the principal payment remains the same. Tables 16.5 and 16.6 depict the difference between payments on a serial and straight serial bond when interest is set at 4% and the amount received from the bond is $8 million.

Table 16.5

Cost of $8,000,000 Serial Bond (4% Interest Rate)

Year	Principal Paid	Interest Paid	Total Paid	Principal Balance
1	666,328	320,000	986,328	7,333,672
2	692,981	293,347	986,328	6,640,692
3	720,700	265,628	986,328	5,919,992
4	749,528	236,800	986,328	5,170,464
5	779,509	206,819	986,328	4,390,955
6	810,689	175, 638	986,328	3,580,266
7	843,117	143,211	986,328	2,737,149
8	876,842	109,486	986,328	1,860,307
9	911,915	74,412	986,328	948,392
10	948,392	37,936	986,328	0
Total	8,000,000	1,863,280	9,863,280	

Table 16.6

Cost of $8,000,000 Straight Serial Bond (4% Interest Rate)

Year	Principal Paid	Interest Paid	Total Paid	Principal Balance
1	800,000	320,000	1,120,000	7,200,000
2	800,000	288,000	1,088,000	6,400,000
3	800,000	256,000	1,056,000	5,600,000
4	800,000	224,000	1,024,000	4,800,000
5	800,000	192,000	992,000	4,000,000
6	800,000	160,000	960,000	3,200,000
7	800,000	128,000	928,000	2,400,000
8	800,000	96,000	896,000	1,600,000
9	800,000	64,000	864,000	800,000
10	800,000	32,000	832,000	0
Total	8,000,000	176,000	9,760,000	

Serial annuity bonds provide for an equal payment each year until the debt is paid. In the early years of a bond, the bulk of the payment is to cover interest charges. In the later years, the bulk of the payment is to reduce the principal.

A *term bond* is paid off with a single payment at the end of the loan period. The public agency must establish a *sinking fund* where funds are deposited over the life of the bond. The interest generated from the funds received from the bond and the annual deposits guarantees payment at the end of the borrowing period. This is a situation where the future value of a sum must be calculated in order to determine how much to allocate to the sinking fund each year. The term bond has fallen into disfavor because of the difficulty of managing the fund and attempting to project interest payments. Most state governments have legislatively abandoned the use of sinking fund bonds.

The second major method of classifying bonds is by the sources of revenue that will be used to repay the debt. Public sport, tourism, and leisure service agencies have undertaken a variety of approaches to bonding.

The most common bonding method used by public agencies is the *General Obligation Bond* (GOB). GOBs are issued by a public agency with the expectation of providing benefits to the entire community. Almost every community, has issued some type of GOB. Because the benefits of GOBs are to the entire community the retirement of the debt is also spread across the entire community. Retirement of debt is most frequently accomplished through increases in real property taxes. General obligation bonds are particularly attractive to investors because they are exempt from federal income tax. In some instances they may be exempt from state and local taxes. Furthermore, GOBs are insured by the full faith and credit of the city, county, or state. This makes them a very secure source of income for an investor, even if the interest rates are not high. The major opposition to GOBs is the increase in property taxes. In public parks and recreation, this has been a particular challenge over the years. Recently, the level

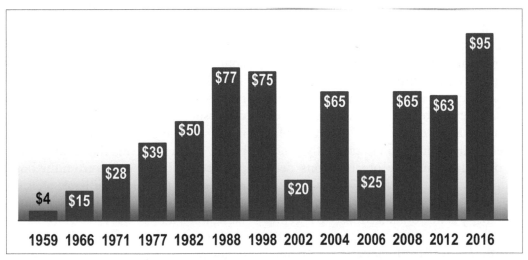

Figure 16.2. Annual Value ($millions) of Fairfax County Park Authority General Obligation Bonds (1959-2016) (Source: Fairfax County Park Authority)

of bonding has increased significantly, as has general public acceptance of the value of parks and recreation. Figure 16.2 illustrates the extent and variability of bond financing for parks and recreation development in one community (Fairfax County, Virginia).

Revenue bonds have received increased attention and emphasis over the past three decades. Revenue bonds are used to finance a revenue-producing facility with the anticipation that revenues from the facility will wholly retire the bond. Increasingly, facilities such as aquatic parks, golf courses, artificial ice arenas, and recreation centers have been financed through this method. A major challenge of the use of revenue bonds is to ensure that there is sufficient revenue to both retire the debt and also to operate and maintain the facility. In some cases, subsidization has been used to finance operations and capital improvements. In most cases, however, the emphasis has been upon the facility generating sufficient revenue to cover both operating and debt retirement expenses.

Certificates of participation are authorized in about 25 states and allow public entities to purchase land and pay for it over a period of time. When a willing seller and a public agency enter into a certificate of participation, the public agency agrees to pay a specific price for the land and to make annual payments for a designated period. A certificate of participation does not require a public referendum and, most importantly, is not counted against the organization's debt limit.

Tax increment financing bonds (TIFs) allow public organizations to secure financing for projects that are enclosed within a political boundary. Commonly used to finance public improvements in development areas (sometimes called redevelopment districts), TIFs have been used to support sport, tourism, and recreation developments. They are most common in urban areas but have been used in some rural areas. Implementation of a TIF plan freezes the assessed valuation of real property within the designated area. It does not freeze the tax rate. Taxes are collected on the property at the base level while investments are made by public agencies, and new businesses are attracted and property values thereby increase. Project costs or bond costs are paid for from additional sales tax revenues, personal income tax revenues, and the increased assessed value of the property. Bonds issued from TIF districts are paid for only on the projected increase of the value of the property, not on the full faith and credit of the city. TIF districts are common throughout the United States and may provide opportunities for the purchase and development of new park land, as well as renovation of existing parks.

Bond banks are usually organized at the state level for the purpose of allowing government entities that might not have sufficient borrowing power or debt rating to secure an acceptable interest rate. Bond banks allow multiple governmental entities to pool their bond requests into a single bond sale. By pooling their resources, smaller governmental agencies can issue a larger bond and secure a more advantageous interest rate. The public entities desiring the bonds are not purchasing them directly from the bond market, but from a bond bank typically established by a state. The Maine Bond Bank, for example, was established by the legislature in 1972 to provide a unique financing program allowing Maine towns, cities, counties, school systems, water districts, sewer districts, or other governmental entities access to national money markets for their public-purpose borrowing needs. The Maine Bond Bank retains a high investment rating and is able to secure bonds at a low interest rate and then purchase bonds from public agencies. Local agencies submit an application to the bond bank, and it is evaluated on the purpose of the bond, estimated cost, construction schedule, state and local valuation, tax levy or user charges, demographic trends, recent financial and debt history, and economic stability. The local agency is able to sell bonds to the bond banks at their lower interest rates.

Other Capital Improvement Revenue Sources

Lease Purchases and Certificates

Lease purchases and certificates are becoming more common among public sport, tourism, and leisure service organizations as a method of financing projects. This alternative allows a public agency to join with private sources to finance major projects. In most cases, a nonprofit holding corporation is created. This nonprofit holding corporation can purchase, develop, and operate the property. Usually, however, the nonprofit organization will purchase and develop the property and lease it to the public entity that will operate it. The lease is an annual or multiyear lease with an automatic renewal and an option for the public agency to purchase the developed land at any time. The leasing organization makes the lease payments from revenue generated from use of the property. Then the nonprofit holding corporation uses the lease payment to retire the principal and interest. When the debt for the property is paid, it can then be given to the public agency, and the nonprofit holding corporation can be dissolved. The nonprofit corporation has no taxing power, but it can help the public agency to avoid a risky and expensive requirement to hold a public referendum on the capital project. In many ways, a lease purchase and certificate program is similar to issuing revenue bonds.

Real Estate Transfer Tax

Real estate transfer tax is levied on the sale of certain classes of property, such as residential, commercial, and industrial. The tax generally increases with the size and value of the property being transferred (sold). Tax rates are controlled by state legislatures, but the revenues from this source of income are generally collected at the county level. It has become a particularly acceptable form of income for public agencies to accommodate the needs that urban growth places upon community services. The allocation of these taxes for natural resources development has become more commonplace. Florida and Maryland were pioneers in requiring that a portion of these taxes be used for park and recreation acquisition and development. Real estate transfer taxes are a fairly reliable source of income, since they are imposed each time property is transferred.

Impact or Dedication Fees

Impact or dedication fees are assessed by local governments in connection with new housing and commercial developments. Their purpose is to defray the cost of providing new or expanded public facilities that are necessary to serve the development. The fees typically require cash payments in advance of the completion of development, are based on a methodology and calculation derived from the cost of the facility and the nature and size of the development, and are used to finance improvements away from, but of benefit to, the development. Local governments throughout the country are increasingly using impact fees to shift more of the costs of financing public facilities from the general taxpayer to the beneficiaries of those new facilities.

The impact or dedication fees supplement local government resources that otherwise have decreased because of diminished state and federal transfers of funds. Local governments have also used impact fees to delay or serve as a substitute for general property tax increases. Impact fees, when based on a comprehensive plan and used in conjunction with a sound capital improvement plan, can be an effective tool for ensuring adequate infrastructure to accommodate growth where and when it is anticipated. In Noblesville, Indiana, for example, the Parks and Recreation Department receives an average of $100 for every new home built. This contributes significantly to the department's annual capital budget.

Revolving Loans

Revolving loans allow an organization to secure a specified amount of money for a specified period of time. A line of credit is authorized, and the sport, tourism, and leisure service organization can then draw off of the line of credit to finance specific projects or equipment purchases. Revolving loans usually carry a higher interest rate than other financial resources. Their value lies in the ability of the organization to have immediate access to a level of funds without requiring an extensive approval process.

Revolving funds have been successfully used with smaller, short-term projects, where debt retirement payments will be made from a secure source. It is not generally considered an effective method for financing major projects.

Mitigation Land Bank

The mitigation land bank has long been a source of development resources for public leisure service organizations. The bank allows developers to either dedicate land in a development for open space preservation or to identify off-site locations they will dedicate. The administering public agency and the developer work together to identify suitable land. The governmental entity may have the authority to create a land bank where developers can substitute money or land in another area of the community for land they are developing. In one Iowa community, the parks and recreation department worked with local developers to acquire a greenbelt along a stream in the community, preserving it for future generations. The use of the land bank is particularly useful when the developer has failed to meet the requirements of land dedication during the development phase of the project.

Special Taxes

Special taxes, such as the transient occupancy tax (also called a bed tax or lodging tax) and the meal tax, can also be used as revenue sources for tourism capital projects. While these funds are typically used to operate destination marketing organizations, they can be and are used to endow grant programs that support local capital projects designed to create a well-balanced tourist destination.

Capital Budgeting in the Commercial Sector

Capital budgeting in the commercial sector is a little different from that in the public or private nonprofit sectors. There are some key differences that need to be highlighted here. Commercial sport and leisure service organizations bond for one of four reasons:

- **Replacement projects.** Investments in new equipment to replace old, worn out, or damaged equipment.
- **Cost-reduction projects.** Replacing existing equipment with new equipment that may operate more efficiently, be more state of the art, or be required to keep up with customer expectations.
- **Safety/environmental projects.** Investments required to comply with safety and/or environmental regulations.
- **Expansion projects.** The expansion of existing services and resources.

All sport, tourism, and leisure service organizations should have a long-range plan or a capital project that corresponds with their corporate vision. Essential components of a capital project proposal include market forecasts, revenue projections, acquisition and construction cost estimates, anticipated operating expenses, and expected profit. The information collected for the capital project proposal helps the organization to have a better understanding of the long-term financial implications of the proposed capital expenditure. Although public and nonprofit sport, tourism, and leisure service organizations may emphasize the merit approach to a capital project, a commercial sport, tourism, and leisure service organization must emphasize the profit approach. The capital budgeting process involves project evaluation and decision making. These are typically approached from an accounting perspective, with emphasis on the net present value, cash flow, and payback period.

Decision Processes

Several different decision tools are used by commercial sport and leisure service organizations to determine the potential contribution of a capital project to the financial health of the organization. One common method is to determine the present value of the returns generated by the project and compare that value to the investment amount. The *net present value* (NPV) is the difference between the present value of returns and the initial investment. In the decision-making process for a capital project, the investor wants to know if additional value is created by undertaking the project. If the NPV is positive, it means that the present value of the investment, and therefore, the project, will add value to the firm and also increase the wealth of the owners. Therefore, the Net Present Value Decision Rule is:

If NPV > 0, then the project meets the standard for approval.

To determine NPV, the organization must anticipate the future cash flow. Cash flow represents earnings before depreciation, amortization, and non-cash charges. For example, a fitness center invests $100,000 in new fitness equipment, supplementing what it already has. It is estimated that, as a result of the investment, an additional cash flow of $22,000 will be realized each year for the next five years. The expected market interest rate (i.e., the interest rate that could be reasonably expected by any other investment carrying the same degree of risk) during those five years is eight percent.

If returns are equal (i.e., the same amount each year), the NPV can be calculated by applying the formula:

$$NPV = RT_C - C$$

Where: R = annual returns, C = the initial investment, and $T_C = (1 - (1 + i)^{-n}/i)$ or the corresponding value found in Table C at the end of this book.

In this example,

$$NPV = \$22,000 \, T_C - \$100,000$$
$$= \$22,000 \, (3.993) - \$100,000$$
$$= -\$12,154$$

The NPV is negative; therefore, the investment is not advisable.

If the annual returns are unequal (which is a more likely scenario), a different way of calculating NPV must be used. If, for example, the $100,000 five-year investment in a market where eight percent interest is expected yields cash flows of $30,000 in year 1, $29,000 in year 2, $26,000 in year 3, $25,000 in year 4, and $18,000 in year 5, then the present values can be calculated by multiplying each year's returns by an appropriate interest factor to determine the present values. The present values are then summed, and the initial investment is subtracted from the total present value of the returns. This results in a calculated NPV. The interest factor to be used is found in Table B at the end of this book. Table 16.7 shows present values for the preceding example.

The cash flows described above and shown in Table 16.7 have a combined present value that is greater than the initial investment. According to the NPV decision rule, this is a good investment.

Figure 16.3 illustrates how NPV is calculated using a timeline. The timeline illustrates the increased revenue at the end of each year, beginning with the $100,000 investment and a market interest rate of 10 percent. In this example, returns during each of the five years are $38,000, $47,000, $58,000, $70,000, and $79,000.

NPV takes into account the time value of money. The time value of money suggests that a dollar invested today is worth more than a dollar in the future, because the dollar received today can earn interest up until the time the future dollar is received, or that inflation will diminish its relative purchasing power over time. To account for the time value of money, the interest factor from Table B is used to determine the present value.

Table 16.7

Sample Data for NPV Decision Using Unequal Returns (8% Interest)

Year	Cash Flow	T$_B$	Present Value
1	30,000	.926	27,780
2	29,000	.857	24,853
3	26,000	.794	20,644
4	25,000	.735	18,375
5	18,000	.681	12,258
Total			103,910

Figure 16.3. Net Present Value Timeline

Another approach to decision-making is to determine the *payback period* (discussed earlier). The payback period is the length of time it takes to recover the initial cost of a project. Payback is usually measured in years. The shorter the payback period, the better the investment. The formula for determining the payback period is illustrated below. This formula is used when the return on the project is expected to be consistent from year to year. If a project cost $100,000, and it expected a $22,000 return each year, it would take 4.55 years to pay for the project.

Cost of Project/Annual Cash Flow = Payback Period

$100,000/$22,000 = 4.55 years

When the return varies each year, as in Table 16.7, simply add up the expected returns for each succeeding year, until the total cost of the project is equaled. In this case, the payback period would be achieved early in the fifth year. There are some disadvantages to the payback period approach to evaluating capital projects. A payback period approach assumes that cash inflows (or revenue) will exceed cash outflows (or expenses). Second, a payback calculation does not usually consider the time value of money. In a payback model, the interest the money could achieve is not considered.

To calculate the payback period while also accounting for the time value of the investment, use the same formula that was used earlier to calculate the IRR. Instead of solving for i (the interest rate), solve for n (number of years). For example, in a 5% investment environment, the payback period for the $100,000 project that generates $22,00 in annual cash flows can more accurately be calculated as follows:

Initial Investment = Annual returns x T_C
$$\$100,000 = \$22,000\ T_C$$
$$T_C = 4.55$$

From Interest Table C (in the appendices), when i=5% and the tabulated value is 4.55, n = just over 5 years.

Using the same technique, the payback period in an 8% market is determined to be almost six years, and in a 2% market the payback period would be less than five years.

Income Sources of Commercial Capital Projects

The same two approaches to financing capital projects in the public sector are also used in the commercial and nonprofit sectors. They are referred to as pay-as-you-go and pay-as-you-use. It was noted earlier in this chapter that the pay-as-you-go approach assumes the availability of all the money needed for the project before it is started. The pay-as-you-use approach incurs debt for the capital investment that is paid off during the use of the asset.

Corporate bonds are another common method of securing funds for capital projects. A corporate bond involves lending money to a publicly held corporation. In return, the lender is promised a fixed rate of return on the investment, with the loan to be repaid in full at a future date (maturity). Corporate bonds are usually issued in multiples of $1,000 or $5,000. Bonds are sold with different maturity dates. Maturity tells the investors when they can expect to get their principal back and for how long they will receive interest payments. For example, a $1,000 bond that matures 10 years in the future can be redeemed at the end of the 10 years for its face value

of $1,000, and the purchaser of the bond certificate will also received fixed interest payments (returns) in each of those years until maturity. If the annual returns are $45, by the end of the 10 years the bond purchaser will have received ten payments of $45 in addition to the $1,000 face value of the bond.

Receipts from the Bond = (10 x $45) +
$$\$1,000 = \$1,450$$

The amount of money that the purchaser receives is not the value of the bond. The money is received in the future (annually for returns and after 10 years for the initial $1,000) and has lost some real value because of inflation or loss of potential investment income from alternate sources. The true value of a bond is calculated by adding the time-adjusted (present) values of the returns to the time-adjusted (present) value of the face value at maturity.

$$\text{Value of Bond} = RT_C + BT_b$$

where R = annual returns, B = the face value of the bond, and T_C and T_B are table values that correspond to the time until maturity (n) and the market interest rate (i).

The market rate refers to the best rate of return that the investor could confidently expect from any other investment opportunity. If an investor is considering purchasing stock that he feels will earn a 6% return over the next 10 years, then he will calculate the value of a 10-year, $1,00 bond that pays $45 annually as follows:

Value of Bond = $RT_C + BT_B$
Value of Bond = $\$45(T_C) + \$1,000\ (T_B)$
Value of Bond = $\$45(7.360)$ + $\$1,000(0.614)$ = ($\$331.2 + \$614$) = $\$945.20$

Note that the calculated value of the bond is less than its face value. The investor will pay no more than $945.20 for the bond because to do so would mean he will earn less money than would be realized through his other 6% investment option. This comparative rate will influence the value of a bond and, therefore, the number of bonds that need to be sold in order to obtain the desired cash for a proposed capital investment. As a general rule, if the coupon rate (annual return/face value of the bond) is less than the market rate, the value of the bond is less than its face value. If the coupon rate is higher than the market rate, the bond value is higher than its face value. In the preceding example, the coupon rate was 4.5% ($45/$1,000) and the market rate was 6%. Therefore, the true value of the bond ($945.20) was less than its $1,000 face value.

Corporate bonds are divided into three groups: short-term notes, which mature in one to two years; medium-term bonds, which mature in five to 12 years; and long-term bonds, which extend beyond 12 years before maturing.

There are three types of corporate bonds. *Mortgage bonds* issue bonds backed by real estate and/or other physical assets. Just as with a home that is mortgaged, if the corporation defaults on the bond, the real estate and/or physical assets are sold to pay the mortgage bond. *Equipment trust certificates* are similar to automobile loans. Traditionally, the corporation provides 20 percent of the cost of the capital project. The balance is then paid off over the next 15 years. When it is paid off, the trustee provides the corporation with a clear title. The final type of corporate bond is an *income

bond.* Income bonds only pay interest if earned, and to the extent it was earned. There is no set time when the bonds must be paid off. Usually, such bonds are issued by firms in bankruptcy. Additionally, the bond holders are frequently the creditors of the bankrupt firm.

Summary

All sport, tourism and leisure service organizations engage in operational budgeting and most are also involved in capital budgeting. Capital budgeting is the process of securing funds for major expense that do not occur regularly and usually result in a long-life resource. The separation of operational and capital budgets helps to maintain consistency in operations and allows appropriate focus on capital needs. There are many sources of capital funds and some are better suited to public organizations than are others. Private nonprofit organizations have their own special capital development opportunities and constraints, and utilize unique criteria in evaluating capital projects. Commercial enterprises view capital projects as financial investments and apply evaluation criteria that reflect the need to realize the best possible return on investment. Useful tools in evaluating a capital investment opportunity include assessments of internal rate of return, payback period, and net present value.

An important source of capital funds can be the sale of bonds. There are several types of bonds and each has advantages and disadvantages in particular situations. Corporate bonds have face values and true values that may not be the same. The true value of a bond to its issuer is what an investor is willing to pay for it.

CHAPTER 17

Business Planning

Introduction

The oft-repeated advice to sport, tourism, and leisure service managers to develop and follow business plans is too commonly relegated to the "nice concept, but not for me" file. For some managers, this ignorance (the act of ignoring the advice) is based on ignorance (a lack of understanding or knowledge). Business plans, it is erroneously believed, are for high-risk, high-volume production companies that depend on major investments and have a high degree of accountability to investors. Just as erroneously, some sport, tourism, and leisure service managers believe that business plans are master planning documents that establish general directions only for the entire organization and are of little direct relevance to specific programs or events. The business plan is an effective tool for the management of sport, tourism, and leisure service organizations. Failure to develop and follow business plans at a variety of levels of operation is a serious management flaw that this chapter is designed to help overcome.

A business plan is a written document that describes all aspects of an enterprise. An enterprise could be a program, service, event, or activity. The business plan differs from a program plan in its inclusion of detailed analyses of resource opportunities, requirements, and management functions. It is especially concerned with (but not limited to) the financial elements of the sport, tourism, or leisure enterprise. It is, in effect, the management "game plan." The business plan is a proven and effective tool for facilitating an internal evaluation of existing or proposed programs or services. It helps those who have dreams and aspirations to objectively determine the desirability and feasibility of their ideas. It helps to identify and consider all conditions that relate to the potential success of an enterprise. Business planning, like other types of planning, forces a manager to seriously consider everything that is necessary for the success of the enterprise. It identifies foreseeable problems and expresses specific commitments to the resolution of those problems. It also identifies available resources and articulates the intended application of those resources to the achievement of stated objectives.

Beyond serving this internal evaluation function, the business plan also helps to meet the information and documentation requirements of external providers of required operational resources. The plan states the objectives to be met by the enterprise and then outlines the chosen approach to meeting those objectives. In so doing, it allows investors, lenders, donors, regulators, suppliers, employees, and customers to develop confidence in the enterprise and, thereby, justify extending credit, permission, patronage, or other support that is needed for success. Readers of the business plan will view it from different perspectives and focus on those elements that are relevant to their interests. Bankers, for example, will read business plans and pay particular attention to descriptions of fixed assets and available collateral. This information helps to determine how well their loans are protected and how ably the borrower can repay loans on schedule and at the agreed-upon rate of interest. Suppliers, such as the owner of a sports stadium, will focus on market and competitive analyses and expect the business plan to demonstrate a reasonable expectation of corporate viability and longevity before entering into a long-term lease

agreement with, for example, a minor league baseball team. Furthermore, prospective major charitable donors will study the management and product/service elements of the business plan of a nonprofit youth-serving agency to learn about how their philanthropic support would be used. In the tourism industry, investors will look carefully at the financial projections in the business plan before deciding about investing in a resort or attraction.

Format of the Business Plan

The following paragraphs describe the essential elements of and a commonly used format for effective business plans. Note that such documents do provide for the demonstration of creativity in presentation, and there is a wide variety of styles used in business plans for sport, tourism, and leisure enterprises.

Title Page

The title page or cover page is used to identify the plan at a glance. Obviously, the name of the enterprise should be boldly displayed. Also, the name, address, and telephone number of the plan's author (or corporate agent for whom the plan was prepared) should be included on the title page. The aesthetic aspects of the cover page do deserve attention, but inordinate energy and resources should not be dedicated to this part of what is really a rather technical document. The entire business plan should be professional in its presentation, both visually and substantively, and the cover page is a good place to demonstrate this standard.

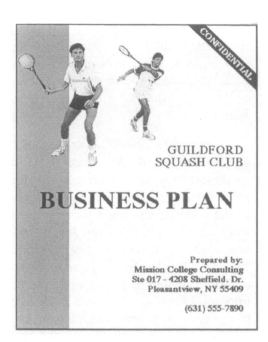

Figure 17.1 Sample Business Plan Cover Page

Inasmuch as business plans articulate ideas that may provide a competitive advantage or should more appropriately be unveiled in a controlled setting, the title page should, where applicable, include a clear notice of the confidential nature of the document. If the business plan is a confidential or restricted-distribution document, then the restrictions should be clearly stated either on the cover or very early on in the document.

Front Matter

Included in the front matter are all those parts of the plan that are organized for ease of reading. Following the title page, a transmittal letter or preface officially introduces the plan to the reader. This brief section (usually less than one page of text) can also be used to "hook" the reader by highlighting some major points of the plan that would be of particular interest. The preface is followed by a table of contents, which offers the reader an outline of the plan by listing all the headings and subheadings. In addition to its value as an overview of the contents of the plan, this table provides references to the locations of various sections in the plan. The front matter might also include a table of tables or a table of figures to further assist the reader in finding key information within the body of the business plan.

Executive Summary

The executive summary is a concise review of plan highlights that enables the reader to quickly get a sense of the nature of the sport, tourism, or leisure enterprise and the resource needs of its management team. It must be brief enough (two to three pages) that even the busiest person could find time to read it, and it should be crafted in such a way as to capture the reader's interest and motivate further exploration and consideration of the plan. Although the executive summary is positioned at the beginning of the business-plan document, its writing should be done after the main body of the plan has been completed. Some business managers have also appended to the Executive Summary a "Fact Sheet," which states, in number form, the following:

1. The name of the sport, tourism, or leisure organization and the program or enterprise covered by the plan.
2. The address and telephone number of the organization representative responsible for the program or enterprise.
3. The type of industry (Standard Industrial Classification) in which the organization operates.
4. The form of agency organization (government agency, proprietorship, partnership, or corporation).

5. The principal product(s) or service line(s) included in the plan.
6. Any registered patents, trademarks, or service marks affected by the plan.
7. The number and names of founders, partners, corporate commissioners, and shareholders.
8. The length of time the enterprise and the organization have been operating as such.
9. The current and/or projected market share.
10. The funds invested in the enterprise to date and their source.
11. Any additional financing required.
12. Proposed terms and payback period for required financing.
13. The total value or net worth of the organization.
14. The names of business advisors (legal counsel, accountant, others).

The Enterprise

The first section of the body of the business plan is designed to provide the reader with a context in which to consider all the information that follows. This important part of the business plan effectively familiarizes the reader with the history of the enterprise and the organization, provides insight into the current situation, and speculates about the future of the enterprise. Historical information is presented in the form of a narrative about how, when, and why the enterprise was or will be started, as well as an identification of the key individuals directing the activity and a description of the principal products or services to be offered. If the business plan has been developed for an existing activity, a discussion of the success experienced thus far should be included. The description of current conditions is limited to relevant circumstances, such as market opportunities, production

capabilities, and competition, while speculation about the future takes the form of vision statements and articulated goals, objectives, and strategies.

The Industry

The preparation of this second section of the body of the document provides an opportunity for careful examination and description of the nature and scope of the industry in which the enterprise will operate. Since it is likely that at least one of the readers of the business plan has little familiarity with the industry or field, this part of the business plan is important because it brings all readers up to the same high level of understanding and awareness that the plan's author has of the environment in which the plan will be implemented. Other readers who are in the industry may already have that understanding, but nonetheless will welcome the author's demonstration of environmental consciousness. The principal characteristics of the industry to be described in the business plan include its size, sales/participation levels, and performance standards. For example, the business plan of a public learn-to-swim program would include a description of the number of such programs offered in the community, region, state, and country. In addition, the total number of program participants, the time of year that courses are typically offered, and the number of badges awarded at each level of instruction would be useful information to offer.

This analysis of the industry will also identify the major participants in the industry and describe their market niches, market shares, strengths and advantages, and weaknesses or disadvantages. The manager of the public swimming program might, for example, explain that aquatic instructional programs in the area are offered by several agencies, including the YMCA, the Boys & Girls Club, and the Community School Corporation. She would then point out that the Boys & Girls Club and the schools do not offer summer programs, and the YMCA has a recreational orientation for its family-based membership. The public agency is targeting young adolescents in the summer season for a highly structured program of aquatic safety training. It will compete with the YMCA to some degree, but it has a competitive advantage through pricing and location.

Further understanding of the industry is promoted by a discussion of industry trends. This requires a careful study of past performances in light of past conditions, as well as speculation about future successes based on an educated guess as to how the relevant operating environment will be. Fortunately, many elements of the sport, tourism, and leisure service industry are closely monitored, and trend analyses are readily available. For example, the trends in aquatic programming are discussed in a variety of publications, such as the regular *Parks & Recreation* magazine special issues on aquatics. The business plan for the learn-to-swim program might emphasize and detail an industry-wide observation that interest in such programs is increasing.

Product/Service Offering

In describing the product or service that will be delivered to consumers, the business plan should focus on its unique features and emphasize its particular advantages. If a novel concept is being introduced, more detail will be required in its description than would be in the description of a product or service with which the reader is already very familiar. In this section of the business plan document, it may be sufficient to describe a proposed three-on-three basketball tournament with just a scant reference to the rules of play and play-down structure and a slightly more descriptive account of the scheduling, setting, and game format to be applied. Conversely, a proposed ice-sculpting competition and winter festival would warrant extensive explanation of the purpose of the event, nature of the activity, schedule of events, qualifications for participation, warm weather alternatives, theme guidelines, site selection, security measures, etc. This is the section of the business plan that is used to ensure that its readers know exactly what the program, service, good, or event is that they are to consider while examining the other important information presented later in the plan.

If the sport, tourism, or leisure product is not in the public domain and is protected by copyright, patent, or other proprietary rights, the nature of that protection should be described in this section. Any contract releases received or awarded should also be identified. It is important for sport, tourism, and leisure service managers to assure the readers of their business plan that the products they "sell" are rightfully theirs to produce or distribute. For example, a sports merchandiser's business plan should state that his invention, the portable heat-generating arena cushion, is patented. If the cushion is to be adorned with the logo of a professional hockey team, the merchandiser will also need to articulate the rights he has to use the logo, as stated in the copyright permission or license agreement.

This part of the business plan also provides an opportunity to discuss the ways in which the product or service under consideration contributes to the realization of organizational objectives. It should include an estimate of the potential for this enterprise to grow, or, if it is a program within a larger set of programs and services, its contribution to the effectiveness, stability, profitability, and growth of the sport, tourism, and leisure organization should be described.

Market Analysis

In the previous section of the business plan, the product was described. Of course, a well-defined product is of little value to the sport, tourism, and leisure service organization if there are no consumers of that product. Potential consumers constitute the market, and understanding the market is vital to the success of the sport, tourism, or leisure enterprise.

The business plan describes the relatively homogeneous group(s) of individuals that might be customers, clients, program participants, or service recipients. This description should clearly establish that the target market is (1) large enough to warrant the offering of a program or service; (2) sufficiently distinct to guide product development, distribution, pricing, and promotion decisions; and (3) accessible to the sport, tourism, or leisure service organization. It may be that the target market is made up of several meaningful market segments; if so, each segment should be described separately. Readers of the business plan will be interested in knowing who and where the market is, what makes individuals in the target market good customer/client candidates, and how successful the organization has been in the past in serving their needs.

It is likely that there will be some form of competition for the attention and resources of the target market. Significant forms of competition include the following:

- Other sport, tourism, and leisure services offered by the organization
- Services and products offered by other sport, tourism, and leisure organizations with access to the same market(s)
- Other discretionary activities available to the target market
- Market inertia

The market analysis includes an assessment of the strengths, weaknesses, advantages, and disadvantages of all major competitors, along with a statement of how the sport, tourism, and leisure service organization plans to address the competitive challenge. Based on the organization's understanding of the market's needs, constraints, and opportunities, as well as an awareness of the competition it faces in the marketplace, it is also expected that this section of the business plan will include a realistic and defensible estimate of the share of the market that can be attracted at different stages of the enterprise's development. It is understood that estimates are nothing more than educated guesses based on relevant information and certain assumptions. The assumptions, therefore, should also be stated.

Marketing Plan

Marketing plans are usually separate, extensive documents that relate market conditions to strategic decisions about product development, sales and distribution, pricing, and promotion. The business plan incorporates a synopsis of the marketing plan and provides the reader with a clear sense of how the organization will manage the marketing of its sport, tourism, or leisure product throughout that product's lifetime. Since some elements of a full marketing plan are addressed in the preceding sections of the business plan, this section will focus on pricing, distribution, and promotion matters:

Pricing. The business plan should discuss the price that will be set for the sport, tourism, and leisure service products of the organization. In addition, the following questions (among others) should be answered:

- How are these prices determined?
- What cost-recovery ratio(s) do these prices reflect?
- How do they compare to those charged by competitors?
- How will these prices contribute to achievement of the organization's financial goals?
- What will be the impact of price changes on consumer responsiveness?

Distribution. How, when, and where the sports, tourism, or leisure service will be delivered to the consumer is also of great interest to the reader of the business plan. This section would normally include descriptions of the service area, season(s) of operation, schedule of marketable events, sales force, and locations of service delivery.

Promotion. The promotions mix (which might include advertising, publicity, personal selling, public relations, and/or sales promotions) should be described in order for the reader to judge the likelihood of the sport, tourism, or leisure service organization reaching its target market and effectively facilitating a desired exchange. The promotions budget should be outlined, along with a process for assessing the impact of the various strategies employed in the promotional plan. Financially oriented readers would be interested in seeing an estimate of the conversion ratio. The conversion ratio is simply an estimate of the consumption (sales revenue or participation) directly resulting from promotion activities in relation to the costs of implementing those promotional activities. For example, the conversion ratio for a $2,500 advertising campaign that increased sales of karate lessons by $12,500 is a respectable 5:1.

Development Plan

If the product around which the enterprise is being established is not fully developed at the time of the business plan's preparation, then this section may be used to report on the status of the product's development. All costs associated with getting the product into a marketable form should be identified, along with development schedules. The improvement, refinement, or expansion of existing or market-ready products may also be considered in this section. Again, development schedules and associated costs should be identified.

Production/Operations Plan

In the production of sport, tourism, and leisure services, there are certain aspects of operation that contribute significantly to the success of the enterprise. They include location, facilities and equipment, and labor. For most businesses, including sport, tourism, and leisure service enterprises, the three most important details are said to be "location, location, location." Consider, for example, the obvious folly of establishing an alpine ski shop in the plains of west Texas, or a mountaineering school in Saskatchewan. A less obvious but equally disastrous mistake might occur in offering a public recreation program at a neighborhood park which, unbeknownst to the recreation agency, has become a place of clandestine drug distribution.

Such mistakes do sometimes occur quite innocently, but the opportunity exists in this section of the business plan to show that every reasonable care was exercised in selecting a location that will contribute to the realization of business goals.

Any facilities and/or major equipment that is required to operate the sport, tourism, or leisure service should be described in the business plan. Sometimes sample floor plans or photographs of buildings and rooms are included to help the reader visualize those physical needs. Recognizing that not all buildings or equipment must be owned by the organization in order for them to be used in production or service delivery, a listing of leased and purchased items should be presented, along with the costs of such properties.

In general terms, the labor requirements should be described. Especially in the delivery of sport, tourism, and leisure services, personnel are key to the success of the enterprise, and the labor needs of the organization deserve careful scrutiny. In this section of the business plan, the number of employees and their general job duties should be discussed. Sometimes, business plans also describe the qualification requirements of employees, their availability (i.e., the number of qualified people in the area that could be hired), compensation and benefits programs, and union affiliations.

Management Team

Even with a good product and a meaningful, identifiable, and accessible target market, a sport, tourism, or leisure service or program can experience limited success because of managers who are not well suited to the enterprise. The business plan provides an opportunity to identify the management team and expound on that team's qualifications for directing the program or service. For many readers of the business plan, this information is as important, or even more important, than the details of the program, market, or financial structure. They believe that the right person managing the enterprise will make sure that the product is good and the financial aspects of the activity are sound.

An organizational chart focusing on the management structure could be used to illustrate hierarchies and functional responsibilities. Whether in chart form or as a narrative, the names of each member of the management team or program leadership staff should be listed, along with brief résumés and annotated job descriptions for each person. More complete résumés and job descriptions can be appended to the business plan if necessary or desirable. The purpose of providing this information is to help readers develop confidence in the management and operation of the enterprise.

It is also customary to discuss the compensation package (salaries, benefits, other contract terms, etc.) that each manager will receive, although such disclosure is often unnecessary when the business plan is used as a planning and evaluation tool for programs and services that are just one part of a larger set of activities conducted by the sport, tourism, or leisure service organization. It should be noted that, if the manager is already on staff and is compensated in a manner consistent with his previous position, declaring the manager's compensation for this enterprise may be a contractual violation, or in some other respect, considered to be inappropriate. If the manager is also the owner, a partner, or a shareholder in the organization, the level of ownership needs to be reported, as do any incentive stock options that may be offered.

In concluding this section, it is appropriate and desirable to list other individuals who are not a direct part of the management team, but may influence it significantly. This list includes consultants, professional mentors, advisors, accountants, bankers, and lawyers. This listing should also indicate the amount of compensation (retainers, consulting fees, stipends, honoraria, etc.) received by these influential advisors for their professional service to the sport, tourism, or leisure service organization.

Financial Plan

One of the main reasons for going through all the work to develop a business plan is to demonstrate the advisability of investment in the particular sport, tourism, or leisure service enterprise. Therefore, it is essential that the plan clearly indicates the level of financial investment that is required. Not only must the business plan state how much money or credit is needed, but it should also describe the type of funding that is needed. For example, the proponent of a new guide fishing enterprise may need $450,000 to acquire equipment, licenses, advertising, etc., but would like to have only $150,000 as debt (i.e., borrowed money) and the remaining $300,000 as equity (i.e., shared ownership). In order to justify the confidence of a lender or an equity investor, the author of the business plan should discuss and include (either in this section or as an appendix) the following financial documents (see Chapter 17 for examples):

Current financial statements (if the enterprise is already in operation). Profit and loss statements and balance sheets for the current and preceding two years should be provided.

Financial projections (for new enterprises). Profit and loss forecasts, pro forma balance sheets, projected cash flow statements, and a break-even analysis for the sport or leisure event (or first three years of an ongoing operation) should be provided. Since these are projections and, as such are subject to the limitations of current knowledge and optimistic expectations of future conditions, effort should be exercised in protecting decision makers from the enthusiasm of the enterprise proponent. It is generally considered wise to be as realistic as possible in making financial projections and then temper that realism with conservatism when estimating income. Conversely, realistic expenditure projections should be tempered with liberalism. In other words, estimate low for revenue and high for expenses.

Ratio analysis. Ratios are quantitative indicators of financial strength and operating success. Chapter 8 provides a detailed discussion of the purposes, applications, and structure of a ratio analyses. It is important to recognize that many ratios can be developed and that their purpose is to facilitate comparison with industry norms. Industry norms are not industry requirements, and deviation from the norm is not necessarily an indication of a problem. Ratio analysis encourages and gives opportunity to reflection and justification of business operations and plans. Include only ratios that are of interest and relevant to the reader. Any ratios that are included in the analysis should be discussed and presented in terms of what they mean for the way that this business will operate.

Appendices

Relevant material may be appended to the business plan. In deciding what to include as an appendix, the information needs of the reader must be the primary consideration. Material should not be included for the sole purpose of making the document thicker. Appended items should be referred to in the body of the plan and may include the following:

- Full résumés of members of the management team.
- Management team job descriptions.
- Product specifications.
- Relevant photographs.
- List of prospective customers or sources of customers.
- List of possible suppliers.
- Consulting reports and market surveys.
- Copies of legal documents.
- Letters of reference.

Summary

The business plan reflects both the dreams and the careful consideration of the sport, tourism, and leisure service organization. It can cover the entire range of services offered by that organization, or just one program or event. Business plans are just as valuable in public and private nonprofit organizations as they are in the commercial sector because they describe how the resources of the organization will be utilized to achieve its corporate objectives. Such an informative guiding document will naturally be of great interest and is, almost without exception, required by potential investors, suppliers, and creditors. Business plans typically include descriptions of the enterprise and its products and production capabilities. Also included are market descriptions and detailed statements disclosing the financial aspects of the enterprise.

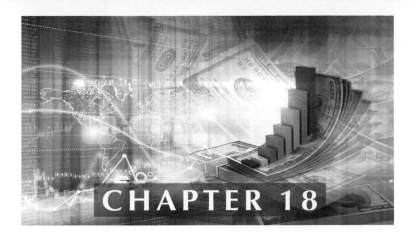

Economic Principles

Introduction

An effective sports, tourism, and leisure service manager is not only capable of establishing, directing, and implementing procedures of sound financial management, but is also aware of the basic economic and accounting principles that relate to those procedures. This chapter introduces some elementary economic concepts that are particularly relevant to financial management in sports, tourism, and leisure service organizations. It should be noted that this is a very basic discussion of a few key principles and in no way is meant to supplant the valuable learning that can be gained from a full course of studies in economics. While financial management and accounting require development of technical proficiency, their parent discipline offers an understanding of the human element of resource allocation. Economics is a social science that

contains specific assumptions about the way people behave as they allocate available resources for the purpose of realizing their wants and needs. Economics involves the measurement and quantification of observed or expected relationships and transactions between economic agents. Individuals, families, teams, government departments, and nonprofit and business organizations are all examples of economic agents.

When, for example, an event manager predicts the attendance at a championship baseball game for which the admission price is $8.00, he applies his understanding of the economic principles of supply and demand. If a public recreation administrator is trying to decide whether investing today in a particular recreation facility or piece of equipment will provide the future returns that she feels are appropriate, she will need to apply her understanding of the economic concepts of inflation, interest, and future values. Furthermore, accounting for the changing value of facilities or equipment over time requires a manager to understand the notion of depreciation, and articulating the benefits of a sports, tourism, or leisure program or enterprise will require an understanding of multipliers, leakage, and inter-industry purchasing as they relate to economic impact assessment.

These key economic principles are important to the effective management of programs, events, attractions, destinations, and facilities. Among other benefits to be gained from studying economics and understanding these few principles is an increased ability to recognize and measure the probable financial outcomes of decisions that might be made with respect to product development, pricing, and promotion. Exploring and understanding these principles can help managers of sport, tourism, and leisure services to see the full effect and impact of specific financial decisions, thereby enhancing their ability to successfully meet their respective financial objectives.

Supply and Demand

The terms supply and demand have more precise meanings than are suggested by their everyday use. In casual conversation, for example, reference is made to the supply of gasoline, and an opinion might be expressed that, after learning about the huge oil reserves in the Persian Gulf, there is a large supply of gasoline—certainly enough to meet the public demand. More correctly, the assertion is that there is a large inventory of gasoline—enough to meet current needs. The difference between inventory and supply is subtle, but important. *Inventory* refers to the quantity of a product or resource that exists. *Supply* refers to the quantity of a product or

resource that the owner is willing to offer or make available at a given price. Oil-producing nations with large petroleum reserves have extensive inventory, but may have a very small supply when the price being offered is only $10 per barrel. Without any change in the inventory of oil, the supply would increase significantly if the price rose to $50 per barrel. Similarly, there is a very small supply of excellent basketball players who will play for a professional team when offered a salary of $5,000 per year. The supply will, however, increase considerably when the annual salary offer goes to $50 million. In this illustration, the number of excellent basketball players did not increase, but the supply for the professional league did. The relationship between quantity made available and the price offered is graphically represented in Figure 18.1 and is referred to as the supply curve.

Figure 18.1. Sample Supply Curve for Athletes in a Professional Sport

From the data presented in Figure 18.1, it appears that there are only about 25 excellent basketball players who are willing to play for a professional team for $20,000 per year. There are, of course, many more equally talented players, but they probably will choose to pursue more lucrative careers for which their college education has prepared them. When the invitation to join the team comes with a $40,000 salary offer, there are many more players (about 40) willing to consider the opportunity. Teams that offer $90,000 per year find an even greater number of excellent players (approximately 70) from whom to recruit. The supply curve illustrates the human behavior expected in situations of exchange. The supply curve shows how the quantities that are available increase and decrease in relation to the prices offered for the product or resource.

In discussing demand, it is common to refer to the amount wanted or needed. The more traveling a team wants to do, the more it wants gasoline for its bus. However, the precise meaning of demand is the amount of a product or resource wanted at a given price. When the consumer price of gasoline is $1.90 per gallon, the team is more inclined to travel, and the quantity of gasoline wanted is greater than when the price is $3.40 per gallon. Similarly, if would-be professional athletes are demanding annual salaries of $20 million to play, the number of teams and the number of player positions will be less than if players could be contracted for $50,000 per year. The relationship between quantity wanted and the price of the resource is graphically represented in Figure 18.2 and is referred to as the demand curve.

Using the demand curve represented in Figure 18.2, it is observed that when players demand $80,000 salaries, the league is only interested in or able to acquire approximately 25 players. If the salaries are only $20,000, perhaps smaller markets can afford to have teams, team rosters can be expanded, and more players (approximately 100) will be needed. As the price goes down, the demand goes up.

Figure 18.2. Sample Demand Curve for Athletes in a Professional Sport

The supply and demand curves shown in Figures 18.1 and 18.2, respectively, appear to be straight lines rather than arc-like curves. The extent of curvature will vary according to the nature of the resource and the behavior of the market. A straight line may, in fact, be the best representation of the price/quantity relationship and is, for convenience and simplicity, used in our discussion of supply and demand. All curves shown in Figure 18.3 can be accurate reflections of either supply or demand.

It might also be observed, when comparing the above supply and demand curves, that the supply and demand curves slope in opposing directions. Supply curves have a positive slope; that is, they show that the quantity made available increases when the price offered increases. Conversely, demand curves have a negative slope. This means that increases in price are associated with decreases in the quantity wanted. If the supply curve and the demand curve for a particular product or service are both drawn on the same field (Figure 18.4), they will intersect at some point. This point is called the equilibrium point. At

Figure 18.3. Examples of Supply and Demand Curves

the equilibrium point, the corresponding price motivates the supplier to make available the same quantity of a resource that is wanted by the consumers at that price. At any price above the equilibrium point, there is insufficient demand (i.e., too much supply). At any price below the equilibrium point, there is inadequate supply (i.e., too much demand).

Supply and demand curves are constructed using data that describe the availability of and the want for resources at different prices. They are the result of experimentation, simulation, and observation of behaviors in similar exchange situations. In the following example, some very simple data will be used to illustrate three different approaches to the estimation of supply and/or demand.

Figure 18.4. The Supply/Demand Equilibrium Point

Estimating Supply and Demand

Data

A marina developer calculated that appropriate revenues could be generated if he offered 20 boat slips for $10 each. If, somehow, his customers could be convinced to pay $90 for a slip, the developer could build a larger facility and realize appropriate revenues by offering 73 boat slips. After studying marina operations at another waterfront in the area, he found that one that charged only $20 was able to attract 100 customers, and another that charged $80 attracted only 25 boat owners. These data are summarized in Table 18.1.

Table 18.1
Summary of Supply and Demand Data for Proposed Marina

Price	Supply	Demand
$90	73	
$80		25
$40	?	?
$20		100
$10	20	

Problems

- How many boat slips should he build if he decides to charge $40 per slip?
- How many customers would want his $40 boat slips?
- At what price will the supply of boat slips equal the demand?
- How many boat slips should he build in order to take full advantage of the demand without creating more capacity than is necessary?

There are two approaches to solving these problems: (1) approximation through graphing, and (2) algebraic calculation. These approaches are illustrated below.

Approximation through Graphing

Using graph paper, plot the known data points and draw the supply and demand curves (Figure 18.5). For a given price, find its intercept on the supply or demand curve and identify the corresponding points on the horizontal axis representing units of supply/demand. For example, at $40, it appears that the supply will be about 40 units and the demand will be for about 75 units.

It also appears that the equilibrium point (where the supply and demand curves intersect) is somewhere around the $60 mark, with supply and demand at that price being approximately 50 units.

Obviously, this method has the advantage of simplicity, but it results in approximate values. In most cases, the approximation is sufficient, especially in consideration of the fact that the supply and demand curves themselves are somewhat imprecise.

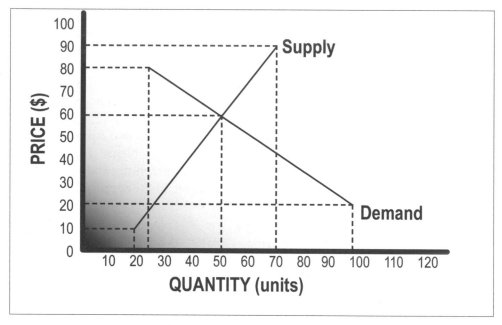

Figure 18.5. Supply/Demand Curve Graph

Algebraic Calculation

The second method provides more precise results, but these too are based on somewhat imprecise values for points along the supply and demand curves. This method involves the use of basic algebra as follows:

Use the formula for calculating any point on a straight line. In this case, the straight lines are slopes.

$y=ax + b$
- where: y is a given price
- x is the quantity supplied or demanded at that price
- a is the slope of the supply or demand curve
- b is a constant

First calculate the slopes of the supply and demand curves:

Slope (supply) = Change in price/Change in quantity

=(90-10) / (73-20)
=1.5

Slope (demand) = Change in price/ Change in quantity

=(80-20) / (25-100)
= -0.8

Next, calculate the constants for both the supply and demand curves.

For the supply curve, use the known coordinates of any point on the line. For example, use $10 and 20 units and a slope of 1.5. Thus:

y = ax + b
10 = 1.5 (20) + b
b = -20

Likewise, for the demand curve, use the known coordinates of any point on the line. For example, use $20 and 100 units and a slope of -0.9. Thus:

y = ax + b
20 = -0.8 (100) + b
b = 100

To estimate the supply and demand when the price is, for example, $40 simply use 40 as the value for y, use the same values for the slope and the constant, and solve for x (ignore the minus sign).

Supply	Demand
y = 1.5x - 20	y = -0.8x + 100
40 = 1.5x - 20	(40) = -0.8x + 100
x = 40 units	x = -75 units

Therefore, if the price is set at $40, the supply will be 40 units, but the demand will be for 75 units. It would be useful to find a price where the supply meets the demand and to know what that supply/demand quantity will be.

With slopes and constants already established, x (the quantity at equilibrium) can be calculated by equating y (price), even though its value is not yet known.

If y(supply) = y(demand), then

1.5x - 20 = -0.8x + 100
x = 52 (the quantity supplied/demanded at the equilibrium point)

To calculate the price at equilibrium, substitute the calculated value for x in either of the equations for supply or demand.

Supply: y = 1.5 (52) - 20
Demand: y = -0.8 (52) + 100
y = $58

It has now been determined that, at a price of $58, the supply and demand will both be 52 units. Note that this result is very close to the result from approximation through graphing ($60 and 50 units) and, in most circumstances, is close enough.)

It is important to note that supply and demand curves are not fixed for eternity. Rather, they reflect the behavior of a certain market or industry at a particular time. Either curve or both curves may change in response to common circumstances or conditions. For example, the pattern of demand for spectator seating at a high school football game may move to the right (i.e., more will be demanded at a given price) if it becomes apparent that the team has a good chance of qualifying for the state championship for the first time in 25 years. Likewise, the curve can move to the left (i.e., less will be demanded at a given price) if the football team consistently loses by 30 or more points to competitors who play their second string for three quarters of the game. Such movements in patterns of demand do not necessarily change the supply curve, but they will likely affect inventory. Refer to the new equilibrium point shown in Figure 18.6 and notice how the number of seats that can be sold and the price at which they can be sold increase solely as a result of change in demand.

Figure 18.6. Illustration of Shifts in the Demand Curve

Not only can shifts in demand occur, but also attitudes about and opportunities for supply can change. For example, a Boy Scout camp may, because of surplus capacity and a generous operating grant, be able to substantially reduce individual participation fees for the usual number of campers. This price reduction also means that the camp administrators will be under pressure to serve more campers because of the increased demand at those lower prices. Figure 18.7 illustrates the impacts of changes in supply conditions.

Figure 18.7. Illustration of Shifts in the Supply Curve

There are many conditions that can influence shifts in supply and demand curves. Generally, they relate to capacity and production opportunity, or to consumer need and sentiment. Some of the most common influences of supply and demand for leisure and sport services are identified in Table 18.2.

Managers of tourism, leisure, and sport organizations who understand the economic principles of supply and demand are well equipped to deal with the relative uncertainties of forecasting revenues and anticipating expenses. They are better able to apply the art of anticipating human behavior in exchange situations to the technical process of budgeting and other aspects of financial management.

Inflation

In discussing the principles of supply and demand, it is evident that decisions with regard to the offering of or desire for inventory reflect the natural desire of both producers and consumers to maximize their returns. Consumers want as much as they can get for the least amount of money, while suppliers want as much money as they can get for the least amount of inventory depletion. Human nature is such that, in a free market economy, this valued drive for maximization results in a gradual increase in the price of goods and services. This phenomenon is called inflation. The impact of inflation is the erosion of the purchasing power of financial resources that do not grow at least at the rate of inflation.

National inflation rates fluctuate. In the last century, there were years that the U.S. national averages were as high as 18% (1918), 14.4% (1947), and 13.5% (1980). There were also several years of very low inflation, such as -10.5% (1921), -9.9% (1932), and -0.4% (2009). Table 18.3 shows the level of inflation observed in the first part of the 21st century. The challenge to the leisure and sport service manager is to protect vital resources from the eroding effects of inflation.

Table 18.2
Common Influences on Supply and Demand for Sport, Leisure, and Tourism Services

Condition	Influence
Increased ability to offer services due to: —new or expanded facilities —new or expanded staff —new equipment —staff with new skills/certification.	Move supply curve to the right.
Reduced capacity of physical plant	Move supply curve to the left.
Realization of greater efficiency due to economies of scale.	Move supply curve to the right.
Revised operational mandate or mission.	Move supply curve in either direction.
Change in market need / problem resolution.	Move demand curve to left if problem resolved or need reduced. New problems or needs move demand curve to the right.
Change in market resources.	Move demand curve to the right if time, money, transportation, etc., more available. Move demand curve to left if constraints increased.
Panic / Perception of scarcity.	Move demand curve to right.
Competition	Move demand curve to the left.

Table 18.3
Average Annual Inflation Rate in the United States (2001-2016)

Year	2001	2002	2003	2004	2005	2006	2007	2008
Rate%	2.8	1.6	2.3	2.7	3.4	3.2	2.8	3.8
Year	2009	2010	2011	2012	2013	2014	2015	2016
Rate%	-0.4	1.6	3.2	2.1	1.5	1.6	0.1	1.3

Interest

Regardless of the source of money that a sport, tourism, or leisure organization acquires and uses in its operation, interest will play a significant role in financial decisions. If the financial resources used by the organization come from lenders or investors, then interest will be paid to them in addition to the original amount borrowed or invested. If the funds used come from internal reserves, then their use will reduce the interest that could have been earned by those reserves. The impact of interest should not be ignored. In fact, this point is emphasized in the unofficial definition: *"Interest—those who understand it, get it; those who don't, pay it."*

Interest is the time value of money. It represents what it costs an economic agent to consume immediately by using funds that it does not have. It represents what an economic agent receives for postponing consumption by lending or investing funds that it does have. Interest is typically expressed as a percentage of an original amount (called principal) that is paid by a borrower or earned by a lender on a per-annum basis. For example, 7% interest on a principal of $2,000 would oblige a borrower to pay the lender the original $2,000 plus $140 interest after one year. The lender may extend the loan period for one more year, after which the borrower would repay the $2,000, plus another $140 (if interest was also

paid after the first year). In this case, the time value of the money was $280. If the borrower did not make the $140 interest payment after the first year, that amount would be considered as an additional loan and be added to the principal to be repaid after the second year. After the second year, the borrower would, in addition to the $2,140 principal, pay an interest charge of $149.80 (7% of $2,140). The total time value of the money when the interest is compounded (i.e., carried over and included in the principal) was $140.00 + $149.80 = $289.80.

Future Value

Unless the owner of money hides it in a sock or under the mattress, that money will be invested and thereby has the potential to grow or increase in value over time. Such is the effect of interest. However, the effect of inflation is the erosion of the purchasing power of money over time. Obviously, it is hoped that the rate of growth will be greater than the rate of inflation. The financial manager works to protect the purchasing power of the sport, tourism, or leisure organization's money. In other words, the financial manager's first goal is to ensure that the future value of a sum is sufficient to overcome the impact of inflation. Earlier in this chapter, it was shown how a sum of money increases in value over time, thanks to interest. The *future value* of an investment can be calculated as follows:

If interest is paid each year for a given number of years, the future value (F) of an original sum is $P+n$ (Pi), where P = the principal (the original amount invested), n = the term (number of years until repayment of the principal), and i = the interest rate. After two years, the value of $2,000 earning 7% paid annually is:

$$F = P+n \ (Pi)$$

$$\$2,000 + 2(\$2,000 \times .07) = \$2,280$$

If the interest is compounded, the future value of the original sum is calculated using a more complicated formula:

$$F = P(1+i)^n$$

Fortunately, table values can be used to avoid calculation of $(1+i)^n$. Interest Table A provides interest factors (TA) to be substituted in a restated formula for the future value of a sum with interest compounded. The restated formula is:

$$F = PT_A.$$

Note that the product of P (the original $2,000 investment) and TA (the table value for $n = 2$ years and $i = 7\%$) is $2,000 x 1.145 = $2,290. This outcome is essentially the same as was earlier determined to be the future value of the sum after two years earning 7% interest.

The foregoing discussion of future values helps the sport, tourism, and leisure organization determine the future value of resources that it currently has and is willing to invest. For example, an agency that plans to fund a future building project by setting aside (investing) $10,000 at the beginning of each year for the next five years is able to calculate the expected balance of that earmarked account at the end of the five-year period.

Assuming a stable interest rate of 8% for five years, the future value of the first amount invested (F1) will be:

$$F1 = P \ (T_A) = \$10,000 \ (1.469) = \$14,690$$

To this amount, add the future value of the next $10,000 installment (F2) invested at 8% for four years:

$$F2 = P(T_A) = \$10,000 \ (1.360) = \$13,600$$

Continue calculating the future values for the remaining installments (while paying attention to the fact that the T_A value should reflect the declining n [years of investment]). Sum the future values to determine the money that will be available for the project after five years.

$$F1 = P \ (T_A) = \$10,000 \ (1.469) = \$14,690$$
$$F2 = P \ (T_A) = \$10,000 \ (1.360) = \$13,600$$
$$F3 = P \ (T_A) = \$10,000 \ (1.260) = \$12,600$$
$$F4 = P \ (T_A) = \$10,000 \ (1.166) = \$11,660$$
$$F5 = P \ (T_A) = \$10,000 \ (1.080) = \$10,080$$
Total $62,630

By setting aside $10,000 per year for the next five years, the organization will have $62,630 for its building project.

Present Value

The calculation of future values requires knowledge of a beginning amount (principal), a term of investment, and the applicable interest rate. There are, however, situations wherein the financial manager has a target future value but needs to know how much to invest at a given rate for a specified term to achieve that target. In a sense, the manager needs to reverse the procedure for determining future value in order to calculate a present value. For illustrative purposes, assume that an athletic team has been invited to travel to and participate in a prestigious tournament in just a little more than two years from now. The team's manager has worked with a transportation agency, hotels, and others to secure a firm price for services needed at the time of the event. The estimated team expenses to be paid at the time of the trip total $40,000. Team members are required to have 50% of the trip funds deposited in the team's interest-bearing account two years before the event. The remainder is payable at the end of the two years, just prior to departure. How much money has to be deposited now? The amount of $20,000 comes to mind quickly, but, after considering what was just discussed about future values, it becomes evident that all that is needed is an amount that in two years will have become $20,000. The question is actually, "What is the present value of the future sum of $20,000?" Using, for example, 6% as the interest rate, the present value can be calculated in the following manner:

$$P = F[1/(1+i)^n] = \$20,000 \, [1/(1+.06)2] = \$20,000 \, (0.890) = \$17,800$$

The team needs to deposit only $17,800 now and $20,000 later to have the full $40,000 at the time of the trip.

Once again, a formula has been introduced that may look a bit intimidating. Fortunately, there is another table that eliminates the need for cumbersome calculations. Interest Table B at the end of this book provides values from the solution of $[1/(1+i)^n]$ when calculating present values.

In the previous illustration, solution of the formula $[1/(1+i)^n]$ generated an interest factor of 0.890. The Table B value corresponding to $i = .06$ and $n = 2$ also generates the interest factor of 0.890. The formula for calculating present value can, therefore, also be expressed as:

$$P = F(T_B)$$

Depreciation

Physical assets used by sport, tourism, and leisure organizations do have a finite life span. With the exception of land, assets such as buildings and equipment eventually wear out or become obsolete because of market or technological developments. The loss of or reduced productivity of these resources is recognized and quantified as *depreciation*. In accounting, depreciation is considered as an expense, and is charged during the same period as is the revenue that the resource generates. Depreciation is recorded as an expense but, since it does not involve a cash outflow, it is also recorded as a reduction in the value of the depreciated fixed asset. At this point, the techniques for calculating depreciation will be presented.

One way of calculating depreciation is to divide the original value (sometimes referred to as the starting book value) of an asset by its expected life span. For example, a $6,000 electronic notice board at a community center may have a five-year life span, after which any repairs needed would be too expensive or may be impossible because of changing technology.

Table 18.4 illustrates the steady reduction in value of the bulletin board during the five years. This is called *straight line depreciation*. Note that the bulletin board has no book value or salvage value at the end of its life span.

Not all assets depreciate to zero value at the end of their projected life spans.

Table 18.4
Annual Starting Values, Depreciation, and Remaining Book Values after Straight Line Depreciation

Period	Starting Book Value	Depreciation Amount	Remaining Book Value
Year 1	$6,000	$1,200	$4,800
Year 2	$4,800	$1,200	$3,600
Year 3	$3,600	$1,200	$2,400
Year 4	$2,400	$1,200	$1,200
Year 5	$1,200	$1,200	$0

Furthermore, only some will depreciate at a constant rate, as was expressed in the preceding example of straight-line depreciation. In reality, many assets will decrease in value more at the beginning of their use than later on, and many will outlast projected life spans, as well as maintain some salvage value, even when obsolete or nonfunctional. *Declining balance depreciation* reflects these realities. With declining balance depreciation, a depreciation rate is set for an asset based on industry standards. This rate affects both the amount of annual depreciation and the salvage value.

To calculate first-year depreciation and remaining book value (salvage value), divide the starting book value of the asset by its life span (a constant value), and then multiply that number by the appropriate depreciation rate. Expressed as a formula:

Depreciation = (Starting Book Value/Life Span) x Depreciation Rate

For example, a $6,000 pitching machine with a five-year life span and 150% depreciation rate would depreciate $1,800 in the first year. This is calculated by dividing the starting value ($6,000) by the lifespan (5 years) and multiplying the result by the depreciation rate of 150% (1.5). The remaining book value, which is also the starting book value for the next year, is calculated by subtracting the depreciation amount ($1,800) from the previous book value ($6,000), leaving $4,200. After the second year, the pitching machine will have depreciated a further $1,260 (($4,200/5) x 1.5) and have a remaining book value of $2,940 ($4,200 – $1,260). As shown in Table 18.5, the final year's depreciation will be much lower (only $432), and there will be a salvage value of $1,009.

Table 18.5
Annual Starting Values, Depreciation, and Remaining Book Values after Declining Balance Depreciation

Period	Starting Book Value	Depreciation Amount	Remaining Book Value
Year 1	$6,000	$1,800	$4,200
Year 2	$4,200	$1,260	$2,940
Year 3	$2,940	$882	$2,058
Year 4	$2,058	$617	$1,441
Year 5	$1,441	$432	$1,009

An important advantage of declining balance depreciation is the tax shelter it offers to profits generated early in an enterprise. Since depreciation is considered an expense, the taxable profits are reduced, but not the cash that is generated from operations. These cash reserves are more critical in the early stages of an enterprise than later, when the depreciation amount is reduced.

Table 18.6 provides a comparison of the depreciation amounts and remaining book values of a $6,000 asset that is straight-line depreciated, and declining-balance depreciated at 150% and 20%. The choice of depreciation method and seemingly small differences in depreciation rates clearly have significant impacts on how the sports, tourism, or leisure service organization accounts for the mortality of its physical resources.

Sensitivity to Changes in Price

Consumers of sport, tourism, and leisure services respond to changes in prices in several different ways. In some cases, an increase in price will result in an increase in consumption because the price increase is thought to be an indication of improved service quality. Most often, however, increases in price have the opposite effect on consumption. When the price goes up, consumption goes down.

The degree to which consumption decreases with a given increase in price will differ between consumer markets. Some groups of consumers are more sensitive to price changes than others, and it is important for the financial manager in sport, tourism, and leisure service organizations to understand and be able to make sound decisions based on an understanding of price-induced fluctuations in demand.

The measure of demand fluctuations is referred to as elasticity of demand. The measure of price-induced demand fluctuations is called price elasticity of demand. More specifically, price elasticity of demand is defined as the percentage change in a quantity consumed that is caused by a percentage change in price. For example, suppose that a 1.0% increase in the admission price results in a 0.5% decrease in sales to a particular market segment. The price elasticity of demand for this market segment and this product would be –0.5.

Table 18.6

Comparison of Depreciation Amounts and Remaining Book Values for Straight Line Declining Balance (150%) and Declining Balance (200%) Depreciation of a $6,000 Asset

Period	Straight Line	150%	200%
Year 1	$1,200	$1,800	$2,400
Year 2	$1,200	$1,260	$1,440
Year 3	$1,200	$882	$864
Year 4	$1,200	$617	$518
Year 5	$1,200	$432	$311
Total Depreciation	$6,000	$4,991	$5,533
Remaining Book Value	$0	$1,009	$467

Allowing that an increase in price practically always results in a decrease in demand, the calculated value of price demand elasticity would always be negative. An important academic/practical contradiction deserves attention at this point. Because elasticities are always negative values (and to avoid confusion when comparing those values) economists usually ignore the negative sign. Thus, an elasticity of −2.5 would be considered greater than −2.4 (in spite of what is learned in elementary school mathematics).

Consider the following illustration, which uses admission price and attendance data from A.J.'s Aussieland Theme Park.

To calculate the price elasticity of demand for any of the four market segments, use the appropriate data from Table 18.7 and apply the following formula:

Price Elasticity=
    Change in attendance/(Sum of attendance/2)

    Change price/(Sum of prices/2)

Example: For the child market segment in 2014-2015, the price elasticity of demand would be:

Price Elasticity =
    (120,000 - 150,000) / ((120,000 + 150,000)/2)

    (3.50 - 3.00) / ((3.00 + 3.50)/2)

    = -1.44

Other elasticities were calculated in an identical manner and are presented in the Table 18.8

Note that the calculated elasticities for the child and senior markets are both "greater" than 1.0 (remember to ignore the minus sign). This means that there was a greater percentage change in attendance than there was in price. As demonstrated by their change in demand, the children and the seniors appear to be relatively sensitive to price changes. In fact, they are so sensitive that the revenue received from increased admission fees paid by the 120,000 remaining customers in 2014 was $30,000 less than the amount received in 2013 from the 150,000 customers who paid the lower fee. Market segments with

Table 18.7
Sample Price and Attendance Data for Four Market Segments

Market Segment	Season	Price	Attendance
Child	2014	$3.00	150,000
Child	2015	$3.50	120,000
Child	2016	$4.00	100,000
Youth	2014	$4.00	105,000
Youth	2015	$5.00	99,500
Youth	2016	$6.00	92,000
Adult	2014	$7.00	60,000
Adult	2015	$8.00	52,500
Adult	2016	$10.00	42,000
Senior	2014	$6.00	35,000
Senior	2015	$6.50	28,000
Senior	2016	$7.00	23,000

Table 18.8
Sample Data and Computed Elasticities for Four Market Segments

Market Segment	Season	Price	Attendance	Elasticity
Child	2014	$3.00	150,000	
Child	2015	$3.50	120,000	-1.44
Child	2016	$4.00	100,000	-1.36
Youth	2014	$4.00	105,000	
Youth	2015	$5.00	99,500	-0.24
Youth	2016	$6.00	92,000	-0.43
Adult	2014	$7.00	60,000	
Adult	2015	$8.00	52,500	-1.00
Adult	2016	$10.00	42,000	-1.00
Senior	2014	$6.00	35,000	
Senior	2015	$6.50	28,000	-2.78
Senior	2016	$7.00	23,000	-2.78

an elasticity of greater than 1.0 are said to be *relatively elastic*. They are markets for which a change in price results in an opposite change in revenue (i.e., increasing prices produces decreasing revenue; decreasing prices produces increasing revenue).

The calculated elasticities for the youth market segment are "less" than 1.0, which indicates that the youth market is relatively insensitive to price changes at A.J.'s Aussieland. Market segments with an elasticity of less than 1.0 are said to be *relatively inelastic*. They are markets for which a change in price results in a parallel change in revenue (i.e., increasing prices produces increasing revenue; decreasing prices produces decreasing revenue).

The adult market is called a *unitary elastic* market segment because price changes, although they cause a decrease in attendance, do not result in either an increase or a decrease in revenues. Unitary elastic markets have a price demand elasticity of approximately 1.0. For the purpose of comparison, the linear demand curves for three markets that share a common point on their demand curves are presented in Figure 18.8.

Figure 18.8. Comparison of Demand Curves for Elastic, Inelastic, and Unitary Elastic Markets

From Figure 18.8, it is evident that markets that are less sensitive to price changes (inelastic) are represented by steep demand curves. Conversely, the demand curves for more price sensitive (elastic) markets will be less sloped.

Economic Impacts

A common strategy for winning support for a major tourism, recreation, or sports development project is the declaration of economic benefits that will be realized in the community by virtue of that particular project. A city council considering the construction of a major sports stadium might be influenced by the promise of hundreds of new jobs in the community and millions of dollars of additional sales, household income, and tax revenues. Because of the influence that such promises may have, it is important for the sport, tourism, and leisure service manager to understand the basics of economic impact analysis and be able to critically evaluate such considerations.

A simple illustration will lay the foundation for this discussion. Assume that Maurice visits the small town of Graham Flats and spends $100 on crafts made and sold locally by Jean. Jean needs a new display case, so she hires Stefan to build one for her. She pays Stefan $80 and spends the remaining $20 at Vicki's produce stand at the Farmer's Market. Stefan pays $35 for materials bought in

New York City, spends $30 on computer software from a mail order company in St. Louis, and buys $15 worth of produce from Vicki. Vicki pays $35 to her lawyer, Susan, who hires Rufus to tend her garden while she attends a professional meeting in Orlando. Rufus is paid $20, while the remaining $15 of Susan's income goes toward her trip. Rufus spends his $20 on garden tools manufactured in Seattle by Ethel & Pen Tool Co. Figure 18.9 diagrams this series of transactions.

Note that, in the above scenario, money was introduced into the Graham Flats economy by Maurice and was respent by several people. Some of the money was spent on locally produced goods and services and some was spent outside the community. Eventually, all the money introduced by Maurice was sent to New York City ($35), St. Louis ($30), Orlando ($15), and Seattle ($20). The exogenous funds had circulated within

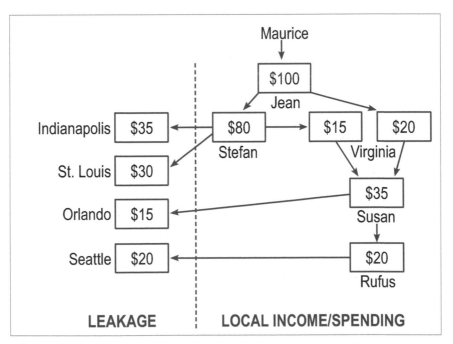

Figure 18.9. *Transaction Series Showing Local Re-spending and Leakage*

the economy and then leaked out through outside spending. However, Maurice's $100 did result in $270 of spending (economic activity) in the community. Its direct impact was multiplied 2.7 times, and it contributed to the employment income of five people in Graham Flats.

Economic impact assessment measures the amount of local re-spending of money that comes into the economy because of a particular event or project. It results in a description of the local income, local sales, and local tax revenues generated by exogenous funds. It results in quantification of the employment created by new income, sales, and tax revenues. Figure 18.10 details the flow of dollars from non-local sources as they move through the local economy and affect government, industry, and household spending activity.

The direct effect of money spent on a major tourism, sports, or leisure project is the local purchasing and employment required for that project. The indirect effect is the local purchasing and employment that results from direct sales and employment income. Induced effects result from third and subsequent rounds of economic activity having their genesis in the project. Economic impact studies are occasionally conducted to provide justification for a "dream" project. Such studies must be viewed with a critical eye, as the results may reflect more of a political will than an economic

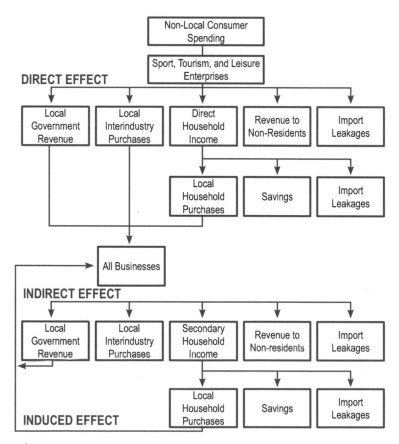

Figure 18.10. Flow of Exogenous Funds through the Local Economy

reality. When evaluating the results of an economic impact study, the sports, tourism, and leisure service manager should consider the following:

- Does the study focus on the impact of money coming from outside the community? This is an important distinction, because the impact of spending local funds is, in most respects, independent of the project. In fact, a project that only stimulates spending of local money may create more import leakage than it does new sales, income, and employment.

- Are the multipliers that are used truly reflective of economic conditions within the community? Extreme caution should be exercised when applying a sales, income, or employment multiplier that was computed for another community that may have a more diverse economic base or may be less subject to seasonal constraints and market fluctuations. While it may be convenient or less expensive, a "borrowed" multiplier just may not fit.

- Are projections of direct spending based on solid market research or on unsubstantiated optimism? Investment decisions that would

require an economic impact analysis are much too important to make on the basis of unreliable or biased information.

Summary

As an introduction to the economic principles that underlie the successful management of financial resources in the sport, tourism, and leisure service organization, this chapter has emphasized the need to develop an understanding and working knowledge of the concepts of supply and demand. Additionally, attention has been devoted to the impact of interest on decisions about present or future use of money. The concepts of depreciation and economic impact assessment were also introduced. The economic principles presented help the financial manager to understand how individuals and society work; that is, they provide insights into basic human behavior. Furthermore, the technical aspects of the discussion also serve as a review of the basic mathematical skills that are needed for procedures discussed earlier in this book. An understanding of basic economics is important to the development of skills and the strengthening of the decision-making ability of financial managers in sport, tourism, and leisure service organizations.

APPENDICES

Interest Table A

n\I	2%	3%	4%	5%	6%	7%	8%	9%	10%	12%	15%
1	1.020	1.030	1.040	1.050	1.060	1.070	1.080	1.090	1.100	1.120	1.150
2	1.040	1.061	1.082	1.103	1.124	1.145	1.166	1.188	1.210	1.254	1.323
3	1.061	1.093	1.125	1.158	1.191	1.225	1.260	1.295	1.331	1.405	1.521
4	1.082	1.126	1.170	1.216	1.262	1.311	1.360	1.412	1.464	1.574	1.749
5	1.104	1.159	1.217	1.276	1.338	1.403	1.469	1.539	1.611	1.762	2.011
6	1.126	1.194	1.265	1.340	1.419	1.501	1.587	1.677	1.772	1.974	2.313
7	1.149	1.230	1.316	1.407	1.504	1.606	1.714	1.828	1.949	2.211	2.660
8	1.172	1.267	1.369	1.477	1.594	1.718	1.851	1.993	2.144	2.476	3.059
9	1.195	1.305	1.423	1.551	1.689	1.838	1.999	2.172	2.358	2.773	3.518
10	1.219	1.344	1.480	1.629	1.791	1.967	2.159	2.367	2.594	3.106	4.046
11	1.243	1.384	1.539	1.710	1.898	2.105	2.332	2.580	2.853	3.479	4.652
12	1.268	1.426	1.601	1.796	2.012	2.252	2.518	2.813	3.138	3.896	5.350
13	1.294	1.469	1.665	1.886	2.133	2.410	2.720	3.066	3.452	4.363	6.153
14	1.319	1.513	1.732	1.980	2.261	2.579	2.937	3.342	3.797	4.887	7.076
15	1.346	1.558	1.801	2.079	2.397	2.759	3.172	3.642	4.177	5.474	8.137
16	1.373	1.605	1.873	2.183	2.540	2.952	3.426	3.970	4.595	6.130	9.358
17	1.400	1.653	1.948	2.292	2.693	3.159	3.700	4.328	5.054	6.866	10.761
18	1.428	1.702	2.026	2.407	2.854	3.380	3.996	4.717	5.560	7.690	12.375
19	1.457	1.754	2.107	2.527	3.026	3.617	4.316	5.142	6.116	8.613	14.232
20	1.486	1.806	2.191	2.653	3.207	3.870	4.661	5.604	6.727	9.646	16.367
21	1.516	1.860	2.279	2.786	3.400	4.141	5.034	6.109	7.400	10.804	18.822
22	1.546	1.916	2.370	2.925	3.604	4.430	5.437	6.659	8.140	12.100	21.645
23	1.577	1.974	2.465	3.072	3.820	4.741	5.871	7.258	8.954	13.552	24.891
24	1.608	2.033	2.563	3.225	4.049	5.072	6.341	7.911	9.850	15.179	28.625
25	1.641	2.094	2.666	3.386	4.292	5.427	6.848	8.623	10.835	17.000	32.919

Interest Table A $(1+i)^n$

Interest Table B

n\I	2%	3%	4%	5%	6%	7%	8%	9%	10%	12%	15%
1	0.980	0.971	0.962	0.952	0.943	0.935	0.926	0.917	0.909	0.893	0.870
2	0.961	0.943	0.925	0.907	0.890	0.873	0.857	0.842	0.826	0.797	0.756
3	0.942	0.915	0.889	0.864	0.840	0.816	0.794	0.772	0.751	0.712	0.658
4	0.924	0.888	0.855	0.823	0.792	0.763	0.735	0.708	0.683	0.636	0.572
5	0.906	0.863	0.822	0.784	0.747	0.713	0.681	0.650	0.621	0.567	0.497
6	0.888	0.837	0.790	0.746	0.705	0.666	0.630	0.596	0.564	0.507	0.432
7	0.871	0.813	0.760	0.711	0.665	0.623	0.583	0.547	0.513	0.452	0.376
8	0.853	0.789	0.731	0.677	0.627	0.582	0.540	0.502	0.467	0.404	0.327
9	0.837	0.766	0.703	0.645	0.592	0.544	0.500	0.460	0.424	0.361	0.284
10	0.820	0.744	0.676	0.614	0.558	0.508	0.463	0.422	0.386	0.322	0.247
11	0.804	0.722	0.650	0.585	0.527	0.475	0.429	0.388	0.350	0.287	0.215
12	0.788	0.701	0.625	0.557	0.497	0.444	0.397	0.356	0.319	0.257	0.187
13	0.773	0.681	0.601	0.530	0.469	0.415	0.368	0.326	0.290	0.229	0.163
14	0.758	0.661	0.577	0.505	0.442	0.388	0.340	0.299	0.263	0.205	0.141
15	0.743	0.642	0.555	0.481	0.417	0.362	0.315	0.275	0.239	0.183	0.123
16	0.728	0.623	0.534	0.458	0.394	0.339	0.292	0.252	0.218	0.163	0.107
17	0.714	0.605	0.513	0.436	0.371	0.317	0.270	0.231	0.198	0.146	0.093
18	0.700	0.587	0.494	0.416	0.350	0.296	0.250	0.212	0.180	0.130	0.081
19	0.686	0.570	0.475	0.396	0.331	0.277	0.232	0.194	0.164	0.116	0.070
20	0.673	0.554	0.456	0.377	0.312	0.258	0.215	0.178	0.149	0.104	0.061
21	0.660	0.538	0.439	0.359	0.294	0.242	0.199	0.164	0.135	0.093	0.053
22	0.647	0.522	0.422	0.342	0.278	0.226	0.184	0.150	0.123	0.083	0.046
23	0.634	0.507	0.406	0.326	0.262	0.211	0.170	0.138	0.112	0.074	0.040
24	0.622	0.492	0.390	0.310	0.247	0.197	0.158	0.126	0.102	0.066	0.035
25	0.610	0.478	0.375	0.295	0.233	0.184	0.146	0.116	0.092	0.059	0.030

Interest Table B $\quad 1/(1+i)^n$

Interest Table C

n\i	2%	3%	4%	5%	6%	7%	8%	9%	10%	12%	15%
1	0.980	0.971	0.962	0.952	0.943	0.935	0.926	0.917	0.909	0.893	0.870
2	1.942	1.913	1.886	1.859	1.833	1.808	1.783	1.759	1.736	1.690	1.626
3	2.884	2.829	2.775	2.723	2.673	2.624	2.577	2.531	2.487	2.402	2.283
4	3.808	3.717	3.630	3.546	3.465	3.387	3.312	3.240	3.170	3.037	2.855
5	4.713	4.580	4.452	4.329	4.212	4.100	3.993	3.890	3.791	3.605	3.352
6	5.601	5.417	5.242	5.076	4.917	4.767	4.623	4.486	4.355	4.111	3.784
7	6.472	6.230	6.002	5.786	5.582	5.389	5.206	5.033	4.868	4.564	4.160
8	7.325	7.020	6.733	6.463	6.210	5.971	5.747	5.535	5.335	4.968	4.487
9	8.162	7.786	7.435	7.108	6.802	6.515	6.247	5.995	5.759	5.328	4.772
10	8.983	8.530	8.111	7.722	7.360	7.024	6.710	6.418	6.145	5.650	5.019
11	9.787	9.253	8.760	8.306	7.887	7.499	7.139	6.805	6.495	5.938	5.234
12	10.575	9.954	9.385	8.863	8.384	7.943	7.536	7.161	6.814	6.194	5.421
13	11.348	10.635	9.986	9.394	8.853	8.358	7.904	7.487	7.103	6.424	5.583
14	12.106	11.296	10.563	9.899	9.295	8.745	8.244	7.786	7.367	6.628	5.724
15	12.849	11.938	11.118	10.380	9.712	9.108	8.559	8.061	7.606	6.811	5.847
16	13.578	12.561	11.652	10.838	10.106	9.447	8.851	8.313	7.824	6.974	5.954
17	14.292	13.166	12.166	11.274	10.477	9.763	9.122	8.544	8.022	7.120	6.047
18	14.992	13.754	12.659	11.690	10.828	10.059	9.372	8.756	8.201	7.250	6.128
19	15.678	14.324	13.134	12.085	11.158	10.336	9.604	8.950	8.365	7.366	6.198
20	16.351	14.877	13.590	12.462	11.470	10.594	9.818	9.129	8.514	7.469	6.259
21	17.011	15.415	14.029	12.821	11.764	10.836	10.017	9.292	8.649	7.562	6.312
22	17.658	15.937	14.451	13.163	12.042	11.061	10.201	9.442	8.772	7.645	6.359
23	18.292	16.444	14.857	13.489	12.303	11.272	10.371	9.580	8.883	7.718	6.399
24	18.914	16.936	15.247	13.799	12.550	11.469	10.529	9.707	8.985	7.784	6.434
25	19.523	17.413	15.622	14.094	12.783	11.654	10.675	9.823	9.077	7.843	6.464

Interest Table C $((1-[1+i]^{-n})/i)$

Index

Related Books

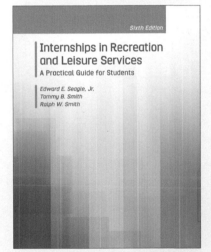